D1359834

SKILL PRACTICE

GRADE

IncentivePublications
BY WORLD BOOK

Many thanks to Charlotte Poulos and Laurie Grupé,
whose adapted exercises are included in this book.

Written by Imogene Forte and Marjorie Frank
Illustrated by Kathleen Bullock
Cover by Brenda Tropinski

Print Edition ISBN 978-1-62950-482-7
E-book Edition ISBN 978-1-62950-483-4 (PDF)

World Book, Inc.
180 North LaSalle Street
Suite 900
Chicago, Illinois 60601
USA

For information about World Book and Incentive Publications products, call **1-800-967-5325,** or visit our websites at **www.worldbook.com** and **www.incentivepublications.com.**

Printed in the United States of America by Sheridan Books, Inc.
Chelsea, Michigan
1st printing June 2016

TABLE OF CONTENTS

Introduction 14

Skills Checklists

    Phonics, Word Recognition, and Reading Skills Checklist............................18

    Spelling, Language, Writing, & Usage Skills Checklist 19

    Social Studies Skills Checklist 142

    Map Skills & Geography Skills Checklist..143

    Science Skills Checklist 210

    Number Concepts & Relationships Skills Checklist 250

    Math Computation & Problem Solving Skills Checklist.........................251

    Geometry, Measurement, & Graphing Skills Checklist 252

Language Arts..**17**

Phonics & Word Recognition Exercises

    Choose Your Adventure! . . . (Beginning, Middle, & Ending Consonants) 20

    Adventure #1   A Bumpy Camel Ride . . . (Middle Consonants) 22

    Adventure #2   Reptile Races . . . (Consonant Blends)................................23

    Adventure #3   A Low-Down Place . . . (S Blends).....................................24

    Adventure #4   A High-in-the-Sky Place . . . (*L* & *R* Blends).........................25

    Adventure #5   Through the Iceberg Maze . . .
    (Beginning & Ending Digraphs)...26

    Adventure #6   Over the Edge . . . (Consonant Blends & Digraphs) 27

    Adventure #7   The Super Ferris Wheel . . . (Double Consonants) 28

    Adventure #8   Snorkeling the Great Reef . . . (Alphabetizing) 29

    Adventure #9   Deep in the Rain Forest . . . (Vowels) 30

    Adventure #10   The Bullfight . . . (Short Vowels).......................................31

    Adventure #11   Clowning Around . . . (Long Vowels) 32

    Adventure #12   Lion-Sized Thrills . . . (Long Vowels with Silent *e*).................33

    Adventure #13   Moose Tracking . . . (Double Vowels) 34

    Adventure #14   Rhino Watching . . . (Vowel Combinations) 35

Adventure #15   A Helicopter Flight . . . (Vowel Combination: *ow*) 36

Adventure #16   Meet the Meat Eaters . . . (Vowel Combinations).................37

Adventure #17   Fire Danger! . . . (Vowel Combinations: Long *a*) 38

Adventure #18   Hurricane Watch . . . (Vowel Combinations: *ai, oa, ou, ea*) 39

Adventure #19   Yodel with a Yeti . . . (*Y* as a Consonant • *Y* as a Vowel)........40

Adventure #20   Stalk a Sasquatch . . . (Silent Letters) 41

Adventure #21   Hunt for Pirate's Treasure . . . (Use Phonics to
Read Whole Words)...................42

Adventure #22   The Sea Turtle Races . . . (Inflectional Endings)...................43

Adventure #23   The Big Jump . . . (Prefixes) 44

Adventure #24   Log Rolling on the River . . . (Suffixes)...................45

Adventure #25   Visit a Desert Hotel . . . (Prefixes & Suffixes) 46

Adventure #26   Nighttime Snooping . . . (Root Words)...................47

Adventure #27   Rodeo Ride . . . (Root Words) 48

Adventure #28   A Swamp Cruise . . . (Syllables) 49

Adventure #29   Tornado Alert! . . . (Syllables) 50

Adventure #30   Volcanic Visit . . . (Contractions) 51

Adventure #31   Go Spelunking! . . . (Contractions) 52

Adventure #32   Alaska Camp Out . . . (Compound Words) 53

Adventure #33   The Wild Boar Chase . . . (Similar Words • Spelling) 54

Adventure #34   A Lot of Hot Air . . . (Homonyms)...................55

Adventure #35   Ski the Alps . . . (Homonyms)...................56

Adventure #36   Track the Mountain Gorilla . . . (Proper Nouns)...................57

Adventure #37   Elephant Ride . . . (Plural Nouns)...................58

Adventure #38   Visit the Crowded Sahara . . . (Possessive Nouns) 59

Adventure #39   Catch a Great Wave! . . . (Synonyms) 60

Adventure #40   Catch a Giraffe Ride . . . (Antonyms) 61

Adventure #41   Galaxy Cruising . . . (Synonyms & Antonyms) 62

Adventure #42   A Scuba Lesson . . . (Multiple Meanings)...................63

Adventure #43   Hike the Great Wall . . . (Word Classification) 64

Adventure #44   Earthquake Inspection . . . (New Vocabulary) 65

Adventure #45   Hot Spots & Cold Spots . . . (New Vocabulary)...................66

Adventure #46   Time Travel . . . (Word Formation)...................67

Reading Skills Exercises

Back to School . . . (Choose Titles) 68

Classroom Rules . . . (Context) 69

Lost Name Tags . . . (Inference) 70

Art and Music Mix-Up . . . (Classifying Words) 71

Find the Hidden Message . . . (Rhyming Words) 72

Benjy's List . . . (Word Meanings) 73

A Picnic Memory . . . (Recalling Information Read) 74

Wise Owl's Shopping Spree . . . (Find Facts and Details) 75

Pick and Pack . . . (Word Identification and Classification) 76

Picnic Tummy Aches . . . (Find Information on a Graph) 77

Being Lost Is No Fun . . . (Main Idea • Inference) 78

Dear Old Golden Rule Days . . . (Main Idea) 79

Word Wizard . . . (Consonant Words • Vocabulary Extension) 80

Word Makers . . . (Word Appreciation) 81

The Great Hit . . . (Context) 82

Math Mix-Up . . . (Sequence) 83

Where Would You Find It? . . . (Context) 84

The Big Game . . . (Identify Characters and Setting) 85

Dressed for Drama . . . (Interpreting Illustrations) 86

Picture Conclusions . . . (Drawing Conclusions) 87

Silly Sentences . . . (Alliteration) 88

Talent Show . . . (Match Sentences with Pictures) 89

A Report on Gilas . . . (Find Facts and Details) 90

Cloud Watching . . . (Word Classification) 91

Playground Fun . . . (Choose Titles) 92

Circus, Circus . . . (Illustrations • Inference) 93

A Deep-Sea Scare . . . (Follow Directions) 94

Rafting on the River . . . (Captions • Main Idea) 95

To Market, To Market! . . . (Match Sentences with Pictures) 96

What's Next? . . . (Make Predictions) 97

Spelling Exercises

Double the Fun . . . (Words with Double Consonants) 98

How Do You Spell Magic? . . . (Confusing Consonants) 99

The Sleepy Letter . . . (Words with Silent *e*) 100

Weighty Words . . . (Words with *ie* or *ei*)..101

Surprise Over the Fence . . . (Words with *s*)..102

Upside-Down View . . . (Words with *o*)..103

Quilting with Qs . . . (Words with *q*) 104

Tracking Down W, X, Y, and Z . . . (Words with *w, x, y,* or *z*)........................105

Getting to Know BIG Words . . . (Big Words) 106

Getting to Know SMALL Words . . . (Small Words) 107

Mistakes in the News . . . (Correct Spelling Errors in Writing)........................108

Places to Know . . . (Proper Nouns) 109

Cracking Some Tough Words . . . (Frequently Misspelled Words) 110

Names to Know . . . (Proper Names) 111

Words That Count . . . (Number Words) 112

Animal Spelling . . . (Animal Words) 113

How's the Fishing? . . . (Identify Correctly Spelled Words)........................114

Checking for Errors . . . (Identify Incorrectly Spelled Words)........................115

Language, Writing, & Usage Exercises

The Carnival Comes to Town . . . (Nouns & Verbs) 116

Milton the Magnificent! . . . (Nouns) 118

A Great Balancing Act . . . (Proper Nouns)..119

Step Right Up! . . . (Plural Nouns) 120

Getting Ready for the Show . . . (Possessive Nouns)........................121

Monkey Action . . . (Verbs) 122

Leaping Through Fire . . . (Complete Sentences)..124

Ring Around Run-ons . . . (Run-on Sentences)..125

Unusual Talents . . . (Questions)..126

Inside the Lion's Mouth . . . (Statements) 127

Ups & Downs . . . (Capitalization) 128

Juggling for Contractions . . . (Contractions)..129

Quotes from the Circus Train . . . (Quotations) 130

Aim for the Ducks . . . (Punctuation)..131

Wonderful Carnival Words . . . (Writing: Descriptive Words)........................132

Come One, Come All! . . . (Writing: Poster) 133

A Three-Ring Circus . . . (Writing: Generating & Organizing Ideas) 134

Fantastic Dreams . . . (Writing: Imaginative Piece) 136

Tina the Terrific . . . (Writing: Finishing a Story) 137

Clowns Up Close . . . (Writing: Character Descriptions) 138

Social Studies **141**

Social Studies Exercises

What's New in the Neighborhood? . . . (Neighborhoods) 144

Where Would You Go? . . . (Places in the Community) 146

Take a Hike . . . or Take a Bike! . . . (Transportation) 148

Don't Ignore the Signs! . . . (Community Signs) 149

Who's in Charge Here? . . . (Community Government) 150

Show Me the Money . . . (Taxes & Community Services) 151

Who Can You Call? . . . (Community Services) 152

Is It a Law? . . . (Rules & Laws) 153

We Do It This Way! . . . (Customs) 154

Do You Really Need That? . . . (Needs & Wants) 155

Workers Wanted! . . . (Jobs in the Community) 156

Making Choices . . . (People's Wants) 157

Do You Really Need It? . . . (Needs & Wants) 158

Job Search . . . (Jobs • Goods & Services) 159

Everybody Is Good at Something . . . (People's Skills) 160

Money Can't Buy Everything . . . (Money) 161

Where Does Our Money Go? . . . (Using Money) 162

Where Did My Money Go? . . . (Using Money) 163

Nature Gets Things Started . . . (Resources & Products) 164

Getting Ice Cream From a Cow . . . (Resources & Products) 165

Map Skills & Geography Exercises

Once Upon a Table . . . (Define a Map • Make a Map) 166

Digging for Treasure . . . (Parts of a Map) 168

Map Mix-Up . . . (Map Titles) 169

Delivery for Bigfoot . . . (Directions on a Map) 170

A Dangerous Delivery . . . (Directions on a Map) 171

Delivery by Dinosaur . . . (Directions on a Map) 172

Who Gets the Milk? . . . (Directions on a Map) 173

Who Ordered the Pizza? . . . (Map Symbols) 174

Map in a Candy Box . . . (Use a Map Key) 176

A New Desert Route . . . (Use a Map Key) 177

Special Delivery . . . (Use a Map Key) 178

Toy Store Confusion . . . (Make a Map Key) 179

Everybody Loves a Party . . . (Recognize Maps) 180

Eliza Bear's Room . . . (Make Maps) 181

Sara in a Hurry . . . (Map Symbols) 182

The First Day of School . . . (Map Key) 183

Weekend Fun . . . (Map Key) 184

Follow the Parade! . . . (Map Key) 185

Wesley's Dream Plate . . . (Make a Map from a Key) 186

Noah Goes North . . . (Directions) 187

A Jungle Trip . . . (Scale) 188

An Underwater Puzzle . . . (Read a Grid) 189

Sara's Garden . . . (Place Things on a Grid) 190

Treasure Island . . . (Read a Map on a Grid) 191

Round or Flat? . . . (Kinds of Maps) 192

Bear County Maps . . . (Kinds of Maps) 193

So Many Bear Places! . . . (U.S. States) 195

Puzzle Time . . . (Recognize U.S. States) 196

The Great Lakes Are Great! . . . (Find Information on a Map) 197

The Bus Ride to Camp . . . (Find Information on a Map) 198

Full Tents . . . (Find Information on a Map) 199

First Prize Map . . . (Landform Map) 200

A Trip to the Farm . . . (Road Map) 201

A Pen Pal in Japan . . . (Product Map) 202

The Weather Reporter . . . (Weather Map) 203

Fishing Friends . . . (Population Map) 204

What's for Dinner? . . . (Read a Chart) 205

A Ride in a Hot Air-Balloon . . . (Read a Chart) 206

Eliza's New Map . . . (Make a Map) 207

Science Exercises

Something's Missing . . . (Plant Parts) 211

Circles Everywhere . . . (Life Cycle of Seed Plants) 212

What Do You Know About Trees? . . . (Identify Parts of Trees) 213

What Do Bees Know? . . . (Flower Parts) 214

Photo-What? . . . (Photosynthesis) 215

Creeping Creatures . . . (Animal Classification) 216

Animals With & Without . . . (Animal Classification) 217

Vertebrates on Wheels . . . (Vertebrate Classification) 218

Mix-Up at the Zoo . . . (Vertebrate Classification) 220

Wormy Questions . . . (Animal Characteristics) 221

Home, Sweet Home . . . (Animal Homes) 222

How Those Animals Behave! . . . (Animal Behavior) 223

Looking for Habitats . . . (Habitats) 224

Eco-Puzzle . . . (Ecology) 226

Who's Who in the Community? . . . (Communities) 227

Too Much Pollution . . . (Pollution) 228

Earth Care . . . (Pollution & Conservation) 229

Places in Space . . . (Earth • Sun • Moon) 230

The Spinning Earth . . . (Day and Night) 231

What's Out There? . . . (Objects in Space) 232

Unsafe! . . . (Safety) 233

When Seasons Change . . . (Seasons) 234

Hot, Cold, or In-Between? . . . (Seasons • Temperature) 235

Body Parts You Can See . . . (Body Parts) 236

Body Parts You Can't See . . . (Body Parts) 237

Disappearing Dinosaurs . . . (Dinosaurs) 238

Old Bones and Fossils . . . (Fossils) 239

A Fish on the Hook . . . (Land and Water) 240

How Much Air? . . . (Air Properties) 242

What You See in the Sea . . . (The Ocean) 243

Whales, Tales, and Other Mysteries of the Deep . . . (Ocean Life) 244

Science Words to Know 245

Number Concepts & Relationships Exercises

Critters in Canoes . . . (Order Whole Numbers) 253

Goofy Golfing Gophers . . . (Comparing Numbers) 254

On the Shelves . . . (Comparing Numbers)..256

Full Tents . . . (Place Value)..258

A Wild Tennis Game . . . (Place Value • Expanded Notation) 259

Under the Bleachers . . . (Counting Money) 260

Snacks at the Ball Game . . . (Comparing Money)..261

Welcome to the Swamp . . . (Ordinals) 262

Ball Team Hang-Ups . . . (Read & Write Whole Numbers;

Match Numerals to Word Names) 264

Trouble Underwater . . . (Read & Write Whole Numbers;

Match Numerals to Word Names) 265

Ant Antics . . . (Order Whole Numbers) 266

Summer Swamp Supplies . . . (Estimate Amounts)..267

A "Weighty" Round-Up . . . (Rounding Whole Numbers) 268

Derby Warm-Up . . . (Patterns & Sequences) 269

A Bad Fit . . . (Relationships Between Numbers)..270

Number Concepts & Relationships Words to Know.......................................271

Math Computation & Problem Solving Exercises

Lost in the Weeds . . . (Addition)..272

Throw Three! . . . (Column Addition) 273

Different Sails . . . (Subtraction)..274

Subtracting Snowballs . . . (Subtraction) 275

Mystery Athlete . . . (Multiplication) 276

How Many Jumps? . . . (Division Facts) 277

Icy Problems . . . (Problems with Money) 278

Swimmer's Line-Up . . . (Fractions) 280

Pizza Party . . . (Mixed Numerals)..281

A Busy Baseball Season . . . (Time • Calendar)...282

Hula Hoop Numbers . . . (Problem Solving)..284

The Great Bug Race . . . (Place Value) 285

Math Computation & Problem Solving Words to Know 286

Geometry, Measurement, & Graphing Exercises

Line Up for Cheers . . . (Line Segments) 287

High-Flying Geometry . . . (Plane Figures) 288

Pool Bottom Geometry . . . (Plane Figures) 289

Flags Everywhere! . . . (Drawing Geometric Figures) 290

Inside the Gym Bag . . . (Solid Geometric Figures) 291

The Topic Is T-Shirts . . . (Congruent Figures)..292

The Great Spaghetti Marathon . . . (Measuring Length: Metric)....................293

Sticks & Stuff . . . (Measuring Length: Metric) 294

The Big Bug Race . . . (Measuring Length: U.S.) 295

Can't Stop Measuring! . . . (Measuring Length: U.S.) 296

Taking the Plunge . . . (Choosing Units of Liquid Capacity: Metric) 297

Who Has the Most Money? . . . (Counting Money) 298

Don't Miss the Sale! . . . (Problems with Money) 299

One Very Busy Family . . . (Time • Calendar) 300

Hot, Cold, or Just Right? . . . (Temperature) 302

Big Gulpers . . . (Reading a Picture Graph) 303

Jungle Time . . . (Telling Time) 304

Geometry, Measurement, & Graphing Words to Know 305

Appendix **307**

Language Arts Skills Test 308

   Part One: Phonics & Word Recognition...308

   Part Two: Reading...312

   Part Three: Spelling..316

   Part Four: Language, Writing, & Usage 318

Social Studies Skills Test...321

   Part One: Social Studies..321

   Part Two: Map Skills & Geography 325

Science Skills Test...328

Math Skills Test 332

   Part One: Number Concepts & Relationships...332

   Part Two: Math Computation & Problem Solving 334

   Part Three: Geometry, Measurement, & Graphing 338

Skills Test Answer Key 342

Skills Exercises Answer Key..344

INTRODUCTION

Do basic skills have to be boring? Absolutely not! Mastery of basic skills provides the foundation for exciting learning opportunities for students. Content relevant to their everyday life is fascinating stuff! Kids love learning about such topics as galaxies and glaciers, thunderstorms and timelines, continents and chemicals, tarantulas and tornadoes, poems and plateaus, elephants and encyclopedias, mixtures and mummies, antonyms and Antarctica, and more. Using these topics and carefully designed practice they develop basic skills which enable them to ponder, process, grow, and achieve school success.

Acquiring, polishing, and using basic skills and content is a cause for celebration—not an exercise in drudgery. *Skill Practice: Grade 2* invites students to sharpen their abilities in the essentials of language arts, social studies, science, and mathematics.

As you examine *Skill Practice: Grade 2*, you will see that it is filled with attractive age-appropriate student exercises. These pages are no ordinary worksheets! *Skill Practice: Grade 2* contains hundreds of inventive and inviting ready-to-use lessons based on a captivating theme that invites the student to join an adventure, solve a puzzle, pursue a mystery, or tackle a problem. Additionally, each illustrated exercise provides diverse tools for reinforcement and extension of basic and higher-order thinking skills.

Skill Practice: Grade 2 contains the following components:

- **A clear, sequential list of skills for eight different content areas**
  Checklists of skills begin each content section. These lists correlate with the exercises, identifying page numbers where specific skills can be practiced. Students can chart their progress by checking off each skill as it is mastered.

- **Over 300 pages of student exercises**
  Each exercise page:
  - . . . addresses a specific basic skill or content area.
  - . . . presents tasks that grab the attention and curiosity of students.
  - . . . contains clear directions to the student.
  - . . . asks students to use, remember, and practice a basic skill.
  - . . . challenges students to think creatively and analytically.
  - . . . requires students to apply the skill to real situations or content.
  - . . . takes students on learning adventures with a variety of delightful characters!

- **A ready-to-use assessment tool**
  Four skills tests follow the skills exercises. The tests are presented in parts corresponding to the skills lists. Designed to be used as pre- or post-tests, individual parts of these tests can be given to students at separate times, if needed.

- **Complete answer keys**
  Easy-to-find-and-use answer keys for all exercises and skills tests follow each section.

HOW TO USE THIS BOOK:

The exercises contained in *Skill Practice: Grade 2* are to be used with adult assistance. The adult may serve as a guide to ensure the student understands the directions and questions.

Skill Practice: Grade 2 is designed to be used in many diverse ways. Its use will vary according to the needs of the students and the structure of the learning environment.

The skills checklists may be used as:

> . . . record-keeping tools to track individual skills mastery;
> . . . planning guides for instruction; and
> . . . a place for students to proudly check off accomplishments.

Each exercise page may be used as:

> . . . a pre-test or check to see how well a student has mastered a skill;
> . . . one of many resources or exercises for teaching a skill;
> . . . a way to practice or polish a skill that has been taught;
> . . . a review of a skill taught earlier;
> . . . reinforcement of a single basic skill, skills cluster, or content base;
> . . . a preview to help identify instructional needs; and
> . . . an assessment for a skill that a student has practiced.

The exercises are flexibly designed for presentation in many formats and settings. They are useful for individual instruction or independent work. They can also be used under the direction of an adult with small groups.

The skills tests may be used as:

> . . . pre-tests to gauge instructional or placement needs;
> . . . information sources to help adjust instruction; and
> . . . post-tests to review student mastery of skills and content areas.

Skill Practice: Grade 2 is not intended to be a complete curriculum or textbook. It is a collection of inventive exercises to sharpen skills and provide students and parents with tools for reinforcing concepts and skills, and for identifying areas that need additional attention. This book offers a delightful assortment of tasks that give students just the practice they need—and to get that practice in a manner that is not boring.

As students take on the challenges of the enticing adventures in this book, they will increase their comfort level with the use of fundamental reading, writing, and language skills and concepts. Watching your student check off the sharpened skills is cause for celebration!

LANGUAGE ARTS

Skills Exercises
Grade Two

SKILLS CHECKLIST
PHONICS, WORD RECOGNITION, & READING

✔	SKILL	PAGE(S)
	Identify and read beginning and ending consonants	20, 21, 23–29
	Identify and read medial consonants	21, 22
	Identify and read beginning and ending consonant blends	23–27
	Identify and read beginning and ending digraphs	26, 27
	Identify double consonants	28
	Put words in alphabetical order	29
	Identify and read short vowels	30, 31
	Identify and read long vowels	30, 32, 33, 37, 38, 39
	Identify and read long vowels with silent *e*	33
	Identify double vowels	34
	Identify and read various vowel combinations	35–39
	Distinguish between *y* as a vowel and as a consonant	40
	Identify and read words with silent letters	41
	Use phonics to read whole words	42
	Identify and read inflectional endings	43
	Identify and use common prefixes	44, 46
	Identify and use common suffixes	45, 46
	Identify and use common root words	47, 48
	Determine syllables in words	49, 50
	Identify and read contractions	51, 52
	Identify and form compound words	53
	Discriminate between words that look similar	54

✔	SKILL	PAGE(S)
	Identify and discriminate between homonyms	55, 56
	Identify and read proper nouns	57
	Identify and read plural nouns	58
	Identify and read possessive nouns	59
	Recognize and use synonyms	60, 62
	Recognize and use antonyms	61, 62
	Recognize and use words with multiple meanings	63
	Classify words according to meaning and use	64
	Learn new words	65, 66
	Form words from other words	67
	Choose titles	68, 92
	Context	69, 82, 84
	Inference	70, 78, 93
	Word identification and classification	71, 76, 91
	Rhyming words	72
	Word meanings	73
	Recall information read	74
	Find facts and details	75, 90
	Find information on a graph	77
	Main idea, inference	78
	Main idea	78, 79, 95
	Consonant blends / vocabulary extension	80
	Word appreciation	81
	Sequence	83
	Identify character and setting	85
	Interpret illustrations	86
	Draw conclusions	87
	Alliteration	88
	Match sentences with pictures	89, 96
	Follow directions	94
	Make predictions	97

SKILLS CHECKLIST
SPELLING, LANGUAGE, WRITING, & USAGE

✔	SKILL	PAGE(S)
	Identify and read beginning and ending consonants	20, 21, 23–29
	Correctly spell words with double consonants	98
	Correctly spell words with confusing initial consonants: *c* & *s*; *c* & *k*; *j* & *g*; *s* & *z*	99
	Identify words spelled correctly	99, 102, 110, 114
	Correctly spell words with silent *e*	100, 101
	Correct words that are spelled incorrectly	101, 106
	Correctly spell words in which the letter *s* is prominent	102
	Identify words spelled incorrectly	102, 115
	Correctly spell words in which the letter *q* is prominent	103
	Correctly spell words in which the letter *o* is prominent	104
	Correctly spell words in which the letters *w*, *x*, *y*, or *z* are prominent	105
	Correctly spell big words	106
	Correctly spell small words	107
	Correctly spell proper names	109
	Correctly spell difficult words	110
	Correctly spell number words	112
	Correctly spell animal names	113
	Identify and write nouns	116–121
	Identify and write verbs	116, 117, 122, 123
	Identify, write, and capitalize proper nouns	119, 128
	Identify and write plural nouns	120
	Identify and write possessive nouns	121
	Identify complete sentences and fix sentence fragments	124
	Recognize and correct run-on sentences	125
	Identify, capitalize, and punctuate statements	127, 131
	Identify, capitalize, and punctuate questions	126, 131
	Identify common contractions and the words that form them	129
	Capitalize words in sentences	128
	Identify different punctuation marks and their uses	130, 131
	Generate and organize ideas for writing	132–139
	Express original ideas clearly in writing	133–136
	Choose effective, interesting words for writing	132
	Write phrases for a poster	133
	Use collected ideas to create a written piece	134, 135
	Write a short imaginative piece	136, 137
	Write character descriptions	138, 139

Choose Your Adventure!

The signs tell about some exciting adventures.
Look at all the signs.
　Circle the **beginning consonants or blends** with red.
　Circle the **ending consonants or blends** with blue.

Welcome to the Worldwide Adventure Company. We have thrilling adventures for everyone.

Sounds good.

Unusual Adventures!
Fight a fire-breathing dragon.
Ride a barrel over Niagara Falls.
Look inside meat-eating plants.
Steer a boat around icebergs.
Surf a monstrous wave.
Rocket through the solar system.
Follow a rare mountain gorilla.
Travel into the past.
Explore deep, dark caves.

Far Off Adventures!
Sahara Desert
Great Wall of China
Deep Amazon Rain Forest
Beautiful Swiss Alps
High Himalayan Mountains
Great Coral Reef
Wild Alaska Wilderness

Name _____

Use with page 21.

Beginning, Middle, & Ending Consonants

Choose Your Adventure, cont.

Search for consonants or consonant blends in the middle of words.
Circle the **middle consonants** or **blends** with green.

Most Unusual Places.....

The coldest spot on Earth
The hottest spot on Earth
The highest spot on Earth
The lowest spot on Earth
Earth's biggest desert
Earth's longest caves

Most Exciting Rides.......

Ferris wheel   helicopter
tornado   parachute
camel   elephant
rocket   time machine
giraffe   bucking bronco

Most Dangerous Adventures.....

Swamp Cruising
Bullfighting
Lion Taming
Alligator Wrestling
Moose Tracking
Chasing the Wild Boar
Tracking the Mountain Gorilla
Hurricane Watching
Log Rolling
Stalking Bigfoot

We're off to ride a camel!

Hold on tight!

blurp

POP POP

The Adventure Company

screech

Name _____

Use with page 20.

21

Beginning, Middle, & Ending Consonants

A Bumpy Camel Ride

When you read about the camel ride, you will see that some words are missing. Choose a word from the **Word Box** to fill in each blank.

Look for the consonants in the middle of the words.

Circle the middle consonants. (There are two in the middle of some words!)

The _____ has two humps.

You will have fun _____ this _____ creature!

You can_____ yourself right between the two humps and hold on tight.

The Bactrian camel has wide flat feet to keep it from _____ into the soft ground.

Bring _____ for warm and cool temperatures.

The grassland home of the camel is sometimes hot like a _____.

At night, it gets close to _____.

On your adventure you may see a suslik, which is an animal like a _____. He digs in _____ or tunnels.

Look out for a poisonous _____!

He is the _____ desert snake!

Adventure # 1
Ride a furry Bactrian camel through the grasslands of Asia. Bring your camera, and be prepared for a bumpy, lumpy ride!

Giddy-up

WORD BOX

viper	desert
camel	freezing
riding	burrows
clothing	fuzzy
sinking	settle
rodent	largest

Name _____

Reptile Races

Adventure # 2

Travel to the desert to watch a race between the Tricky Lizard and the Sticky-Tongued Snake. Which one will get the *yummy* first prize?

Which one do *you* think is *the* fastest?

The Tricky Lizard can only follow words that begin with the **tr** blend. Color his path to the prize **green.**

The Sticky-Tongued Snake can only follow words that begin with the **st** blend. Color his path to the prize **yellow.**

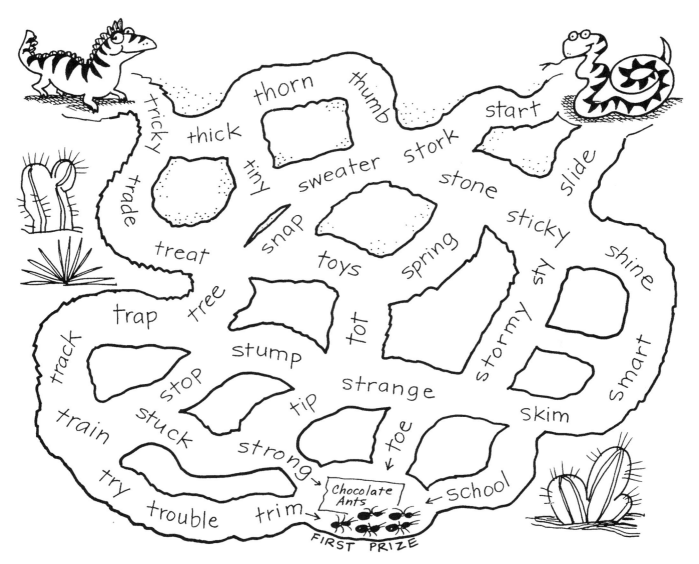

tricky
thick
thorn
thumb
start
trade
tiny
sweater
stork
stone
slide
treat
snap
sticky
shine
trap
tree
toys
spring
sty
stormy
smart
track
stump
tot
skim
stop
tip
strange
train
stuck
strong
toe
school
try
trouble
trim
Chocolate Ants
FIRST PRIZE

Which animal has the shortest path? (Circle one.)   **snake**   **lizard**

Name _____

Consonant Blends

A Low-Down Place

The trench is filled with **s** blends that can be used to begin words.

Make a word by writing an **s** blend at the beginning of each word on the right.

Adventure # 3

You bring the camera! We'll bring the submarine! You can explore the lowest spot on Earth!

sk

squ

sc

sw

sl

st

sm

sn

sp

The lowest spot known in the Pacific Ocean is the Challenger Deep in the Mariana Trench. The Challenger Deep is 35,840 feet (10,924 meters) below the surface.

The Adventure Co. Submarine

1. _____ ick

2. _____ ile

3. _____ arf

4. _____ at

5. _____ iff

6. _____ irrel

7. _____ ate

8. _____ ray

9. _____ ail

10. _____ im

11. _____ oon

12. _____ ip

13. _____ unk

14. _____ eep

15. _____ ash

16. _____ oop

17. _____ ing

18. _____ op

Name _____

A High-in-the-Sky Place

Adventure # 4

It will be a hard climb for our airplane, but you'll love the view! If you dare, fly with us to the highest point on Earth.

The mountain is filled with **l** and **r** blends that can be used to begin words. Make a word by writing one of the blends at the beginning of each word.

1. _____ own
2. _____ ue
3. _____ ite
4. _____ ing
5. _____ og
6. _____ oat
7. _____ ass
8. _____ ain
9. _____ ippery
10. _____ ate
11. _____ eek
12. _____ y
13. _____ ip
14. _____ ide
15. _____ ong
16. _____ ow
17. _____ ick
18. _____ op

Mt. Everest, in Nepal, is 29,035 feet (8,850 meters) tall. It is called the world's highest mountain.

The Adventure Company

bl
cr
pl
cl
gl
fr
sl
br
dr
fl
wr
tr
pr

Name _____

L & R **Blends**

Through the Iceberg Maze

Adventure # 5

Bring warm clothes and be ready for a challenge.
We're heading across an icy ocean, and we have a lot of icebergs to dodge.

Color icebergs blue if the words begin or end with these digraphs: **sh, th,** or **ch.**

Draw a path across the water that passes near these icebergs.

wing

chip

bush

mink

math   skin

sock   chin

stuck   thumb   scale   jump

milk

shop   catch   brisk

worst   sang

wish

risk   duck

birch

scoot   with

Draw a circle around these beginnings and endings:
ng   nk   ck
lk   st
mp   sk
sc

The Adventure Co. Sea Craft

Name _____

Beginning & Ending Digraphs

Copyright © 2016 World Book, Inc./
Incentive Publications, Chicago, IL

Over the Edge

The words in the barrel were shaken up so much that they have split apart.

Use a crayon or marker to circle the parts that belong together.

Write the words on the lines.

ju mp cr
fl oat dr ink ash
sw im scr pr owl
str ike eam tri ck

1. _____

2. _____

3. _____

4. _____

5. _____

6. _____

7. _____

8. _____

9. _____

Name _____

Consonant Blends & Digraphs

The Super Ferris Wheel

The words on the seats have double consonants in them.

Circle the double consonants in each word.

Then choose the best word to fit in each sentence.

sunny

chilly

cotton

terrific

funny

arrow

puddle

worry

giggle

furry

wedding

1. I was beginning to _____ about this ride.

2. We're glad it is a bright _____ day at the fair.

3. The wind is a little _____ way up high.

4. I should have worn something warmer than a _____ shirt.

5. We started to _____ when we got near the top.

6. Look! Someone is having a _____ right here at the fair!

7. It's _____ how small people look down below.

8. This was an exciting, _____ ride!

Name _____

Double Consonants

Snorkeling the Great Reef

Draw a line to connect the names in alphabetical order.

Then you will see another sea creature.

What is it?

Adventure # 8

Learn to snorkel! Watch some of the most interesting creatures beneath the sea!

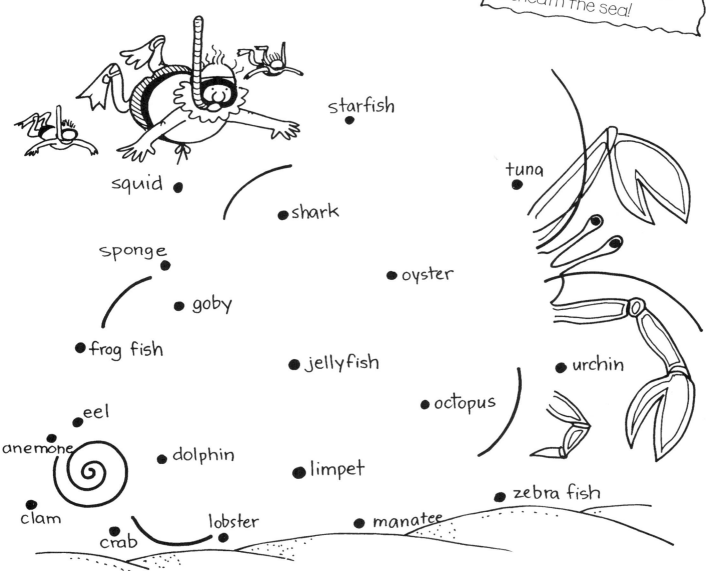

starfish

squid

shark

tuna

sponge

oyster

goby

frog fish

jellyfish

urchin

octopus

eel

anemone

dolphin

limpet

clam

zebra fish

lobster

manatee

crab

Name _____

Alphabetizing

Deep in the Rain Forest

The rain forest is filled with unusual plants and lost vowels.

Write the missing vowels into the words in the picture.

Then write the first vowel from words 1, 3, 5, and 7 into the blanks in number 11.

You'll spell the name of a very long jungle animal.

Name _____

The Bullfight

When the bullfighter enters the ring, he must go carefully toward the bull.
Color a path for him that follows the words with short vowel sounds.

run sun bull

crowd cheer red

cape fight fear trip

careful pay snort shoe fall rip cone

skip cloak

horns mud hop crazy

rosy flop

cheer flick

able stop

Adventure # 10
Are you really brave
enough for this?
Fighting an angry bull
is a tough job.
Get your red cape
ready, and be fast on
your feet!

Name _____

Short Vowels

Clowning Around

Follow all the directions.
Then circle all the words with
long vowel sounds.

Adventure # 11

Did you ever think you would like to join a circus?
Here's your chance to spend some time at the circus.
Start off your visit by getting to know a clown.

1. Draw a bow in the clown's hair.

2. Draw a smile on her face.

3. Draw a kite in the air.

4. Draw a string from the kite to her hand.

5. Draw an ice cream cone in her other hand.

6. Color her nose red.

7. Color her cape green.

8. Draw a rose on each shoe.

9. Draw a cupcake in her pocket.

10. Draw a balloon for her pet.

Color the clown carefully.

Name _____

Lion-Sized Thrills

Help make the lion's cage strong enough to hold the lion.
Color the squares in the cage where the words have long vowels with a **silent e** at the end (such as **cage, bite, bones,** and **cute**).

Adventure # 12
Here's a really thrilling circus adventure! Learn how the lion tamer tames a fierce lion.

If you find at least 20, you'll keep the lion tamer safe and healthy.

sting	tame	drool	beet	drone	paws	rate	cage	shop	help	fun	cake
page	whip	tooth			stale	furry	smile	maul	dine	boot	
slope	door	bee	ate		mate	tail	claws	page	lock	key	
sea	cape	roar			June	sneer	cone	chair	white	door	
rose	black	sleep			ape	plate	sharp	yelp	twist	rage	

Name _____

Long Vowels with Silent *e*

Moose Tracking

Adventure # 13

Tracking the wild moose is quite a skill.
You can learn to follow moose in the north
woods of Canada and Alaska.
No shooting is allowed—except with a camera!

As you read about the moose, look for words with double vowels.

Write these words on the lines. Write each word only once. How many different words can you find?

More tourists.

There is a big, goofy-looking moose on the loose in the deep woods of northern Canada. Look! Can you see his trail of moose prints? What huge feet he has! The track of each foot is six inches long. He needs these large feet when he moves through cool pools and ponds looking for food. He likes to feed on plants and never eats toadstools or beetles. The moose is very quiet, so he is hard to find. This moose lives in Canada. Moose live in Alaska, too! But this moose would probably never live in a zoo. He would rather be free!

List the words that you found.

1. _____   8. _____   15. _____
2. _____   9. _____   16. _____
3. _____   10. _____   17. _____
4. _____   11. _____   18. _____
5. _____   12. _____   19. _____
6. _____   13. _____   20. _____
7. _____   14. _____

There are ____ different words with double vowels.

Name _____

Double Vowels

Rhino Watching

Read about the rhino and his bird friends.
Look for words that have vowel combinations
that give a **long e** sound.
(This sound can be made by **e, ee, ie,** or **ea.**)
Circle the words that have a **long e** sound.

Adventure # 14
Come to Africa to watch
the great rhinoceros.
You'll find out that the rhino
has some important friends.

The rhinoceros is an odd-looking beast that is said to be related to early dinosaurs. These days, there are not many rhinos left in Africa. Some hunters seek them out and kill them to take their large horns.

Their friends, the egrets (pronounced ee-grets), come in flocks to sit on the backs of the rhinos and other large animals. The egrets sit on the animals' backs and wait for them to kick up insects with their feet. Then the egrets quickly fly down to eat up the insects. This is a good friendship, because the birds get a meal and the rhinos get rid of bothersome insects.

Name _____

A Helicopter Flight

Adventure # 15

Get on board our Adventure helicopter!
You'll have the most exciting ride.
We'll follow the crow through the clouds to his lunch.
Everywhere he goes, we'll go, too!

Color the clouds with words having the sound made by **ow** in the word **crow.**

Draw a path for the crow that follows those clouds.

down

clown

tow

town

low

crown   know   brown

plow

cow

mow   how

show

growl

grow   now

prowl   snow   flow

Name _____

Vowel Combination: *ow*

Meet the Meat Eaters

Meat-eating plants give off sweet-smelling, sticky nectar.

The smell attracts insects and other small creatures.

The sticky stuff keeps them from getting away!

Adventure # 16
Visit meat-eating plants around the world!
But keep your fingers in your pockets!

Use the vowel combinations in the plants to finish the words before the plant snaps shut!

1. p____n

2. c____ght

3. fr____ndly

4. d____dly

5. ____t

6. h____t

7. m____t

8. ____ch!

9. b____t

10. m____l

11. p____son

12. retr____t

13. m____th

14. gl____

15. h____rs

16. t____ch

17. ab____t

18. ag____nst

ea

oa

oi
ai
au

ue
ou
ie

Don't worry! These plants don't eat humans.

Name _____

Vowel Combinations

Fire Danger!

Adventure # 17
Take a trip into the long-ago past to battle a fire-breathing dragon. Get into your knight's metal suit and don't forget to bring a sword!

To tame the dragon, circle all the vowels or vowel combinations that make a **long a** sound (such as in **tame**).

Hint: look for **ai, ey, ay,** and **a with a silent e** at the end of the word!

Fire!

Rules for Fighting a Dragon

1. Don't expect the dragon to be playful.
2. Take a sharp sword.
3. Don't be afraid.
4. Don't step on its tail.
5. Wave your sword wildly.
6. Aim straight for its heart.
7. Shout, "Hey! Go away!"
8. Escape before it's too late.

Name _____

Vowel Combinations: Long *a*

Hurricane Watch

Solve each riddle with a word that has something to do with a storm.

Each word has a vowel combination of **ea**, **ai**, **ou**, or **oa**.

Adventure # 18

Hurricane Matilda is storming in.
We can watch the storm, but not from the boat.
We'll get to shore and find a safe place for watching.

Riddle 1

Get me out of the water
When the wind starts to blow.
Row me right to the shore,
And don't be slow!

I am a _____.
(I rhyme with "float.")

Riddle 3

Don't play here today
With your shovel and pail!
You'll get swept out to sea
And get pounded with hail.

I am the _____.
(I rhyme with "peach.")

Riddle 2

We're crashing waves.
We toss ships around.
We wash over beaches
And cover the ground.

Our sound is _____.
(It rhymes with "crowd.")

Riddle 4

I pour from the skies
And drench the land.
I blow in your windows
And soak into the sand.

I am the _____.
(I rhyme with "pane.")

Name _____

Vowel Combinations: *ai, oa, ou, ea*

Yodel with a Yeti

Adventure # 19

Come hiking in the high Himalayan Mountains!
Old stories called legends say that a great, white creature can be seen there.
He's called a Yeti (or an abominable snowman).
You also might hear some yodeling in the mountains. (Is it the Yeti?!!)
You can even learn to yodel yourself.

Yodel-lay-dee-hoo!

Yodel-lady back at you.

today   yes   try   Yeti
lucky
yodeled   yelled
yellow
easily   yummy   snowy
fly   yank   silly
yikes!

The words on the mountain all have at least one **y**.
Sometimes **y** is a consonant, such as in **yet** or **yell**.
Sometimes **y** is a vowel, such as in **spy, key, stay,** or **funny**.
When **y** is a vowel, it helps make a **long a, long i,** or **long e** sound.
Write the words in the correct place below.
You will need to write one word in both places.

Words with **y** as a consonant:

_____ _____

_____ _____

_____ _____

_____ _____

Words with **y** as a vowel:

_____ _____

_____ _____

_____ _____

_____ _____

Name _____

Stalk a Sasquatch

Adventure # 20

It is said that a big hairy creature with huge feet
stalks the woods of the Northwest United States.
Join the searchers for the Sasquatch (also
known as Bigfoot).
You must walk in silence.
Listen for the sound of big feet walking.

Color the footprints that contain
silent letters.
This will show you the path to follow.

silent
forest
comb
ketchuP
lamb
write
knead
limb
follow
plumber
wren
plum
waiting
dinner
wrist
creature
post
woods
crumbs
cot
bag
feet
know
climb
step
trees
shiver
elbow
watch
stalk
knob
tons
walk

START HERE

come along!

Name _____

Silent Letters

Hunt for Pirate's Treasure

Adventure # 21

Bring a shovel and a sack for treasure. We'll provide the map! Take a trip to the deserted Island of the Bones and dig for pirate's treasure.

What is in the treasure chest?

Look for words in the puzzle that name things that could be inside the chest. Circle any possible "treasures" you find.

(Words can be left to right, right to left, up and down, or down and up!)

```
B  H  T  E  E  T  O  S  I  S
O  Y  D  N  A  C  X  H  E  L
O  Y  S  T  E  R  S  O  S  E
K  D  W  O  R  M  S  E  P  W
S  I  L  V  E  R  C  S  O  E
L  A  U  N  D  R  Y  M  O  J
O  M  G  M  U  D  S  A  N  D
C  O  O  K  I  E  S  R  S  U
A  N  L  S  E  N  O  B  I  G
O  D  D  B  O  T  T  L  E  S
R  S  H  E  L  L  S  E  Z  Y
C  O  C  O  N  U  T  S  G  R
```

There are 20 "treasures" in the puzzle. How many did you find?_____

Name _____

Use Phonics to Read Whole Words

The Sea Turtle Races

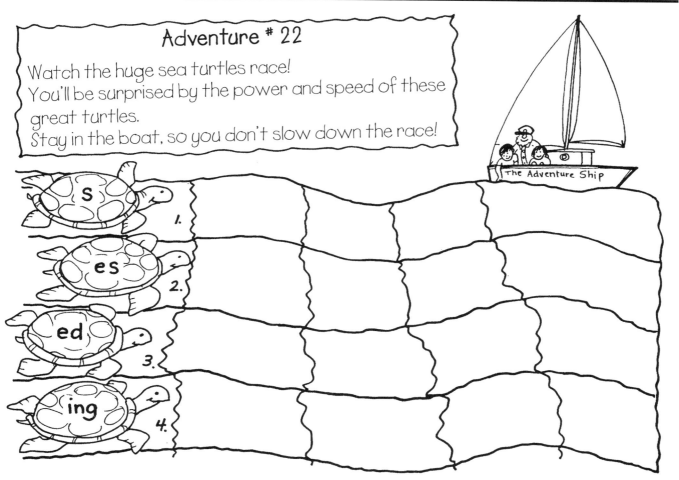

Adventure # 22

Watch the huge sea turtles race!
You'll be surprised by the power and speed of these great turtles.
Stay in the boat, so you don't slow down the race!

The Adventure Ship

Write the correct ending in each blank in the sentences. Use **s, es, ed,** or **ing.**
Each time you use an ending, color one part of its lane.

1. Will you be watch_____ the race today?

2. Leatherback turtles have weigh_____ up to 1,500 pounds.

3. Turtles have thick heavy legs for walk_____.

4. Some turtles have liv_____ to be 100 years old!

5. Who shout_____ the loudest during the race?

6. We have been wait_____ a long time for the race.

7. Turtle number one trick_____ them every year.

8. I pick_____ the winner!

Which turtle gets the farthest? _____

Name _____

Inflectional Endings

The Big Jump

Unpack your parachute and get ready for the jump of your life! Follow all the safety rules.

Finish the words by adding one of the prefixes from the parachute.

Each time you use a prefix, color its section. Be sure to color each section a different color.

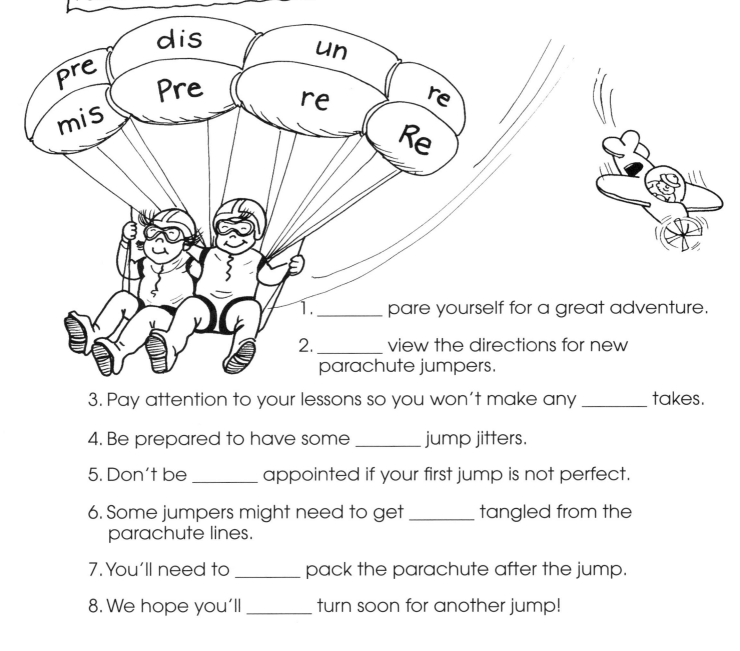

Prefixes on parachute: pre, mis, dis, Pre, un, re, re, Re

1. _____ pare yourself for a great adventure.

2. _____ view the directions for new parachute jumpers.

3. Pay attention to your lessons so you won't make any _____ takes.

4. Be prepared to have some _____ jump jitters.

5. Don't be _____ appointed if your first jump is not perfect.

6. Some jumpers might need to get _____ tangled from the parachute lines.

7. You'll need to _____ pack the parachute after the jump.

8. We hope you'll _____ turn soon for another jump!

Name _____

Prefixes

Log Rolling on the River

Adventure # 24

The slippery, rolling logs are the only way across the Raging Rapids River. The river is deep and cold, and it moves fast. Watch your step!

Choose the correct suffix to complete each word in the sentences.

Use the suffixes in the box at the bottom of the page.

Each time you finish a word, color that log.

1. The logs are the only poss_____ way to cross the river.

2. Choose the logs wise_____.

3. Don't be care_____ as you cross.

4. The rushing waters are very danger_____.

5. The water is more power_____ than you might think.

6. It would be fool_____ to think this is easy.

7. It is import_____ to move quick___.

8. Show your friendli_____ by offering help to someone else.

9. Is this a good way to spend your vaca_____?

10. There will be much excite_____ when you get across.

ment	ous	ness	less	ant
ful	ly	ible	ish	tion

Name _____

Suffixes

Visit a Desert Hotel

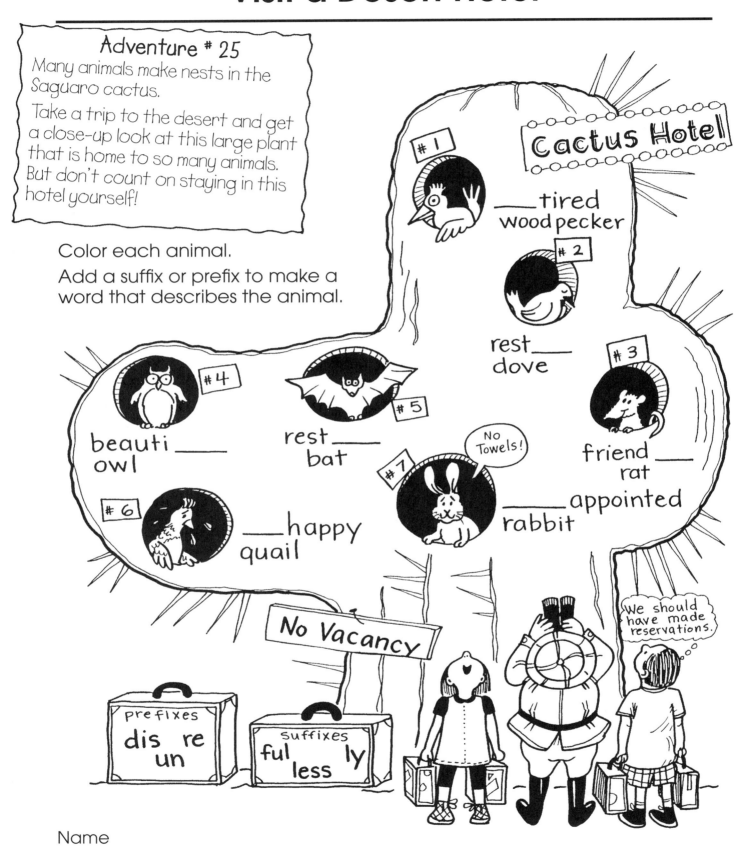

Adventure # 25

Many animals make nests in the Saguaro cactus.

Take a trip to the desert and get a close-up look at this large plant that is home to so many animals. But don't count on staying in this hotel yourself!

Color each animal.

Add a suffix or prefix to make a word that describes the animal.

Cactus Hotel

#1 ___tired woodpecker

#2 rest___ dove

#3 friend___ rat

#4 beauti___ owl

#5 rest___ bat

#6 ___happy quail

#7 ___rabbit No Towels!

___appointed

No Vacancy

prefixes dis re un

suffixes ful less ly

We should have made reservations.

Name _____

Nighttime Snooping

A **root word** is a word that was there before prefixes or suffixes were added.

Look at the bold word in each of these sentences about nocturnal animals.

Decide what the root word is.

Write it on the line.

1. The platypus is such an **unusual** animal. _____

2. Koala bears have **disappeared** from many areas. _____

3. The **poisonous** leaves of the eucalyptus tree do not harm koalas. _____

4. **Quietly** the desert shrew moves through the desert. _____

5. The Tasmanian devil is the **strangest** animal. _____

6. A marsupial mouse lemur sleeps **peacefully** all day. _____

7. Australia is home to some of the **largest** bats. _____

8. It's **unbelievable** how possums can spend so much time upside-down! _____

9. A Victoria koala lives in the **coldest** part of Australia. _____

10. Stay around for daylight, and watch the **powerful** kangaroos jumping. _____

Name _____

Rodeo Ride

Read the word at the top of each group.
Draw a lasso around the word that is
the correct root word.

Remember: A **root word** is the word
without any prefixes or suffixes added to it.

> **Adventure # 27**
> Ride a bucking bronco!
> Learn to lasso an untamed calf!
> Bring your riding boots and
> prepare to get saddle sores!

1. unstoppable

stop   able

unstop

stoppable

2. dangerous

danger

dan

dang

3. working

or

work

king

I'm as skillful with a lasso as a real cowgirl.

4. disagreeable

disagree

agreeable

agree   dis

5. blameless

am less blame

6. finest

fine   fin   nest

7. neighborhood

neigh   bor

neighbor

8. careful

full   are   care

9. untamed

un   tame

tamed   tam

This bronco is full of wildness!

snort snort

10. unfriendliness

unfriendly   friendly

friendliness   friend

I hope I don't mistakenly lasso myself!

Name _____

Root Words

A Swamp Cruise

Read all the words the characters are saying.
Pay attention to the number of syllables in the words.
Write one word on each line in the boxes below.

Welcome to Mosquito Swamp.
Don't fall out of the canoe, little explorers.
You might lose your hat in the river.
This wild alligator has dangerous teeth.
Taming him would be an impossibility!
Perhaps we should exit the swamp now.

Don't you want to wrestle?

one-syllable words:	two-syllable words:	three-syllable words:
_____	_____	_____
_____	_____	_____
_____	_____	_____
_____	_____	_____

Write a word with four syllables. _____

Write a word with six syllables. _____

Name _____

Syllables

Tornado Alert!

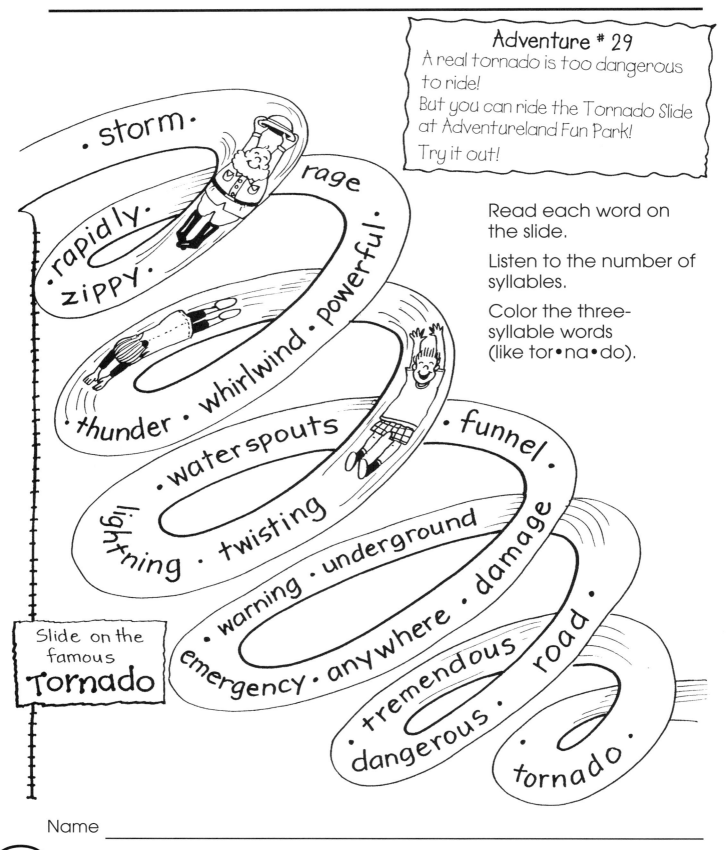

Adventure # 29

A real tornado is too dangerous to ride!

But you can ride the Tornado Slide at Adventureland Fun Park!

Try it out!

Read each word on the slide.

Listen to the number of syllables.

Color the three-syllable words (like tor•na•do).

Slide on the famous **Tornado**

storm • rapidly • zippy • rage • powerful • whirlwind • thunder • waterspouts • lightning • twisting • funnel • warning • underground • damage • anywhere • tremendous • road • emergency • dangerous • tornado

Name _____

Volcanic Visit

Each sentence has two words that can form a contraction.
Color the matching contraction in the puzzle.
What word appears? _____

Puzzle words: don't, be, is, you're, you'll, weave, who's, couldn't, we've, isn't, there, shouldn't, aren't, they're, art, we'll, your, you've, K a, M

1. This volcano is not Mt. St. Helens.

2. Who is living near the active volcano?

3. The last visitors could not find the crater.

4. Many volcanoes are not finished changing.

5. We hope you are bringing a lunch with you.

6. You should not hike on an erupting volcano.

7. We will stay away from any lava flows.

8. They are getting too close to the side of the volcano!

9. You have found a vent at the side of the volcano.

10. We have seen some amazing sites at this volcano.

11. We do not know where the magma chamber is located.

12. You will enjoy hiking on the volcano when it stops acting up.

Name _____

Contractions

Go Spelunking!

In each sentence below, combine the two words in **bold type** to form a contraction.

Write the contraction on the line.

Then color the part of the cave that matches the sentence.

1. **They will** walk through the opening into the cave. _____

2. **She will** move carefully down the path._____

3. **I have** just found a stalagmite on the floor of the cavern._____

4. We expect **you will** see some bats hanging in the corners._____

5. **Do not** forget to carry two lights at all times. _____

6. **You would** be smart to wear a helmet into the cave. _____

7. **We will** count the stalactites hanging from the ceiling._____

8. **It is** always good to see the light again when you leave the cave. _____

Name _____

Contractions

Alaska Camp Out

1. Add a word from the woodpile to form a compound word on each tent.

2. Then write 10 more compound words made from words in the woodpile. You can use words in more than one compound word.

1. _____

2. _____

3. _____

4. _____

5. _____

6. _____

7. _____

8. _____

9. _____

10. _____

Name _____

Compound Words

The Wild Boar Chase

1. Chase the wild boar through the maze of words.

2. Color only the spaces with words that are spelled correctly.

3. Then write the numbered letters on the lines at the bottom to find the name of some things in Borneo that are very large.

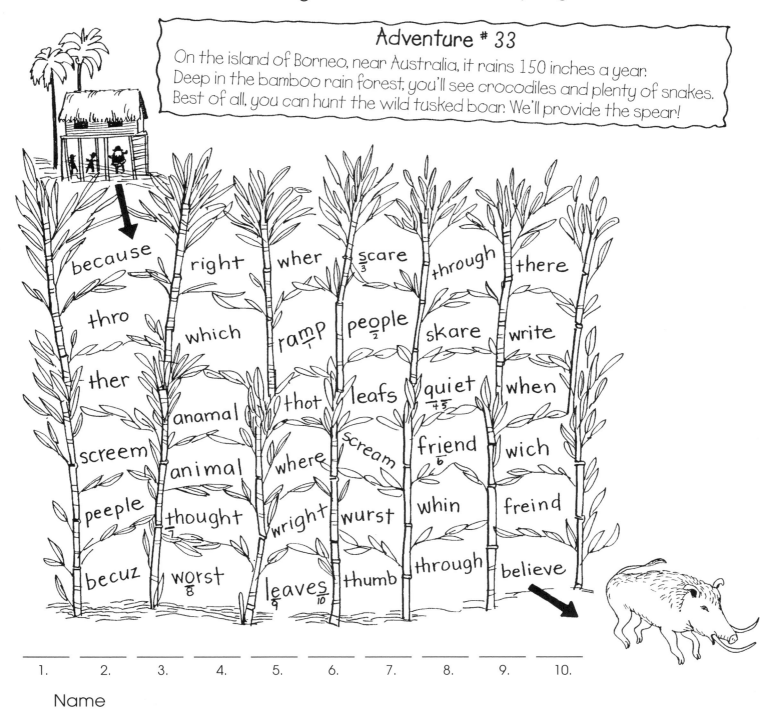

Adventure # 33

On the island of Borneo, near Australia, it rains 150 inches a year. Deep in the bamboo rain forest, you'll see crocodiles and plenty of snakes. Best of all, you can hunt the wild tusked boar. We'll provide the spear!

because   right   wher   scare (3)   through   there

thro   which   ramp (1)   people (2)   skare   write

ther   anamal   thot   leafs   quiet (4 5)   when

screem   animal   where   scream   friend (6)   wich

peeple   thought (7)   wright   wurst   whin   freind

becuz   worst (8)   leaves (9)   thumb   through   believe

1. ___ 2. ___ 3. ___ 4. ___ 5. ___ 6. ___ 7. ___ 8. ___ 9. ___ 10. ___

Name _____

Similar Words • Spelling

A Lot of Hot Air

The balloon is decorated with homonyms.

Homonyms are words that sound the same but are spelled differently.

1. Choose a homonym from the balloon to write in each blank.

2. Circle the homonym that you choose.

3. Then color the design on the balloon.

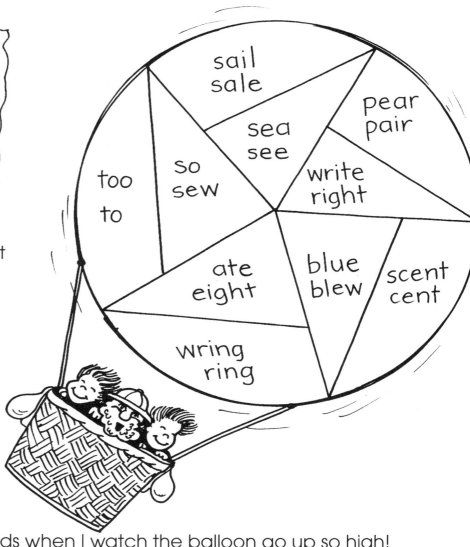

1. I _____ my hands when I watch the balloon go up so high!

2. While I waited for my turn, I _____ my whole lunch.

3. The _____ was the best part of my lunch.

4. Would it be hard work to _____ designs on the balloon?

5. Will we _____ over the _____ today.

6. We'll enjoy the fresh _____ of the air, _____.

7. I'll _____ postcards while I float through the air.

8. I heard the wind _____ one balloon very fast yesterday.

Name _____

Ski the Alps

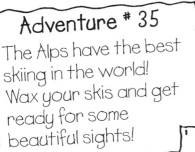

Adventure # 35

The Alps have the best skiing in the world! Wax your skis and get ready for some beautiful sights!

The answers to the mountain puzzle are all homonyms.

Homonyms sound alike, but do not look alike. One word in each clue sentence is the wrong homonym.

Write the correct homonym into the puzzle.

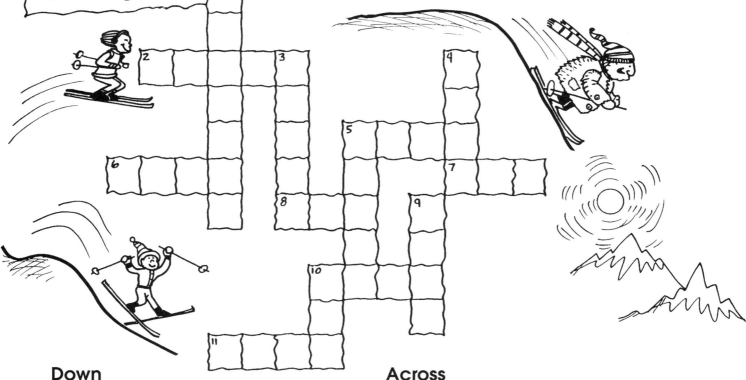

Down

1. The king rained for twenty years.

3. Good shoppers always look for sails.

4. The wind blue down a tree.

5. Let's take a ride in a plain.

9. "Please come hear."

10. This morning there was do on the grass.

Across

2. I have ten pears of socks.

5. She will pair the potatoes.

6. The storyteller told a tall tail.

7. Which weigh do we go?

8. She rowed her boat in the see.

10. I sent a letter to my deer aunt.

11. They new the truth.

Name _____

Track the Mountain Gorilla

Proper nouns name special people, places, or things.

They start with capital letters.

Circle the proper nouns that should be capitalized.

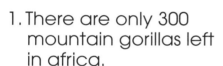

Adventure # 36

A mountain gorilla is not easy to find. It is a member of an endangered species. We'll take you to a place where you can track one down (just to look at). Then we'll search around the world for other endangered species.

1. There are only 300 mountain gorillas left in africa.

2. A scientist named dr. kenwick studies endangered animals.

3. The city of ashland, oregon, is the home of the national forensic laboratory where scientists work to protect endangered animals.

4. Many species of birds in new zealand are endangered.

5. On saturday we'll go to the library to read about the spanish lynx.

6. During the month of april we will travel to mexico to see more animals.

7. We'll return to the united states to visit the florida panther.

Name _____

Proper Nouns

Elephant Ride

The elephant is filled with nouns (names of things).
Plural nouns name more than one of something.

Most names are made plural by adding **s**.

If a noun ends in **sh, ss, ch, z,** or **x**, add **es** to make it plural.

Add **s** or **es** to make these words plural.

If you add **s,** color the section **gray.**

If you add **es,** color it **any other color.**

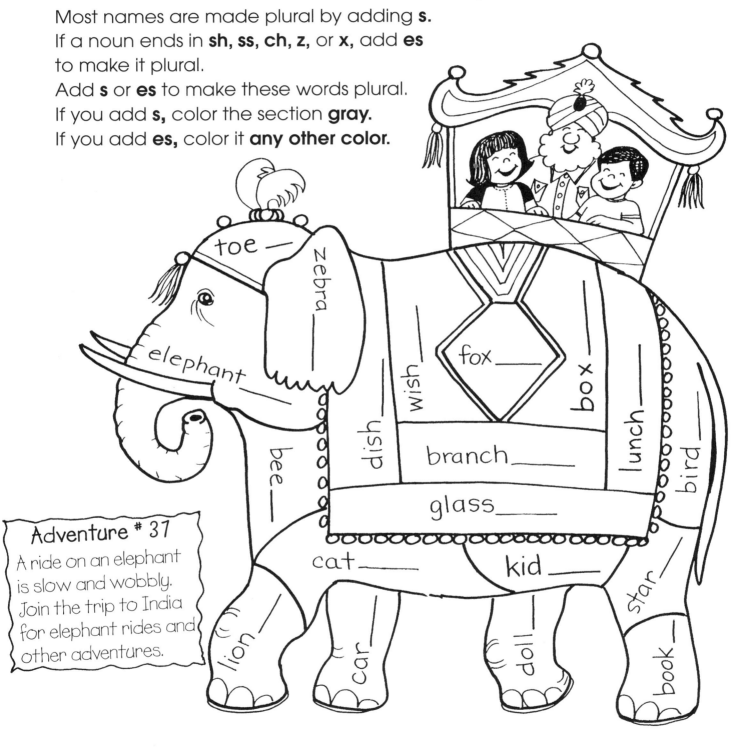

Adventure # 37

A ride on an elephant is slow and wobbly. Join the trip to India for elephant rides and other adventures.

toe ____
zebra ____
elephant ____
bee ____
dish ____
wish ____
fox ____
box ____
lunch ____
bird ____
branch ____
glass ____
cat ____
kid ____
star ____
lion ____
car ____
doll ____
book ____

Name _____

Visit the Crowded Sahara

We write the animal's name in a special way to show that it owns something.

This makes the name a **possessive noun.**

Add **'s** to each animal's name to show that something belongs to it.

Adventure # 38
It's the largest desert in the world!
You see open spaces for hundreds of miles.
But if you look closely, you will see that it is filled with animals.
Come meet some of the interesting animals of the Sahara!

jerboa

addax

chameleon

scorpion

1. The desert scorpion _____ sting is as poisonous as the bite of a cobra.

2. The sand cat _____ paws have thick fur under its feet to keep it from sinking into the soft sand.

3. A prickly desert hedgehog _____ favorite meal is a scorpion after it bites off the stinger in its tail.

4. The jerboa _____ jump can cover eight feet in a single bound.

5. The addax _____ hooves are wide so it can travel quickly over the soft sand.

6. The chameleon _____ long, sticky tongue allows it to catch insects easily.

7. A male sandgrouse _____ trick for feeding its young is to sit in water until his belly feathers are soaked to the skin. Then the chicks drink from his feathers.

8. The vulture _____ job is to clean up dead animals.

You might want to take notes on these wild and crazy guys!

Name _____

Possessive Nouns

Catch a Great Wave!

Here's how to catch a great wave.
Look at the word each surfer is saying.

Then write three synonyms for that word in the "talk balloons."

Synonyms are words that mean the same thing!

Adventure # 39
The Pacific Ocean is the place for the great waves! If you want to learn to surf, this is the place to come.

Great!

Huge!

Scared!

Name _____

Catch a Giraffe Ride

Adventure # 40

In the grasslands of Africa, the grass is taller than you are.

That's why it's a good idea to catch a ride on a giraffe.

His long legs will keep you up out of the grass so you can see the sights!

WORDS

OPPOSITES

1. tall   1. _____
2. thin   2. _____
3. happy   3. _____
4. dirty   4. _____
5. together   5. _____
6. dangerous   6. _____
7. top   7. _____
8. weak   8. _____
9. young   9. _____
10. close   10. _____

The young giraffe wonders if you can think of opposites **(antonyms)** for all these words.

Each time you write an opposite, color a spot on the giraffe.

Name _____

Antonyms

Galaxy Cruising

Adventure # 41

Cruise the galaxy in our deluxe star cruiser.
See all the planets! Search for new stars!
Look for black holes and wormholes!
Look out for meteors and asteroids!

Find pairs of stars that are
synonyms (same meaning).
Color them yellow.

Find pairs of stars that are
antonyms (opposites).
Color them red.

Name _____

Synonyms & Antonyms

A Scuba Lesson

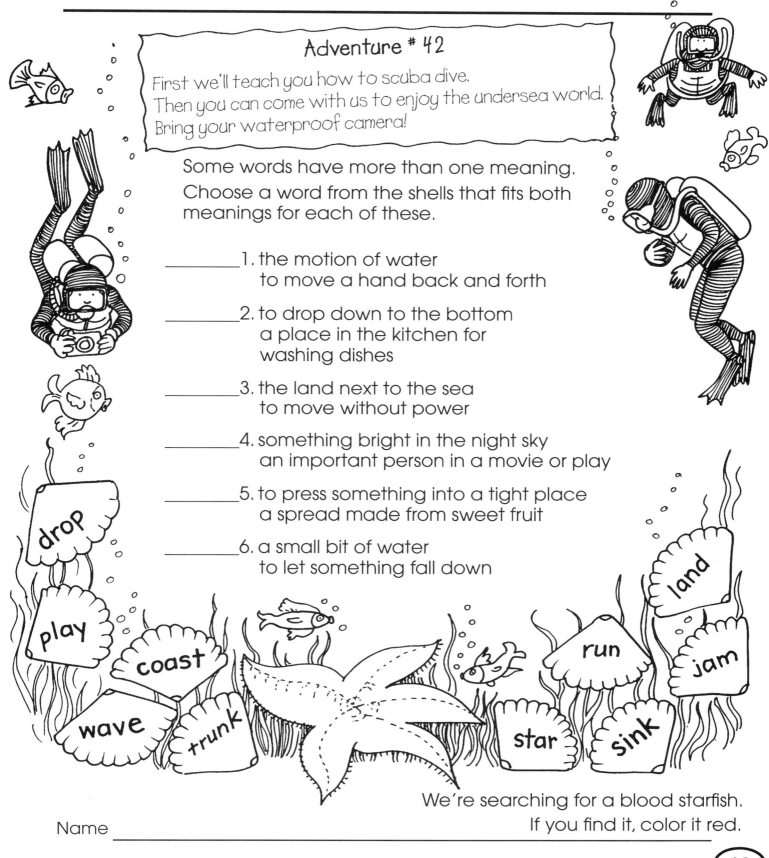

Adventure # 42

First we'll teach you how to scuba dive.
Then you can come with us to enjoy the undersea world.
Bring your waterproof camera!

Some words have more than one meaning.
Choose a word from the shells that fits both meanings for each of these.

_____ 1. the motion of water
to move a hand back and forth

_____ 2. to drop down to the bottom
a place in the kitchen for
washing dishes

_____ 3. the land next to the sea
to move without power

_____ 4. something bright in the night sky
an important person in a movie or play

_____ 5. to press something into a tight place
a spread made from sweet fruit

_____ 6. a small bit of water
to let something fall down

drop

play

coast

wave

trunk

land

jam

run

star

sink

We're searching for a blood starfish.
If you find it, color it red.

Name _____

Multiple Meanings

Hike the Great Wall

Adventure # 43

It is one of the great wonders of the world. You must see the Great Wall of China. It is 1,500 miles long— the largest project ever built!

Look at the groups of words along the wall. What do the words within each group have in common?

Write a label that describes the words in the group.

Write the labels in the boxes below the word groups.

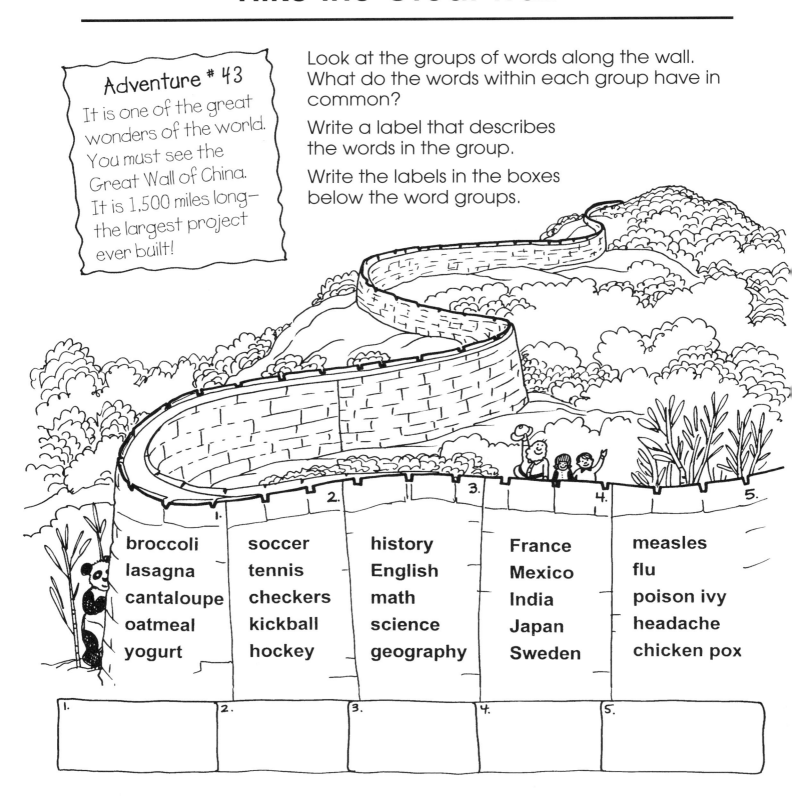

1.	2.	3.	4.	5.
broccoli	soccer	history	France	measles
lasagna	tennis	English	Mexico	flu
cantaloupe	checkers	math	India	poison ivy
oatmeal	kickball	science	Japan	headache
yogurt	hockey	geography	Sweden	chicken pox

1.	2.	3.	4.	5.

Name _____

Word Classification

Earthquake Inspection

crust
shockwave
fault
emergency
tremo
seismograph
magma

landslide
plates
disaster
tsunami
aftershock
fire

Find these earthquake words in the puzzle. Circle them and read them.

Ask a teacher or parent to help you find out what they mean.

(Words may be found reading up, down, forwards, backwards, or diagonally!)

Remarkable !

Spectacular !

Immense !

Adventure # 44
Visit the site of an earthquake. Learn what to do to protect yourself in an earthquake!

Name

Copyright © 2016 World Book, Inc./
Incentive Publications, Chicago, IL

New Vocabulary

Hot Spots & Cold Spots

Adventure # 45

Get packed to visit the hottest and coldest spots on Earth. We'll take you to both! Which place would you like to visit first?

Collect some "hot" words and "cold" words.
There are a few to get you started.
You write the rest!

The hottest temperature measured, on a desert in North Africa, is 136°F !

The coldest temperature recorded is −127°F in Vostok, Antarctica.

Hot

steamy
sweaty
broil
humid

_____
_____
_____
_____
_____
_____
_____

Cold

winter
shiver
frosty
blizzard

_____
_____
_____
_____
_____
_____
_____

Name _____

New Vocabulary

Time Travel

Did you know that the word dinosaur means terrifying lizard?

POP

The Adventure Company
Time Machine

Adventure # 46

No other adventure company offers this trip!
Take a ride in our amazing time machine.
Go back in time to the days of dinosaurs.
See the Tyrannosaurus rex alive—for yourself!

Now that you've run into the greatest dinosaur of all time, why don't you borrow its name for a while?

Write at least 18 words that use letters from this name.

You might be able to make many more!

TYRANNOSAURUS REX

1. _____

2. _____

3. _____

4. _____

5. _____

6. _____

7. _____

8. _____

9. _____

10. _____

11. _____

12. _____

13. _____

14. _____

15. _____

16. _____

17. _____

18. _____

Name _____

Word Formation

Back To School

It is the first day of school in Happy Hollow Forest. The students are busy finding out about the fun things the teacher has planned for them.

Check the title for each learning center.

☐ Reading, Writing, and Math
☐ Welcome to School
☐ Mighty Math

☐ Write Here
☐ Good Students Work Hard
☐ Library Lingo

☐ Wet and Wild
☐ Find Out About Plants
☐ Plants and Animals

☐ Time to Read
☐ School Is Fun
☐ Eat a Balanced Lunch

Name _____

Choose Titles

Classroom Rules

Wise Owl insists that all students read his list of classroom rules on the first day of school. He gives a test to make sure that they understand these rules.

Help the students stay out of trouble. Read the rules on the chart and answer the questions.

1. Listen attentively when the teacher is speaking.
2. Remain seated during class.
3. Raise your hand before addressing the class.
4. Return all free reading books to the book table when you finish using them.
5. Gum chewing is not permitted under any circumstances.
6. Complete all homework assignments neatly and turn them in on time.
7. Be on time.
8. Use good manners and low voices while eating.

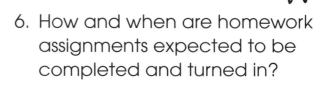

1. Which rule tells the students not to walk around during class? ____

2. What is another word that could be used to mean the same thing as "attentively" in rule #1?
   _____

3. Which rule applies to cafeteria behavior? _____

4. What rule tells students not to be late for school? _____

5. What words in rule 3 tell the student what to do before speaking to the class? _____

6. How and when are homework assignments expected to be completed and turned in?
   _____
   _____

7. Where are free reading books kept in the classroom?
   _____

8. When are the students allowed to chew gum?
   _____

Name _____

Context

Lost Name Tags

The teacher has a problem. All the students' name tags are lost.
Read the clues to help the teacher find out the students' names.
Write each student's name on his or her name tag.

Mr. Wise Owl

1. The student with the big hair bow is named Suzie.

2. Pauli has on tennis shoes.

3. Flossie is sitting next to Pauli.

4. Bella always looks as if she is about to fly away.

5. The lunch box belongs to Benjy.

6. You never see Becky without a book.

7. Champie wears glasses.

Name _____

Art and Music Mix-Up

Ms. Bella Blue Jay is getting ready for class. The art supplies and musical instruments are all mixed up.

Help her straighten them out by finding the following words hiding in the storage chest.

Circle the words that name art supplies and **draw a box around** the ones that name musical instruments.

Bella Blue Jay's Chest

tuba

brushes

piano

palette

tambourine

paper

crayons

clarinet

paint

xylophone

violin

harmonica

saxophone

drum

easel

pencils

guitar

tempera

keyboard

markers

Sketch Pad

How many musical instruments are in the storage chest? _____

How many art supplies are in the chest? _____

Name _____

Classifying Words

Find the Hidden Message

Wise Owl gave his students the puzzle below to solve.
See if you can solve it for them.
Follow the directions to find the hidden message.

1. If **school** rhymes with **cool,** color the #1 spaces.
2. If **ball** rhymes with **tall,** color the #2 spaces.
3. If **pencil** rhymes with **pickle,** color the #3 spaces.
4. If **book** rhymes with **look,** color the #4 spaces.
5. If **map** rhymes with **tap,** color the #5 spaces.
6. If **lunch** rhymes with **bunch,** color the #6 spaces.
7. If **blue** rhymes with **bike,** color the #7 spaces.
8. If **sun** rhymes with **sky,** color the #8 spaces.
9. If **slide** rhymes with **glide,** color the #9 spaces.
10. If **spoon** rhymes with **fork,** color the #10 spaces.

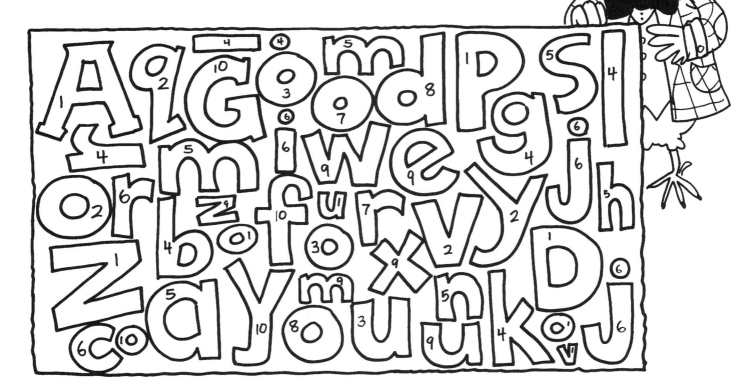

Name _____

Benjy's List

Benjy is trying to find out all he can about his new school.
Help him to locate the things on his list.
Circle the answer that tells where he would find . . .

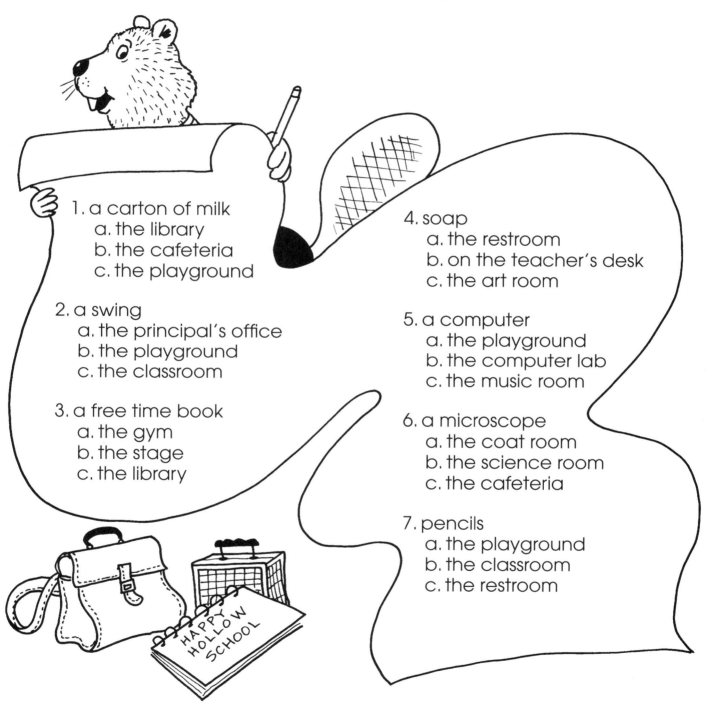

1. a carton of milk
   a. the library
   b. the cafeteria
   c. the playground

2. a swing
   a. the principal's office
   b. the playground
   c. the classroom

3. a free time book
   a. the gym
   b. the stage
   c. the library

4. soap
   a. the restroom
   b. on the teacher's desk
   c. the art room

5. a computer
   a. the playground
   b. the computer lab
   c. the music room

6. a microscope
   a. the coat room
   b. the science room
   c. the cafeteria

7. pencils
   a. the playground
   b. the classroom
   c. the restroom

Name _____

Word Meanings

A Picnic Memory

This picture was made at the Happy Hollow School Picnic.

Study the picture carefully before covering it with a sheet of paper.

Complete the sentences.

Then uncover the picture to check your answers.

1. _____ students are enjoying the picnic.

2. The fruit basket is filled with _____ .

3. There are three _____ in the stream.

4. A _____ is perched on the lily pad.

5. Three students are playing _____ .

6. There will be plenty of _____ to drink.

7. A good title for this picture would be

_____ .

Name _____

Recalling Information Read

Wise Owl's Shopping Spree

Wise Owl is buying food for the class picnic.

He has made a checklist of food he wants to buy for the picnic.

Read his shopping list.

Then answer the questions.

Shopping List:
popcorn
apples
pizza
cookies
potato chips
lemonade
sandwiches
grapes
carrots
paper plates
napkins
watermelon

Circle the correct answer.

1. What kind of fruit is on the list?	oranges	apples	pears
2. What kind of drink is on his list?	soda	tea	lemonade
3. What needs to be cooked?	lemonade	apples	pizza
4. Are bananas on the list?	yes	no	
5. What will he need that is not on the list?	cups	plates	napkins
6. Does Wise Owl plan to buy ice?	yes	no	
7. Does Wise Owl plan to buy anything that is not food?	yes	no	
8. Are potato chips on the list?	yes	no	
9. How many fruits are on the list?	five	two	three
10. What is the name of the vegetable on the list?	beans	carrots	tomatoes

Name _____

Find Facts and Details

Pick and Pack

Hooray! Today is Picnic Day at Happy Hollow School.

Help the students pack for the picnic. Cross out the word in each group that does not belong.

1. **FRUIT**
   apple
   banana
   potato

2. **FOOD**
   sandwich
   chips
   pencil

3. **SPORTS**
   ball
   jump rope
   microscope

4. **PICNIC SUPPLIES**
   plates
   cups
   notebook

5. **COOKIES**
   chocolate
   spice
   hamburger

6. **DRINKS**
   lemonade
   water
   forks

Name _____

Word Identification and Classification

Picnic Tummy Aches

At the picnic, the students ate too much food.
Now they all have tummy aches.

The graph shows how much
of each food they ate.
Read the graph to answer the questions.

Circle the correct answers:

1. Which food was eaten the most?
   cookies   sandwiches

2. How many sandwiches were eaten?
   20   10   26

3. Which food was eaten the least?
   pizza   chips   sandwiches

4. How many pizzas were eaten?
   8   12   10   9

5. How many jugs of lemonade
did the animals drink?
   26   9   20

6. How many cookies were eaten?
   10   8   26   20

7. The animals ate only 8:
   sandwiches   pizzas   cookies

8. How many bags of chips were eaten?
   9   10   20

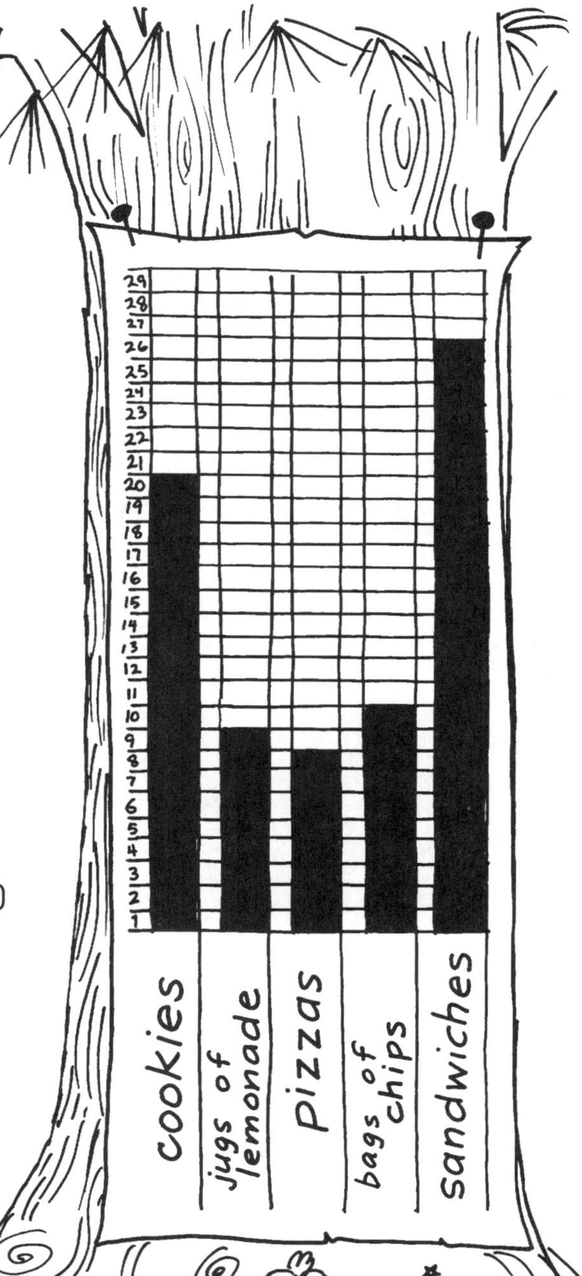

Name _____

Find Information on a Graph

Being Lost Is No Fun

Suzie and Becky wandered away from the group.
Something happened that they did not plan!

Read the story to find out what happened.

Suzie and Becky are so frightened.

They have lost their friends.

They don't know where they are.

They hear a roaring noise.

Now they are even more frightened.

Suzie sees a big, furry shape.

Becky sees two big red eyes
staring at them.

They run fast.

They want to get away from the
roaring sound and red eyes!

1. Circle the main idea of the story.
   a. Two friends run fast.
   b. Two friends are planning a camping trip.
   c. Suzie and Becky get lost in the woods and become very frightened.

2. Draw in the circle what you think frightened the friends.

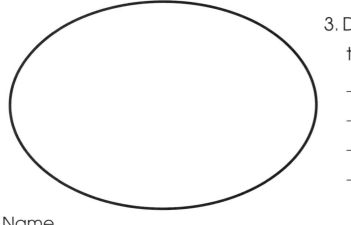

3. Describe what you think the thing
   that frightened them looks like.

   _____
   _____
   _____
   _____

Name _____

Main Idea • Inference

Dear Old Golden Rule Days

Read the poem about a school of long ago. Finish the picture.

Then select the sentence that gives the main idea of the poem.

School Days! School Days!
Dear old Golden Rule Days
Reading, writing, and arithmetic
Taught to the tune of a hickory stick.
Teachers right, kids are wrong.
All work, no play, obey the teacher,
Break no rules, study, study all day long.

Golden Rule:

SCHOOL HOUSE

Draw: A clock on the wall
A hickory stick for teacher
Three books on teacher's desk
An apple for the teacher beside the books

Put an X in the box that tells the main idea of the poem.

☐ Students must obey all school rules.

☐ This school is strict.

☐ The teacher has a hickory stick.

Would you enjoy attending this school? _____

Name _____

Main Idea

Word Wizard

Cherie Chipmunk calls herself a word wizard.

She likes to make up word games to play with her friends.

She almost always wins the games. See if you can win this one.

I'm finished!

Rules for Cherie Chipmunk's Word Game

1. See how many words you can write that begin with the consonant blend **ch–**
2. Each word must be at least four letters long.
3. No letter may be used more than once in a word.
4. Give yourself one point for each word.
5. Compare your score with Cherie's.

chick

_____

_____

_____

_____

_____

_____

_____

_____

_____

_____

_____

_____

_____

```
SCORE BOX

Cherie: ___22___

You: _____
```

Name _____

Consonant Words • Vocabulary Extension

Word Makers

Cherie asked Ricki to play the word maker game. It's an easy game.

All you have to do is change one letter at a time to make new words in each word box.

Make at least five for each word and try for more. The first one is done for you.

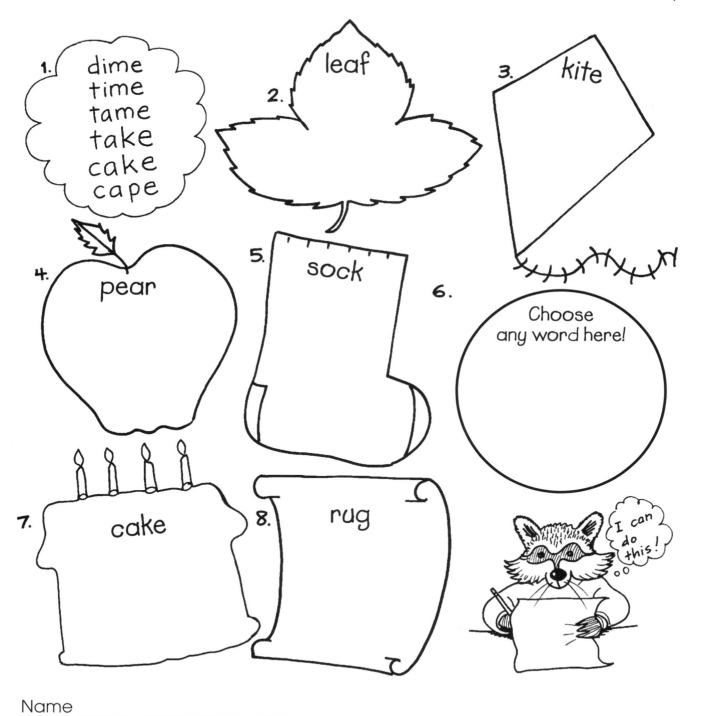

1. dime
   time
   tame
   take
   cake
   cape

2. leaf

3. kite

4. pear

5. sock

6. Choose any word here!

7. cake

8. rug

I can do this!

Name _____

The Great Hit

Pauli plays baseball for the Happy Hollow team. The story is about his greatest hit.

The story has some missing words. Choose a word from the word box to fill in each empty space.

The Great Hit

Pauli wanted this to be his best game.

He practiced hitting the _____ every_____ .

"Today I will _____ a home run," he said.

He was right.

"Whack!" Pauli got a _____ hit.

The ball sailed _____ up _____ the air.

It went right over the _____ and right into

Ms. Bella Jay's _____ .

He got a home _____ .

Oh no! I can't look!

Word Box

fence	hit	ball
great	day	into
high	window	run

Name _____

Math Mix-Up

As Pauli tried to explain the math assignment to Flossie, things got mixed up. Flossie could not understand the assignment.

What did Pauli really say?
Fix the mixed-up sentences, and write each one correctly.

1. addition subtraction we studying are and

2. the are page 21 on problems

3. problems 22 are there all in

4. assignment due the tomorrow is

5. study together let's

I don't get it!

Name _____

Sequence

Where Would You Find It?

Would you find a playmate in the principal's office?

Would you find a pencil sharpener in a salad?

Would you find a sandwich in a book?

Ricky Raccoon is trying to decide where to find these things he will need for school.

He needs to know the words first.

Help him read the words.

Then circle the words that tell where he can find each thing!

Where would you find . . .

1. a sandwich
a. in a book
b. in a drum
c. in a lunch box

2. a book
a. in the library
b. in spaghetti
c. on a slide

3. a playmate
a. in the closet
b. on the playground
c. in the principal's office

4. a jacket
a. in the garden
b. in the ocean
c. in his closet

5. shoe laces
a. in his sneakers
b. in the trash can
c. on the teacher's desk

6. a pencil sharpener
a. in the classroom
b. in a salad
c. in a barn

Name _____

The Big Game

The Happy Hollow soccer team wins lots of games. The whole school looks forward to the games.

Last week's game was the first one of the season. Read about this game, then answer the questions.

The Happy Hollow News

SPORTS PAGE

The big soccer game took place on Friday.
Pauli was captain of the team.
Flossie made sure all the equipment was ready.
Suzie brought lemonade for everybody.
The ball field by the creek never looked better.
The sun was shining, and it was a beautiful day.
The cheerleaders cheered when the game started.
The team played well.
Unfortunately, they lost the game.
The cheerleaders were sad; one even cried.

Our soccer team works _so_ hard!

1. When did the soccer game occur?	Monday	Friday	Wednesday
2. Who was the captain of the team?	Pauli	Ricki	Benjy
3. What was Flossie's job?	coach	equipment manager	cheerleader
4. What did Suzie bring?	cookies	candy	lemonade
5. Where was the ball field?	in the forest	by the creek	in the meadow
6. What kind of day was it?	dark	rainy	sunny
7. What made the cheerleaders sad?	team lost	sun	rain

Name _____

Identify Characters and Setting

Dressed for Drama

These students are dressed for the class play.
The name of the play is *The Forest Queen.*

Read all the clues to find out what character each will play.
Write the correct name below each creature.

CLUES

The queen wears a crown.

The prince has on sneakers.

The princess loves jewelry.

The thief is standing
next to the prince.

The Queen's maid carried
the Queen's pillow.

1. Which character has the most
   interesting costume?

   _____

   _____

2. What are the qualities of the costume
   that make it most interesting?

   _____

   _____

Name _____

Picture Conclusions

Finish each of the two picture stories by drawing conclusions in the blank spaces.

Name _____

Drawing Conclusions

Silly Sentences

Suzie Squirrel scribbles silly sentences in serious situations.
They are made up of words that repeat the same sound over and over.

The Happy Hollow students love her fun sentences.
They especially like ones made with their own names.

Read each sentence below and listen to the sounds.
Circle the letters in each sentence that make the repeating sound.

Say these seven silly sentences.

1. Benjy the brown beaver bounced boxes, bats, and billiard balls.

2. Flossie the funny frog found fifty-five frosty flutter flies flying frantically.

3. Pauli Porcupine's pet pig planned a pickle party for Polly parrot.

4. Suzie Squirrel squiggled and squirmed and sipped silly sodas.

5. Becky Bunny brought Benny Beaver big bags of back-to-basics books.

6. Chippie Chipmunk courageously climbed the crooks, crannies, and crevices of cumberland canyon.

7. Ricki Raccoon raced repeatedly around the round red room.

8. Make up a silly sound sentence with your own name!

_____

_____

Name _____

Talent Show

Preparations for The Happy Hollow Talent Show are underway.
Ms. Bella Blue Jay is in charge.

Help Ms. Bella match each student with his or her talents.
Draw a line from each picture below to
the matching picture.

Sammy Skunk reads poetry.

Flossie Frog sings opera.

Benjy Beaver plays the harp.

Pauli Porcupine tap dances.

Suzie Squirrel dances ballet.

Becky Bunny is a gymnast.

Ricki Raccoon plays the harmonica.

Draw yourself
to show your
special talent.

Name _____

Match Sentences with Pictures

A Report on Gilas

Read about the Gila monster and find out what it is.
Chippie wrote this report for science class.
Harry the Gila monster isn't really a monster.
Circle the correct answers.

Gila Monsters by Chippie

Gilas are big lizards.

They live in North America in hot places.

They can live a long time without food.

This Gila has a big head and a thick tail.

Its skin is black with pink and yellow spots.

The bite of a Gila monster is poisonous.

Gila monsters move slowly.

1. What is a Gila monster?   snake   lizard   turtle

2. What kind of tail does it have?   curly   thin   thick

3. What colors are its spots?   red   pink and yellow   purple

4. How does it move?   rapidly   in circles   slowly

5. What do you think is the most interesting thing about a Gila?

_____

_____

Name _____

Find Facts and Details

Cloud Watching

Flossie is a little bit lazy.
She is lying on her back watching clouds instead of doing homework.
She is surprised to see words in the clouds.

Read the labels on the clouds.
Circle the word in each cloud that does not belong.

1. **crunchy**
crackers celery
milk
popcorn peanuts

2. **smooth**
milkshake clean sheets
baby's skin
hairbrush whipped cream

3. **cold**
popsicle ice
milkshake
snowflakes fire

4. **fluffy**
feather rock
cotton candy
clouds pillow

5. **sticky**
glue cotton
peanut butter
honey syrup

6. **hot**
stove
sunburn
steam oven
ice cream

Name _____

Word Classification

Playground Fun

This group of friends is enjoying some playground fun.
Look at the pictures to see what each one is doing.
Circle the best title for each picture.

1. Down the Slide

   Chippie Rests

   Sunshine and Fresh Air

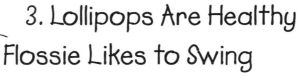

2. Fun on the Seesaw

   Up and Down

   Two on the Playground

3. Lollipops Are Healthy

   Flossie Likes to Swing

   A Rainy Day

4. Becky at Bat

   Time for the Game

   Becky has a Ball

Name _____

Choose Titles

Circus, Circus

The circus is coming to Happy Hollow.
Look at the pictures of all the circus acts.
Then answer the questions.

Circle your answer.

1. What part of the show do you like best?

   elephant tricks   lion tamer   clown

   dog tricks   trapeze   tightrope

                          fire eater

2. What job do you think is the most dangerous?

   lion tamer   trapeze artist   tightrope walker

   clown   fire eater   elephant trainer

3. What animal do you think has the hardest job?

   lion   cat   dog   elephant   bear

Name _____

Illustrations • Inference

A Deep-Sea Scare

Benjy made up this deep-sea picture story.

Follow all the directions to
finish Benjy's picture.

1. Give a name to the diver.
   Write it on the line below her.

2. Draw some gold in the chest.

3. Color the lobster red.

4. Color the octopus purple.

5. Color stripes on the fish.

6. Color all the bubbles blue.

Count the crabs.
How many are there?

Draw something scary near the diver.

name the diver

Name _____

Follow Directions

Rafting on the River

Becky's friends sent her pictures of their raft trip.
She wrote a story about the pictures.

**We are in a raft.
We are starting down the river.**

This is fun! The river is wild.

Oops! We tip over. We get very wet.

We are three wet, tired dogs.

Circle the best answer in each box.

1. This story tells	2. This story is	3. A good title is
how to get wet	sad	Three Bad Dogs
about a raft trip	fun	Two on a Raft
how to be tired	scary	A Wet and Wild Ride

Name _____

Captions • Main Idea

To Market, To Market!

The Happy Hollow students love Farmer Joe.

Solve the riddles to find out what they buy from the market.

Write the word that finishes each poem.

1. I have a pit inside. I'm red like a berry.
I'm good in pies.
Just call me a
_____

2. I come in a jar
I cost only a nickel.
I'm long and green.
Call me a
_____

3. I'm red and round.
I'm not a potato.
I'm good in salads.
I am a
_____

4. My color is yellow.
I rhyme with "horn."
I have an ear.
My name is
_____

5. I wiggle a lot.
I like to squirm.
Fish like me for dinner.
I am a
_____

Name _____

Match Sentences with Pictures

What's Next?

Ricky is writing stories for a class book.

Help him figure out good endings for his stories.

Write your ideas on the lines.

1. A great dragon is breathing fire.

   He is moving toward the castle.

   What will happen next?

   _____

   -

   _____

2. The cookie jar was full, but now it's empty.

   There are muddy footprints in the kitchen.

   What will happen next?

   _____

   -

   _____

3. The scorpions are sleeping in the jar.

   Someone left the top off the jar.

   What will happen next?

   _____

   -

   _____

4. The garbage can is full.

   Ricky's cousin is in the back yard.

   What will happen next?

   _____

   -

   _____

Name _____

Make Predictions

Double the Fun

The McFrog twins have more than double the ice cream they usually get!
Their cones are full of double-good words, too.
All the words in the cones are missing pairs of double letters.
Find the right pair for each group of words. Write the letters in the blanks.

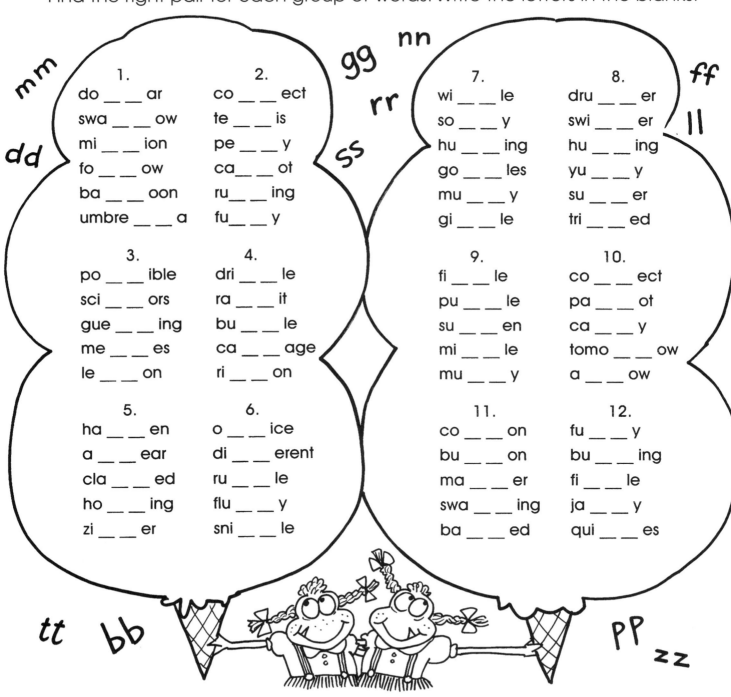

mm *dd* *gg* *nn* *rr* *ss* *ff* *ll*

1.
do _ _ ar
swa _ _ ow
mi _ _ ion
fo _ _ ow
ba _ _ oon
umbre _ _ a

2.
co _ _ ect
te _ _ is
pe _ _ y
ca _ _ ot
ru _ _ ing
fu _ _ y

3.
po _ _ ible
sci _ _ ors
gue _ _ ing
me _ _ es
le _ _ on

4.
dri _ _ le
ra _ _ it
bu _ _ le
ca _ _ age
ri _ _ on

5.
ha _ _ en
a _ _ ear
cla _ _ ed
ho _ _ ing
zi _ _ er

6.
o _ _ ice
di _ _ erent
ru _ _ le
flu _ _ y
sni _ _ le

7.
wi _ _ le
so _ _ y
hu _ _ ing
go _ _ les
mu _ _ y
gi _ _ le

8.
dru _ _ er
swi _ _ er
hu _ _ ing
yu _ _ y
su _ _ er
tri _ _ ed

9.
fi _ _ le
pu _ _ le
su _ _ en
mi _ _ le
mu _ _ y

10.
co _ _ ect
pa _ _ ot
ca _ _ y
tomo _ _ ow
a _ _ ow

11.
co _ _ on
bu _ _ on
ma _ _ er
swa _ _ ing
ba _ _ ed

12.
fu _ _ y
bu _ _ ing
fi _ _ le
ja _ _ y
qui _ _ es

tt *bb* *pp* *zz*

Name _____

How Do You Spell Magic?

Milton the Magician is pulling words out of his magic hat instead of rabbits. In each pair or group of words, one has used the wrong letter to make the sound **s** or **z** or **k** or **g.**

Circle the word from each pair that has the right spelling.

4. sircle
   circle

5. crasy
   crazy

6. size
   sise

7. abcent
   absent

8. cloudy
   kloudy

20. jentle
    gentle

9. giant
   jiant

19. krayon
    crayon

10. gym
    jym

18. city
    sity

11. jelly
    gelly

17. cool
    kool

12. jiraffe
    giraffe

16. kolor
    color

15. catch
    katch

14. tease
    teaze

13. eyes
    eyze

1.
majic
magic
magik

2.
surprise
surprize

Presto!

3.
circus
cirkus
sircus

Name _____

The Sleepy Letter

What a strange dream Jake is having!
Usually he dreams in pictures, but tonight he is dreaming of words.
Some of the words have a sleepy letter that makes no sound—the silent **e.**
Read each word. If it contains a silent **e,** color that section of Jake's dream.

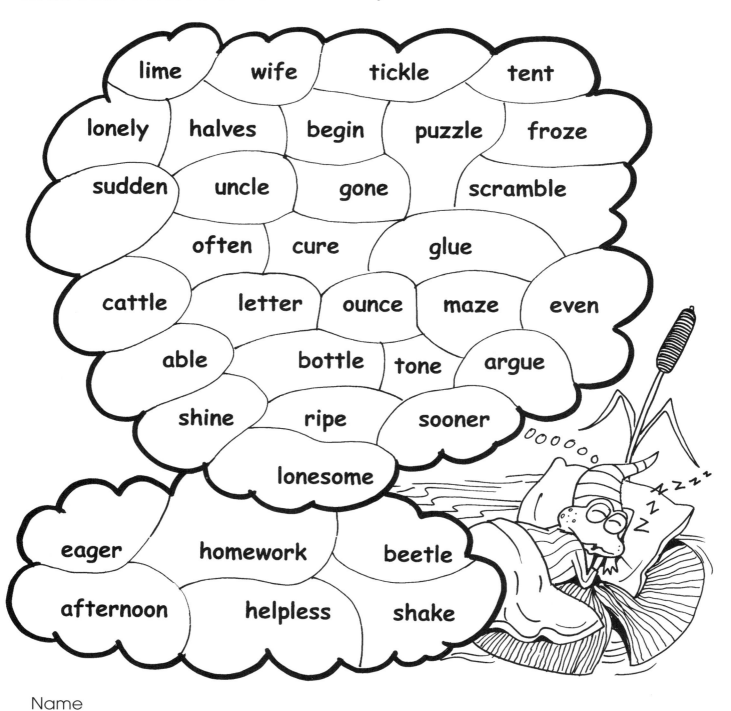

lime · wife · tickle · tent
lonely · halves · begin · puzzle · froze
sudden · uncle · gone · scramble
often · cure · glue
cattle · letter · ounce · maze · even
able · bottle · tone · argue
shine · ripe · sooner
lonesome
eager · homework · beetle
afternoon · helpless · shake

Name _____

Words with Silent e

Weighty Words

Waldo is having trouble with his weights! His spelling is in trouble, too!
Maybe it's because he has forgotten the spelling rule on the barbells.
Review the rule about using **i** and **e** in spelling words.
Then use the rule to find the words below Waldo that are
spelled correctly.
Circle them in red.
The words above Waldo are rule-breakers! They do not follow the **ie** rule.
Choose the right spelling for each one. Circle it in red.

1. height   3. either   5. foriegn
   hieght   iether   foreign

2. weird   4. neither   6. cieling
   wierd   niether   ceiling

RULE:
i comes before e,
except after c

or when sounding like A, as in "neighbor" or "weigh"

lie   neice   veil   vein   cieling   weight

their   piece   grieve   biege   brief   peice

breif   eight   freight   nieghbor   believe   pie

recieve   reign   riendeer   sleigh   die   neighborhood

Name _____

Words with _ie_ or _ei_

Surprise Over the Fence

Snoopy Sissy Skunk is spying on something over the fence.

What is it? Read the words in the puzzle to find out.

All the words contain the letter **s.** Some of them
are spelled wrong.

Color the correct word spaces green.

Color the wrong word spaces red or blue.

Sassy
mesy
misster
sandwitches
Mississippi
sirup
possable
mising
fussy
bussines
disease
sisster
hissing
salid
pleese
sword
seeweed
singel
scissors
surprize
seeson
sausage
sixthe
stranjer
strawberrys
sucess
seventey
sentances
studants
sneeze
snooze
necessary
sixtene
slushey
sientists

Words with s

Name _____

Upside-Down View

The Opossum family spends all day upside down. Oftentimes, they are asleep.

When they wake up, they have a view of words that contain **o**'s.

They like words with **o,** since they have some themselves!

Put the **o**'s into all the words they see. This will help you spell those words right.

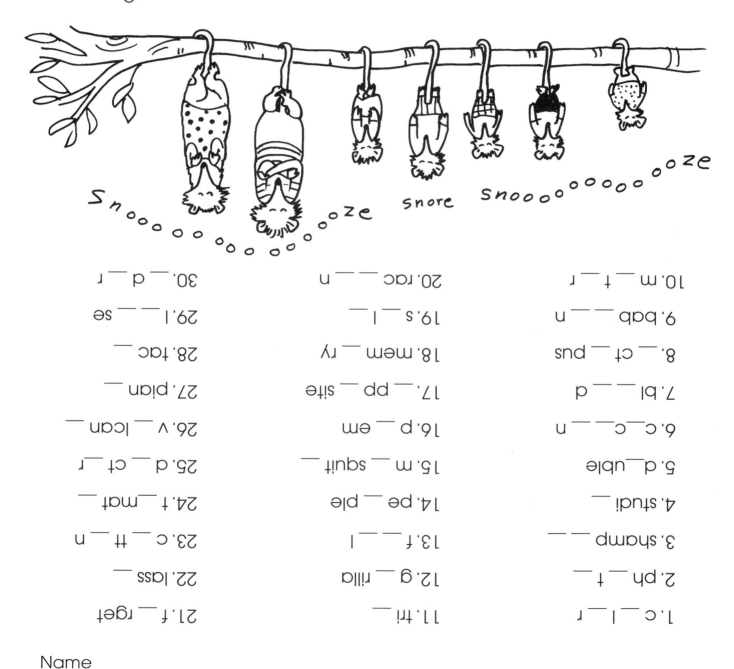

1. c_l_r
2. ph_t_
3. shamp__
4. studi_!
5. d_uble
6. c_c__n
7. bl__d
8. _ct_pus
9. babb_n
10. m_t_r

11. tri__
12. g_rilla
13. f__t_l
14. pe_ple
15. _m_squit_
16. p__em
17. _pp_site
18. mem_ry
19. s_l_
20. rac__n

21. f_rget
22. lass_
23. c_tt_n
24. t_mat_
25. d_ct_r
26. v_lcan_
27. pian_
28. tac__
29. l__se
30. d__r

Name _____

Words with o

Quilting with Qs

Grandma Quail's quilt is full of words with the letter **q.** Can you spell them?
Follow the clues to write a word that belongs in each square.

Then color the quilt.

If a square has a word that begins with **q,** color the
square green. If **q** is not at the beginning of the word,
color the square yellow.

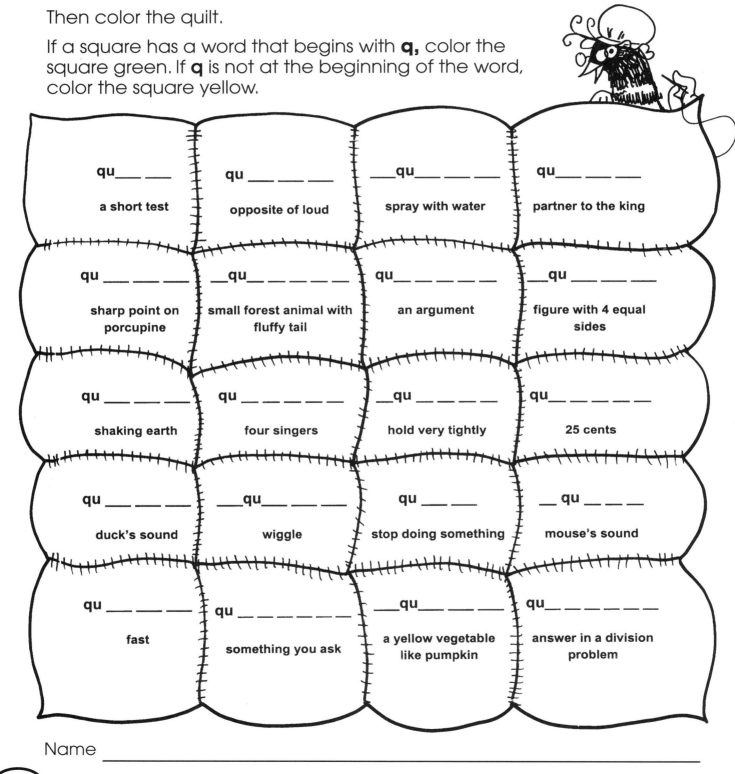

qu___ ___

a short test

qu ___ ___ ___

opposite of loud

___qu___ ___ ___

spray with water

qu___ ___ ___

partner to the king

qu ___ ___ ___

**sharp point on
porcupine**

___qu___ ___ ___ ___

**small forest animal with
fluffy tail**

qu___ ___ ___ ___

an argument

___qu ___ ___ ___ ___

**figure with 4 equal
sides**

qu ___ ___ ___

shaking earth

qu ___ ___ ___ ___

four singers

___qu ___ ___ ___

hold very tightly

qu___ ___ ___ ___

25 cents

qu ___ ___ ___

duck's sound

___qu___ ___ ___

wiggle

qu ___ ___

stop doing something

___ qu ___ ___ ___

mouse's sound

qu ___ ___ ___

fast

qu ___ ___ ___ ___ ___

something you ask

___qu___ ___ ___

**a yellow vegetable
like pumpkin**

qu___ ___ ___ ___ ___

**answer in a division
problem**

Name _____

Words with q

Tracking Down W, X, Y, and Z

Sometimes words with **w, x, y,** or **z** can be tricky to spell.

Clever Detective Sherlock Foxy is tracking down some problem words with these letters. Every word has **w, x, y,** or **z**.

Fill in the missing letters in these words to spell them correctly.

1. We __ __ __ sday

2. wond __ rf __ l

3. waff __ __

4. __ __ isper

5. awf __ l

6. whol __

7. wick __ d

8. w __ __ stle

9. ex __ ept

10. ex __ ct

11. exp __ ct

12. mixt __ re

13. ex __ ra

14. ex __ iting

15. yo __ k

16. yaw____

17. yes __ __ __ day

18. r __ yme

19. s __ rup

20. cr __ zy

21. m __ stery

22. __ ize

23. __ ipper

24. doz __ n

25. fr __ __ ze

26. squ __ __ ze

27. fizz __

28. c __ zy

29. laz __

30. ye __ __ ow

31. j __ zz

32. __ ero

33. wea __ __ er

34. w __ w!

Name _____

Getting to Know BIG Words

Tiny Tina loves big words.
She has all of these huge words spelled right on her spelling test.
Answer the questions about Tina's favorite big words.

explosion

extraterrestrial

Mississippi

superhuman   ridiculous

kindergarten

EXCEPTIONAL   dictionary

multiplication

hippopotamus   earthworm

outrageous

somersault

tremendous   emergency

underground   restaurant

1. Which words have an **ous** ending?

   _____

2. Which words have **ion** in them?

   _____

3. Which words have the vowel combination **au** in them?

   _____

4. Which words are compound words?

   _____

5. Which word has 3 sets of double letters?

   _____

Name _____

Getting to Know SMALL Words

Big Bruce Bear loves tiny words.
Unfortunately, his spelling is not as sharp as his claws!
Every word on Bruce's list is spelled wrong. Write each word correctly.

1. mowse

2. fone

3. tiney

4. inche

5. opin

6. meny

7. wich

8. evry

9. varry

10. whin

11. wuld

12. buzy

13. jist

14. furst

15. fith

16. evin

17. uze

18. dere

19. allso

20. talke

21. mabe

22. bern

23. bie

24. ofen

25. wunce

26. nune

27. wuz

28. culd

29. anser

30. wo'nt

Name

Small Words

Mistakes in the News

The news headlines are a bit confusing to Bruno this week.
Maybe it's because of all the spelling errors.
Fix the mistakes in the headlines.
Write each one over in the space below the headline.
Spell the words right!

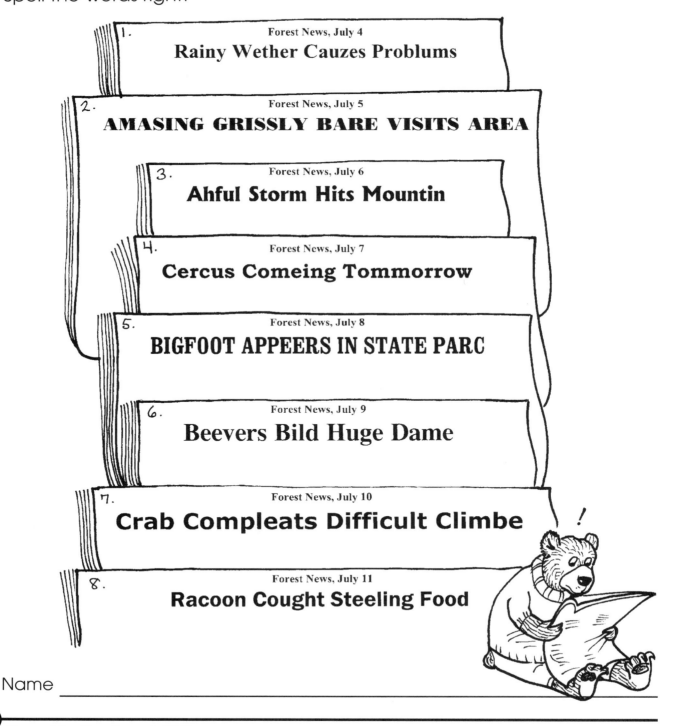

1. Forest News, July 4
Rainy Wether Cauzes Problums

2. Forest News, July 5
AMASING GRISSLY BARE VISITS AREA

3. Forest News, July 6
Ahful Storm Hits Mountin

4. Forest News, July 7
Cercus Comeing Tommorrow

5. Forest News, July 8
BIGFOOT APPEERS IN STATE PARC

6. Forest News, July 9
Beevers Bild Huge Dame

7. Forest News, July 10
Crab Compleats Difficult Climbe

8. Forest News, July 11
Racoon Cought Steeling Food

Name _____

Correct Spelling Errors in Writing

Places to Know

Look at all the places Wilbur wants to visit. Where will he go first?
He's checking the board to see what flights are leaving today.
Oops! Some of the letters are missing from the place names.
Finish the names to spell them right.

DESTINATIONS

1. Dis_____land
2. Cal_____nia
3. N___ Y___k City
4. Golden Gate B_____
5. Mex_____
6. At_____ Ocean
7. P_____ Ocean
8. Fl_____da
9. Austr_____
10. C____ada
11. Wa_____ D.C.

12. M_____ W___ Galaxy
13. Grand C_____n
14. South _____ica
15. R_____y Mount____s
16. Ch_____ago
17. _____aska
18. Mount E_____st
19. S_____ Pole
20. Eur_____ (continent)
21. Af_____ (continent)
22. Ant_____ (continent)

Name _____

Copyright © 2016 World Book, Inc./
Incentive Publications, Chicago, IL

Proper Nouns

Cracking Some Tough Words

Chester has strong claws, but even he is having a hard time cracking these tough words today.

Help him decide which spelling is correct for each word.

Circle the correct spelling with a red marker or crayon.

1. a. choclate
   b. chocolate
   c. chocalate

2. a. vegtable
   b. vegetable
   c. vegatable

3. a. pepel
   b. peple
   c. people

4. a. suprize
   b. surprize
   c. surprise

5. a. scissors
   b. sissors
   c. scisors

6. a. tongue
   b. tonge
   c. tounge

7. a. memarize
   b. memorise
   c. memorize

8. a. bananna
   b. bannana
   c. banana

9. a. busness
   b. business
   c. buisness

10. a. twelfth
    b. twelth
    c. twelveth

11. a. friendly
    b. freindly
    c. friendley

12. a. lafter
    b. laufter
    c. laughter

13. a. adress
    b. address
    c. addres

14. a. puzzle
    b. puzzel
    c. puzel

15. a. calender
    b. callender
    c. calendar

16. a. suppoze
    b. suppose
    c. supose

17. a. kichen
    b. kitchin
    c. kitchen

18. a. regaler
    b. regular
    c. reguler

19. a. exercise
    b. exersise
    c. exercize

Name _____

Frequently Misspelled Words

Copyright © 2016 World Book, Inc./
Incentive Publications, Chicago, IL

Names to Know

For her new computer game, Ella needs to know how to spell some important names of days, months, and holidays.

She has a start on these names. Help her finish them.

Write the missing word or word part to spell each word correctly.

NAME GAME

A. Days of the Week

S _____

M _____

T _____

W _____

T _____

F _____

S _____

B. Months

Jan _____

Feb _____

Au _____

Sep _____

Nov _____

C. Holidays

1) December day for presents

_____

2) day for hearts and chocolates

_____

3) a day to be thankful

_____

4) U.S. Independence Day

F _____ of J _____

5) day to celebrate mom

M _____ 's D _____

6) celebration of birthdays of George Washington and Abraham Lincoln

Pr _____ s'
Day

Name _____

Proper Names

Words That Count

Mrs. Rabbit never loses count of her children.
How many children does she have?
Write the number (in words). _____
Write all of these numbers in words. Spell them carefully!

A. 1,000,000 _____

B. 1,000 _____

C. 500 _____

D. 101 _____

E. 13 _____

F. 40 _____

G. 55 _____

H. 77 _____

I. 38 _____

J. 19 _____

K. 14 _____

L. 80 _____

M. 16 _____

N. 67 _____

O. 2nd _____

P. 5th _____

Q. 3rd _____

R. 9th _____

Name _____

Number Words

Animal Spelling

Reba's telephone book has the names and numbers of all her animal friends.

Since she is a good speller, all the names are spelled right.

Angela Ant	445-2020	Lannie Lizard	622-0864
Cassie Cougar	662-1010	Moe Monkey	622-8653
Egbert Eagle	554-8763	Maurice Mule	445-1357
Ellie Elephant	622-9999	Ronald Rabbit	445-1065
Gonzo Giraffe	455-9753	Rebecca Raccoon	552-1753
Gus Grasshopper	662-9999	Reba Rattlesnake	552-8765
George Gorilla	455-9081	Ralph Rooster	999-9876
Gustus Goose	622-1111	Peter Parrot	224-0001
Gail Gopher	445-0897	Polly Porcupine	544-8675
Kit Kangaroo	455-5678	Todd Turtle	622-1975
Lonnie Lion	455-8888	Zoie Zebra	455-2468

Find the names that match these numbers.

Write the last name of the animal friend. Spell it right.

Usually an animal name does not need a capital letter, but these are the proper names of Reba's friends. So, begin each one with a capital letter.

A. 622-0864 _____

B. 662-9999 _____

C. 544-8675 _____

D. 455-5678 _____

E. 622-8653 _____

F. 622-9999 _____

G. 455-9753 _____

H. 552-1753 _____

I. 622-1975 _____

J. 554-8763 _____

K. 445-1065 _____

L. 224-0001 _____

M. 552-8765 _____

N. 445-0897 _____

O. 445-1357 _____

P. 455-2468 _____

Name _____

Animal Words

How's the Fishing?

How many fish has the Rabbit family hooked today?

Find out by looking for words that are spelled right.

Draw a line with a hook to "catch" each word that is spelled right.

How many did you catch? _____

- careful
- befour
- **drawer**
- trubble

- **opin**
- accident
- **bacon**
- famus
- empty

- visiter
- evry
- **voice**
- uncle
- memary
- music

- somebody
- recess
- wiggel
- next
- arownd
- **quiet**

- length
- **queston**
- fourty
- **just**
- wether
- kitchen

- speshal
- cought
- heart
- nise
- wrong
- gladly

- ocean
- littel
- visiter
- does'nt
- odor
- natur

- puzzel
- **taught**
- pleaze
- wiegh

- **musterd**
- jelley
- hundred
- **fever**

Name _____

Identify Correctly Spelled Words

Checking for Errors

Some of the words on Franky's checkerboard are spelled right.
Some of the words are spelled wrong.
In each square, circle the words spelled wrong.
Use a red crayon or marker.
If a square has one wrong, color it blue.
If a square has two wrong, color it yellow.
If a square has three or more wrong, color it red.

a. anamals addition alley arownd		b. basball batheing becuz beautiful	c. every always importent exactly
	d. diferent against figure possible	e. mountins usally measure mustard	
f. finaly sudenly building musik		g. circle bought clotheing puzzle	h. yellow general probaly dollar
	i. exercise million sombody regalar	j. eigher wether laddar famus	
k. laughed jealous quiet pleeze		l. togethar trubble choose vacation	m. captain election docter people
	n. expect sience freind resess	o. afraid suger cotten children	

Name _____

Identify Incorrectly Spelled Words

The Carnival Comes to Town

A **noun** names a person, place, or thing.

See the daring circus acts! Hop on the thrilling rides! Watch hilarious clowns!

Take a chance on winning great prizes! The carnival has come to town!

Look at the carnival on these two pages (pages 116 and 117). Choose the things that you would like to see and do. Write a list of your top 10 choices!

Top 10 Things to See

Write 10 nouns naming things you want to see.

1. _____
2. _____
3. _____
4. _____
5. _____
6. _____
7. _____
8. _____
9. _____
10. _____

Name _____

Use with page 117.

Nouns & Verbs

The Carnival Comes to Town, cont.

A **verb** shows action. It tells what someone is doing.

Top 10 Things to Do
Write 10 verbs telling actions you want to do.

1. _____
2. _____
3. _____
4. _____
5. _____
6. _____
7. _____
8. _____
9. _____
10. _____

Name _____

Use with page 116.

Nouns & Verbs

Milton the Magnificent!

A **noun** names a person, place, or thing.

Milton wants to pull a surprise out of his hat. What will it be? Find the noun in each sentence and put a red line under it. Write the first letter of the noun in the matching blank below. Then draw the surprise in Milton's hand!

Abracadabra!

1. She is a good friend.
2. She never needs an umbrella.
3. She is not a zebra.
4. She has never lived in a zoo!
5. She's afraid of yaks.
6. She often sleeps in the kitchen.

7. She is not an iguana.
8. She has a sticky, pink tongue.
9. Her teeth are tiny and sharp.
10. She hates eating eggs.
11. Her curious nose sniffs everything!

___ ___ ___ ___ ___ ___ ___ ___ ___ ___ ___
1   2   3   4   5   6   7   8   9   10 11

Name _____

A Great Balancing Act

The seals do a fantastic balancing act.

They can bounce and balance many balls at one time.

Look at the nouns on the balls. Which ones are proper nouns?

Give every proper noun a capital letter, and then color its ball.

A **proper noun** names a particular person, place, or thing. It begins with a capital letter.

bellview School

mrs. clown

seals

carnival

dallas, texas

valentine's day

leo the lion

october

monday

july

zebra

brooklyn bridge

rizzo the clown

main street

milton

trapeze

magician

friday

colorado river

thanksgiving

Name _____

Proper Nouns

Step Right Up!

A plural noun names more than one of something.

"Step right up!" "Win great prizes!" "It's so easy!"

Listen to the shouts along the carnival arcade. Look at all the prizes to win.

Clyde Clown would like to win more than one!

Write the plural form of each noun in the box under the picture.

mouse

bunny

bear

knife

camera

butterfly

puppy

turtle

fish

glass

radio

monkey

duck

pennant

hippo

Name _____

Getting Ready for the Show

These cute little clowns are all dressed up
for tonight's show.
It took a long time to get them ready.
Let's see what they are wearing!

Finish the sentences below.

Add **'s** in each space to show that
the clown owns something.

Add **'s** to
most nouns
to show
ownership.

Bubbles   Bebe   Bonnie   Bobby

1. Bubbles is holding Bobby _____ bear.

2. Can you count Bebe _____ buttons and Bonnie _____ bows?

3. Whose name is on Bobby _____ bib?

4. Bubbles likes his bottle better than Bebe _____ bonnet.

5. Look! Isn't Bobby _____ balloon big?

6. Bonnie _____ booties are big enough for Bubbles.

7. There are spots on every clown _____ cheeks.

8. Everyone admires Bobby _____ hairdo.

Color the clowns and their costumes!

Name _____

Possessive Nouns

Monkey Action

A **verb** shows action. It tells what someone is doing.

What is more fun than a barrel of monkeys? Not much!

This barrel holds a puzzle about the actions of monkeys.

Every word in the puzzle is a verb.

Use the clues and the words in the **Word Box** (on page 123) to find the right answers for the puzzle.

Name

Use these clues to finish the puzzle on page 122.
Every answer is a verb.

Down

1. Mongo always _____ and laughed at the other monkeys.

2. Have you noticed how much monkeys __scratch__ under their arms?

3. Morey Monkey always _____ the toes of the other monkeys.

9. Oops! He slipped out of the barrel and _____ to the ground.

10. Sometimes the monkeys _____ around in their food!

13. Did you see that monkey _____ a banana across the cage?

Across

4. How high can that monkey _____ ?

5. Watch her do a _____ off the bar!

6. When the monkey got a can of soda pop, all he did was _____ it.

7. Did the zoo keeper _____ Morey when the lunch was passed out?

8. Monkeys are noisy. They screech and __chatter__ .

11. Minnie _____ when the monkeys tease her.

12. Oh, no! That's too high! Don't _____ !

14. That flip turned into a _____ .

15. Monkeys _____ up bananas very fast.

WORD BOX

toss
shake
chatter
scratch
roll
gobble
tickles
reach
sobs
skip
tumbled
flip
flop
jump
teased

Name _____

Use with page 122.

Verbs

Leaping Through Fire

It's so much fun to watch this act!
Waldo has trained his dogs to leap through burning hoops.
The dogs don't even act afraid (except for one).
Finish each sentence fragment to make it a complete sentence.

A **complete sentence** has a naming part and an action part.

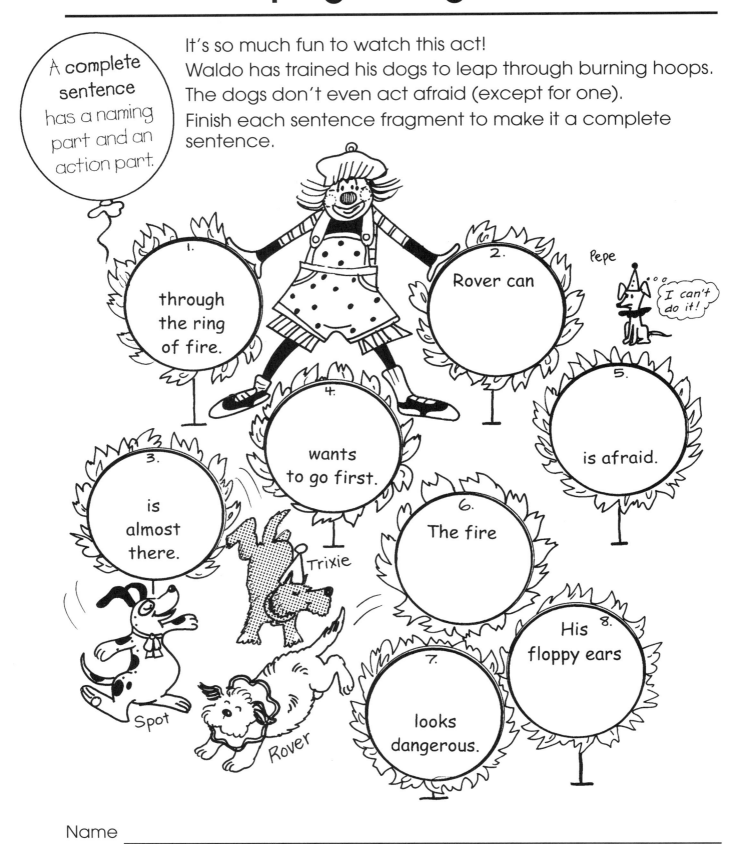

1. through the ring of fire.

2. Rover can

Pepe

I can't do it!

4. wants to go first.

Trixie

5. is afraid.

3. is almost there.

Spot

Rover

6. The fire

7. looks dangerous.

His floppy ears 8.

Name _____

Complete Sentences

Ring Around Run-ons

The ring toss is a favorite game of the Clown-Around Kids. Zeke and Zelda are always arguing about who is the best. Today they are trying to get rings around the bottles that have certain numbers. Help them out!

A **run-on** sentence runs two complete sentences together.

First, decide which sentences are run-ons. Fix them!

Then draw a ring around the bottles with the numbers of the run-on sentences.

1. Zeke threw the rings wildly, without aiming.

2. Zelda threw three rings around three bottles then she got a prize.

3. A radio was the prize she chose it was the best prize of all.

4. Even though Zeke was not careful, he won two games.

5. Step right up play the most exciting game throw rings around bottles

6. Did Zelda spend all her money did Zeke win anything?

7. Who won twenty free rides on the roller coaster?

8. Would Zeke be happy if he won the stuffed boa constrictor?

9. Only one ring went on the bottle the other nine flew out of the booth.

10. Who is the best at the ring toss anyway is it Zeke or Zelda?

How many rings did you draw?_____

Name _____

Unusual Talents

Ellie, the elephant, might have some unusual talents.
It is possible she can do the things her friends say she can,
but we can't be sure!

Change each statement about Ellie into a question to show
that you wonder if she really does have these talents!

A question asks something. It ends with a ?

oh, oh, oh

Ellie walks on the high wire.

Does Ellie walk on the high wire?

Can I believe my eyes?

Write each statement as a question.

1. That is Ellie on the high wire.

_____

2. It is true that the elephant can fly.

_____

3. Ellie can juggle pies.

_____

4. Ellie knows how to ride a unicycle.

_____

5. The elephant jumped through a ring of fire.

_____

6. Ellie ate all the cotton candy.

_____

Name _____

Inside the Lion's Mouth

A **statement** is a telling sentence. It ends with a period.

Would you have the nerve to do this? Is Rollo being brave or foolish?

Read the story to find out what is going on!

As you read the sentences that tell the story, look for statements.

If a sentence is a statement, put a check on the line at the beginning of the sentence and a period at the end of it.

_____ 1. "Who is afraid of me"

_____ 2. This is the question Lester the lion asked the clowns

_____ 3. Everyone was silent

_____ 4. The clowns were so afraid, they couldn't even talk to the lion

_____ 5. They thought he might eat them if they said they were afraid

_____ 6. They thought he might eat them if they said they were **not** afraid

_____ 7. What happened then

_____ 8. Rollo offered his banana to the lion

_____ 9. Do lions like bananas

_____10. Let's hope so

_____11. Lester and Rollo became friends

_____12. Rollo showed the other clowns how much he trusted Lester by putting his head in the lion's mouth

_____13. Was this a good idea

_____14. What do you think happened next

Name _____

Statements

Ups & Downs

The Cannonball has more ups and downs than any ride at the carnival. Can you hear the screams?

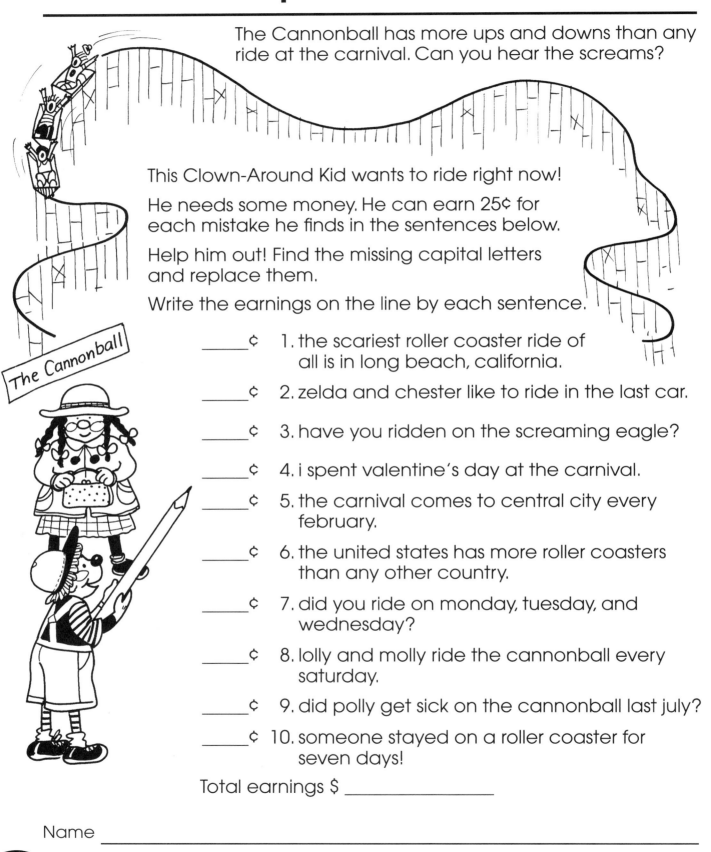

This Clown-Around Kid wants to ride right now!

He needs some money. He can earn 25¢ for each mistake he finds in the sentences below.

Help him out! Find the missing capital letters and replace them.

Write the earnings on the line by each sentence.

The Cannonball

_____ ¢   1. the scariest roller coaster ride of all is in long beach, california.

_____ ¢   2. zelda and chester like to ride in the last car.

_____ ¢   3. have you ridden on the screaming eagle?

_____ ¢   4. i spent valentine's day at the carnival.

_____ ¢   5. the carnival comes to central city every february.

_____ ¢   6. the united states has more roller coasters than any other country.

_____ ¢   7. did you ride on monday, tuesday, and wednesday?

_____ ¢   8. lolly and molly ride the cannonball every saturday.

_____ ¢   9. did polly get sick on the cannonball last july?

_____ ¢ 10. someone stayed on a roller coaster for seven days!

Total earnings $ _____

Name _____

Juggling for Contractions

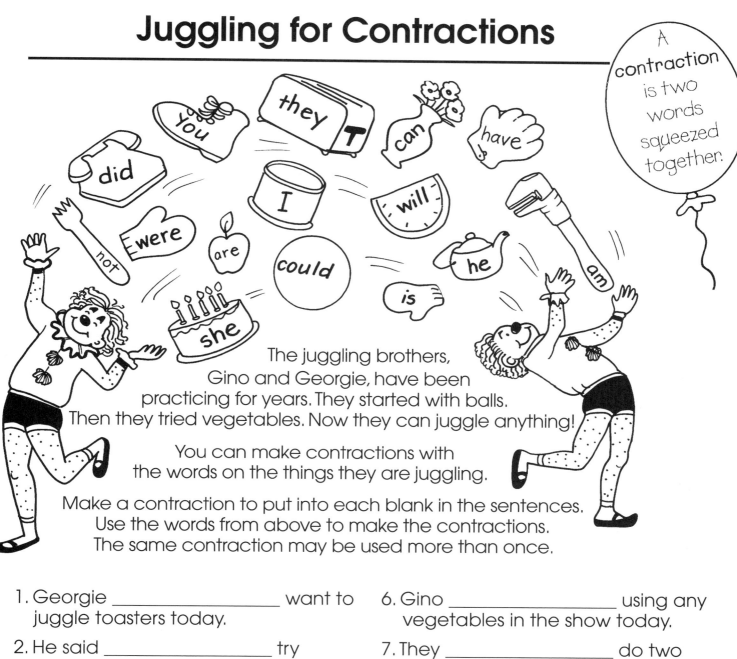

A contraction is two words squeezed together.

The juggling brothers, Gino and Georgie, have been practicing for years. They started with balls. Then they tried vegetables. Now they can juggle anything!

You can make contractions with the words on the things they are juggling.

Make a contraction to put into each blank in the sentences. Use the words from above to make the contractions. The same contraction may be used more than once.

1. Georgie _____ want to juggle toasters today.

2. He said _____ try again tomorrow.

3. "_____ start with five things each," said Gino.

4. The cake _____ fall to the ground once.

5. "_____ the best!" cried the audience.

6. Gino _____ using any vegetables in the show today.

7. They _____ do two shows today.

8. The show _____ last past four o'clock.

9. _____ they learn to juggle long ago?

10. "I _____ take my eyes off them!" said one visitor.

Name _____

Quotes from the Circus Train

The people on the train all have some comments to make about the ride! Everything they are saying can be turned into sentences called quotations. Here's how! Tell who is speaking, and tell his or her exact words.

Put those exact words inside quotation marks. Put a comma after the quotation, unless it has a question mark or an exclamation point or is the end of the sentence.

Use the quotations above to finish these sentences.

1. _____ "Can we go faster?" _____ asked Bubbles.

2. The engineer shouted, _____

_____

3. _____ wondered Mrs. Clown.

4. Danno said, _____

5. _____ hollered the twins.

Name _____

Aim for the Ducks

How many ducks can the clowns hit at the arcade?
If they can hit all the ducks in two rows, they will win the prize of their choice!
Help them by following the directions below.

Find all the places where punctuation marks are missing and write them in.
Each time you use a mark, color a duck that has that punctuation mark.
Try to color at least two whole rows for the prize.

1. Ellie ate peanuts cotton candy and a funnel cake
2. Did you want to ride the Octopus
3. Oh no Now it's raining
4. Did the clown lose her nose
5. Hurry The show is starting
6. Please don't feed the monkeys
7. Mop Pop and Glop are clowns
8. The elephants stole the peanuts
9. Watch out for the tiger
10. Could you tame a lion
11. I can't wait to see the fire-eater
12. Well I think I have the tickets

Name _____

Punctuation

Wonderful Carnival Words

If you go looking, listening, and sniffing around the carnival, you will find some wonderful carnival words! These are words you could use to describe the sights, sounds, feelings, smells, and experiences of the carnival.

Look at each of the carnival pictures. Write some interesting or unusual words to describe each thing.

Yikes!

1. _____
2. _____
3. _____
4. _____
5. _____
6. _____

OOOPS!

1. _____   4. _____
2. _____   5. _____
3. _____   6. _____

Mmmmm!

1. _____   4. _____
2. _____   5. _____
3. _____   6. _____

Yawn!

1. _____   4. _____
2. _____   5. _____
3. _____   6. _____

Name _____

Writing: Descriptive Words

Come One, Come All!

A poster is a great way to attract people to come to an event!
Make your own poster to tell about one of the acts in the carnival or one of the carnival rides.

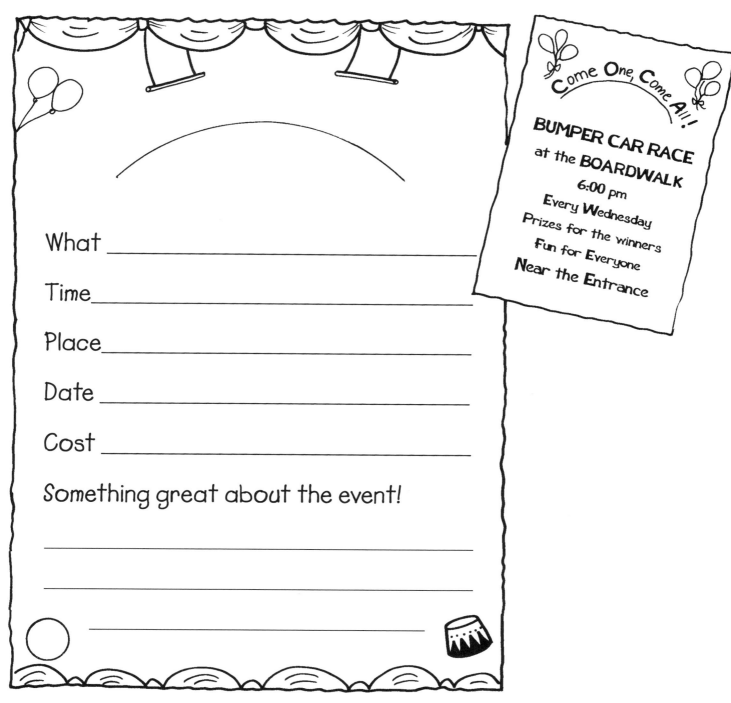

What _____

Time _____

Place _____

Date _____

Cost _____

Something great about the event!

_____

_____

_____

Come One, Come All!

BUMPER CAR RACE
at the **BOARDWALK**
6:00 pm
Every Wednesday
Prizes for the winners
Fun for Everyone
Near the Entrance

Name _____

Writing: Poster

A Three-Ring Circus

A carnival is like a three-ring circus!
There is so much going on—all at once.
Collect some ideas about things that go on
at the carnival.
Write down words and phrases—as many as
you can think of.

FOODS I ATE...

FUNNY THINGS I SAW...

RIDES I TRIED...

Use some of your good ideas to write a story on the next page (page 135).

Name _____

Writing: Generating & Organizing Ideas

A Three-Ring Circus, cont.

Write your story on the lines below.

Tell what you did during a day at the carnival.

Include things you saw, did, and ate.

After you write your story, draw a picture to go along with it!

Draw a picture here.

_____

(Title)

_____

_____

_____

_____

_____

_____

_____

_____

Name _____

Use with page 134.

Writing: Generating & Organizing Ideas

Fantastic Dreams

Snoozy is dreaming about a great trapeze trick he could do.
What would your dream trick be?

Draw yourself doing the wildest trick you can
imagine! Then write about it on the lines below.

Name _____

Writing: Imaginative Piece

Tina the Terrific

What is so terrific about Tina, the trapeze artist?
Read the beginning of her story.

Then finish it in an interesting way that will
make others enjoy reading it!

Our Tina....

When Tina was only two years old, she amazed her
mom and dad. She amazed the neighborhood!
She hung upside down in tall trees. She jumped
down from high places. She even leaped off their

_____ .

She couldn't wait _____

_____

_____

_____

_____

_____

_____

_____

_____

_____

_____

Name _____

Writing: Finishing a Story

Clowns Up Close

Take a close-up look into the faces of the clowns!

Aren't they interesting characters?

A clown's face can tell you something about the personality of the clown.

Is the clown lazy, grumpy, silly, hungry, sad, happy, curious, troublesome, mischievous, or bothersome?

Try to match each clown with a name that shows the clown's personality.

Baby Cakes   Sweet-tooth Lou   Chatty Charo

Sorrowful Sam   Granny Annie   Angry Andy

Smart Art   Weary Willie   Silly Sid

Name _____

Use with page 139.

Writing: Character Descriptions

Clowns Up Close, cont.

Choose one of the clowns to write about. Write a description or story about the clown. Describe the clown's looks, tricks, activities, thoughts, or personality.

_____
_____
_____
_____
_____
_____
_____
_____
_____
_____
_____

Write a story telling something your clown did.

Draw a clown face.

_____
_____
_____
_____
_____
_____
_____

Name _____

Use with page 138.

Writing: Character Descriptions

SOCIAL STUDIES

Skills Exercises
Grade Two

SKILLS CHECKLIST
SOCIAL STUDIES

✔	SKILL	PAGE(S)
	Examine and define neighborhoods	144, 145
	Locate own home in the universe	144, 145
	Use a map of a neighborhood	144, 145
	Use map skills to locate places and find information on maps	144–147
	Identify and find places in a community	146–147
	Identify and describe services in the community	146, 147, 151, 152
	Identify different kinds of transportation and their uses	148
	Recognize signs found in the community	149
	Identify current officials of local and federal governments	150
	Recognize some features of local government	150, 151
	Identify some ways local taxes may be spent	151
	Differentiate between rules and laws	153
	Recognize that people follow customs; define custom	154
	Differentiate between needs and wants	155
	Identify some kinds of jobs in the community	156, 159
	Describe and distinguish between people's needs and wants	157, 158
	Differentiate between goods and services	159
	Identify different skills that people have	160
	Describe some ways money is used in a community	161
	Explore concepts of managing and using money	162, 163
	Determine the resources used to make a product	164, 165
	Identify products and resources	164, 165

SKILLS CHECKLIST
MAP SKILLS & GEOGRAPHY

✔	SKILL	PAGE(S)
	Define a map as a representation of a real place	166, 167
	Use maps to locate things and places	166–178
	Identify and use a variety of maps	166–179
	Identify the parts of a map (title, labels, scale, key, compass)	168
	Choose a title for a map	169
	Use directions to locate things on a map	170–173
	Identify directions on a map	170–173
	Compare locations on a map	171–173, 176
	Use maps to find information and answer questions	171–178
	Identify and draw map symbols	174–176, 179
	Use map symbols to find things on a map; match symbols to words	174–179
	Read a map key and use it to locate things on a map	174–179
	Make a map key	179
	Define and recognize maps	180
	Identify and use a variety of maps	180, 183–188, 191–204
	Make simple maps	181, 186, 207
	Use maps to locate things	182–184, 187, 191, 192, 194–199, 201, 202
	Identify and draw map symbols; match symbols to words	182–186
	Identify parts of a map: titles, key, scale, and compass rose	182–188
	Read and use titles and labels on a map	182–188, 192–207
	Use map symbols and keys to find things on a map	183–186, 190–191, 197–199, 201–204
	Use maps to find information and answer questions	183–188, 192–204
	Make a map from a key	186
	Follow compass directions to find things on a map	187
	Identify directions on a map (N, S, E, W)	187
	Compare locations on a map	187, 192, 194–197, 198, 199, 201, 206
	Use a simple scale to determine distances on a map	188
	Find and place objects on a simple grid	189–190
	Read a map on a grid	191
	Identify N Pole, S Pole, and equator on a map or globe	192
	Recognize continents and oceans on a world map	192
	Recognize and identify different kinds of maps	192, 193, 200–204
	Locate own state on a U.S. map	194, 195
	Recognize names and shapes of some states in the U.S.	194–197
	Recognize landforms on a map	200
	Find information on charts or tables	205, 206

What's New in the Neighborhood?

A **neighborhood** is a place where people live. Every neighborhood has homes. The homes in this neighborhood are very close together.

There's a new kid in the neighborhood!

Help Abby find her way around.

Use the map to answer the questions about her new neighborhood.

Jefferson Ave.

Ninth Street

Tenth Street

PARK   LIBRARY

Madison Ave.

Abby's home

Washington Ave.

1. How many streets must Abby walk on to get to school?_____

2. How many blocks is the library from Abby's home? _____

3. How many blocks does Abby live from the café?_____

4. What direction is the park from Abby's home? _____

5. What street is the market on?_____

6. What streets pass the fire station?_____

   and _____

Name _____

What's New in the Neighborhood? cont.

There's a new kid in this neighborhood, too!

Help Mario find his way around.

Use the map to answer the questions about his new neighborhood.

7. How many homes are in Mario's new neighborhood? _____

8. Who is Mario's closest neighbor? _____

9. Which direction will Mario walk to get to school? _____

10. Who lives closest to the pond? _____

11. Will Mario need to cross the creek to visit Tom Brown? _____

12. How many homes are on Blueberry Highway? _____

Name _____

Use with page 144.

Neighborhoods

Where Would You Go?

Where would you go to catch a fish, eat a pizza, or get a tooth fixed?

Towns and cities are full of places you can go to get things or do things.

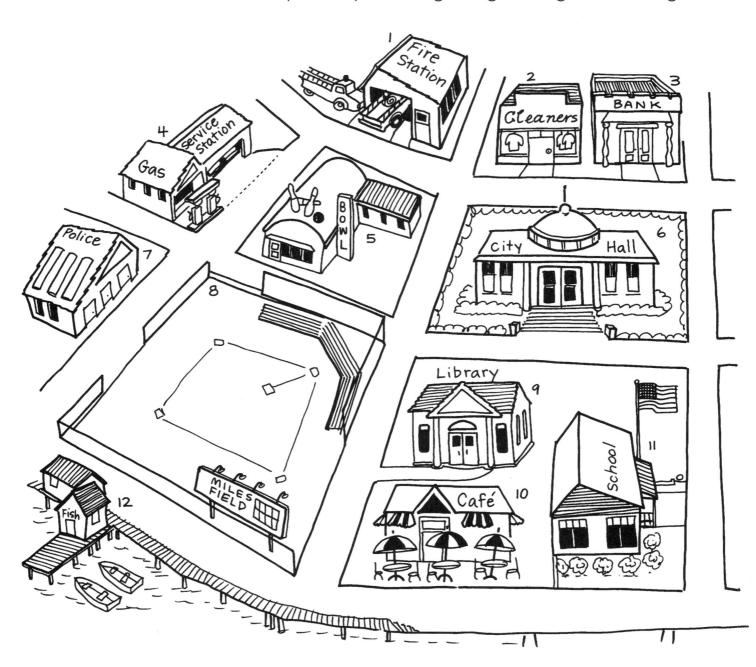

Use the map of this town to decide where you would go to get or do the things listed on the next page (page 147).

Name _____

Places in the Community

Use with page 147.

Where Would You Go? cont.

Write the number of the place that you would go to . . .

1. borrow a book _____

2. get a car repaired _____

3. save some money _____

4. swing on a swing _____

5. see a baseball game _____

6. buy a dog collar _____

7. eat a pizza _____

8. get your tooth fixed _____

9. buy a new coat _____

10. attend a math class _____

11. practice your diving _____

12. practice your bowling _____

13. get a jacket cleaned _____

14. get rid of old newspapers _____

15. have knee surgery _____

16. drink a milkshake _____

Name _____

Use with page 146.

Places in the Community

Take a Hike . . . or Take a Bike!

There are many ways to get around a town.
You might choose your feet, a bike, a train, or a helicopter!
Look at the different kinds of transportation Abby finds in her town.
Which kind should she use for each place she wants to go?

Write the number to tell what Abby might use to . . .

1. get across the river _____

2. get across town _____

3. get out of town _____

4. get to the airport _____

5. take a baby for a stroll _____

6. look around the park _____

7. see the town
   from up in the air _____

8. visit Molly two
   blocks away _____

9. visit Grandma
   1000 miles away _____

10. get some
    good exercise _____

11. travel around town
    on sidewalks _____

12. enjoy an afternoon
    on the river _____

Name _____

Transportation

Don't Ignore the Signs!

They don't talk, but they tell you all kinds of important things!
Most of them are not even very big, but they give big messages!

We would be in big trouble without signs to let us know
what's what, what's where, what to do, and what not to do!
Every community has lots of signs.

Draw a line to match each of these with the word that
tells its meaning.

school crossing

poison

steep stairs

telephone

no smoking

wash your hands

slippery pavement

handicapped access

first aid

rest rooms

NO DOGS ALLOWED

Uh, oh!

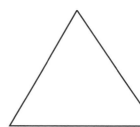

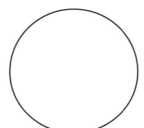

Design a sign that
would give each
of these messages.

no littering

zoo

quiet

Name _____

Who's in Charge Here?

Valerie Tyler won the election! She is the new mayor of Grover City.
Roberto Sanchez is a new member of the city council.
What will they do in their new jobs?

The **city council** is a group of people who have been elected by the citizens of the city to make rules and laws for the community. The council talks about problems and tries to solve them. They listen to citizens to hear what is important to them.

Agenda
- ✓ traffic problems
- ✓ plans for saving water
- ✓ build a new swimming pool?
- ✓ new skateboarding rules
- ✓ listening to citizens

The **mayor** helps to see that the laws are followed. He or she works with the council and many others to run the city.

1. Who is your mayor? _____

2. How long has he or she been the mayor? _____

3. How often does your community elect a mayor? _____

4. What group makes laws or rules in your community? _____

_____

5. Find the names of two people in that group. _____

and _____

Name _____

Show Me the Money

Where does the money go?
The citizens of Grover City want to know what happens to their tax money.
In most cities people pay taxes to help pay for services that everyone uses.
Here's how some of the money gets used in Grover City.

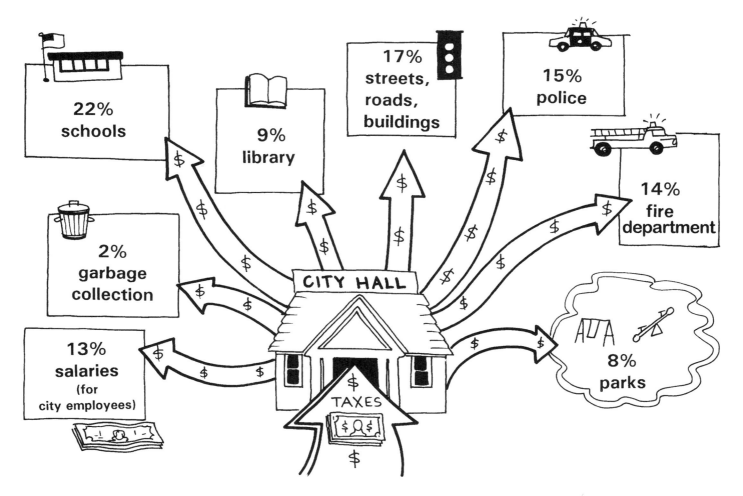

What percent of the money goes to . . .

1. schools? _____
2. library? _____
3. pay for city employees? _____
4. streets, roads, & buildings? _____

Which service gets . . .

5. 8%? _____
6. 15%? _____
7. 2%? _____
8. 14%? _____

Name _____

Who Can You Call?

Help!

There are many community services that can help you with different needs.
Which one should you call for each problem below?
Draw a line to match each need with the place that meets it.

1. You need help finding a fact for your history homework.

2. You see a fire out your window.

3. You find a lost child in the street.

4. You want to use the park picnic area for your soccer team party.

5. You see water gushing out of a pipe in the street.

6. Someone has been badly hurt.

7. You need to find a zip code.

8. Your garbage has not been picked up for three weeks.

9. There is a dangerous dog loose in your neighborhood.

10. The electricity has gone out on your street.

Post Office

Police

Garbage Collection

Library

Power Company

Ambulance

Woof! Woof!

Animal Control

Water Services

Fire Department

Parks Office

Name _____

Community Services

Is It a Law?

A **LAW** is a rule for a community. Everyone in the community must obey the laws. There are punishments for people who break laws.

A **RULE** is a statement about how people should behave.

It is not a good idea to throw food, but is there a law against it?

Figure it out! Learn the difference between a rule and a law.

Communities need both to help keep people safe and healthy and to help people live together, solve problems, and make decisions.
Look at each sign, and decide if it is a rule or law. Color the signs that show laws.

Name _____

We Do It This Way!

Families, communities, and other groups have customs.
A **custom** is a special way of doing things.

Every summer, Mario's family has a lightning bug party.

They invite all the neighbors to come for an after-dark picnic. They eat good food, play games, and catch lightning bugs. (Then they always set the lightning bugs free!)

Circle the customs that you have taken part in.

Thanksgiving dinner

Mardi Gras celebration

going trick-or-treating

fireworks on July 4th

dressing up for a costume party

decorating Easter eggs

telling stories around a campfire

hanging the flag

breaking a piñata

lighting a menorah

reading a bedtime story

hanging stockings on a fireplace

decorating a Christmas tree

making valentines

making snow angels

Name _____

Do You Really Need That?

Abby and Mario are packing for a camping trip.

They are going with their dads to spend two weeks living out in the woods.

What do they really need for survival?

Look at the things Abby and Mario are packing.

Color the things that are needs.

Needs are things humans must have in order to live (like food, clothing, shelter, air, water, and love).
Wants are things people would like to have but do not really need for survival.

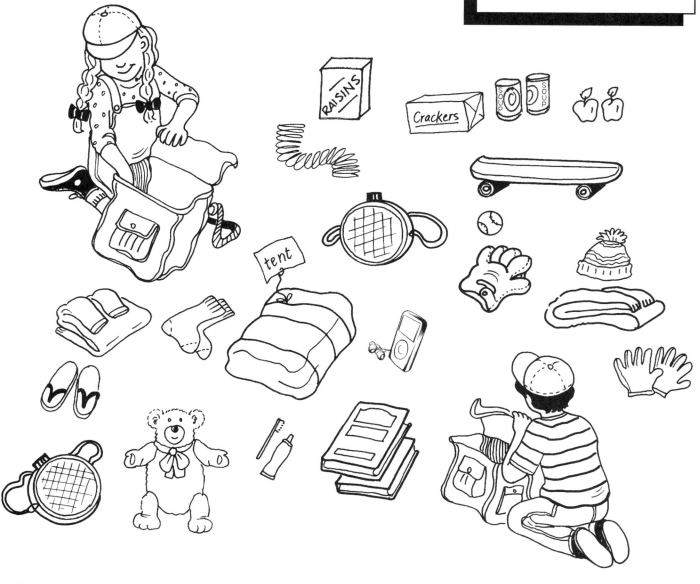

Name _____

Needs & Wants

Workers Wanted!

The Grover City community bulletin board has ads for job openings.
Who can fill the jobs?
Write the number for each job next to the person who should apply for it.
Use the workers named in the box below.

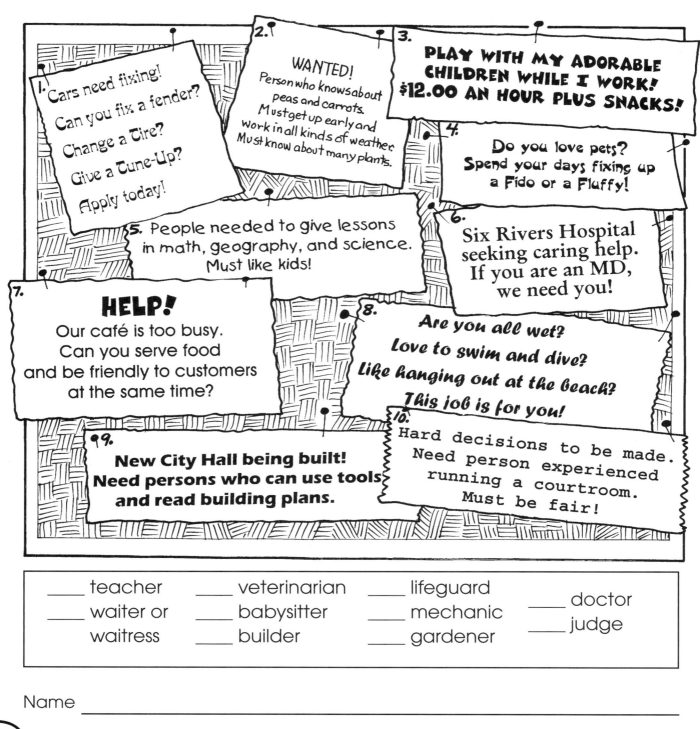

1. Cars need fixing! Can you fix a fender? Change a Tire? Give a Tune-Up? Apply today!

2. WANTED! Person who knows about peas and carrots. Must get up early and work in all kinds of weather. Must know about many plants.

3. PLAY WITH MY ADORABLE CHILDREN WHILE I WORK! $12.00 AN HOUR PLUS SNACKS!

4. Do you love pets? Spend your days fixing up a Fido or a Fluffy!

5. People needed to give lessons in math, geography, and science. Must like kids!

6. Six Rivers Hospital seeking caring help. If you are an MD, we need you!

7. HELP! Our café is too busy. Can you serve food and be friendly to customers at the same time?

8. Are you all wet? Love to swim and dive? Like hanging out at the beach? This job is for you!

9. New City Hall being built! Need persons who can use tools and read building plans.

10. Hard decisions to be made. Need person experienced running a courtroom. Must be fair!

_____ teacher

_____ waiter or waitress

_____ veterinarian

_____ babysitter

_____ builder

_____ lifeguard

_____ mechanic

_____ gardener

_____ doctor

_____ judge

Name _____

Making Choices

These kids are looking at a catalog of many things to buy.
They know they can't have everything they want.
They must choose things they want the most.
Color the five things you would want the most.

If your mom or dad wanted five things,
would they be the same things that you want?
Circle five things you think your mom or dad would want.

Name _____

Do You Really Need It?

Both kids say they **need** some things.
Only some of the things are real **needs;** the other things are **wants.**
Color the bubbles that name real **needs.**

1. I need a new skateboard.

2. I need a warm coat.

3. I need food to eat.

4. I need chocolate cake.

5. I need a dollhouse for my dolls.

6. I need a place to live.

7. I need friends and family to love.

8. I need a toy robot with wings and wheels.

9. I need cartoons to watch on television.

10. I need fresh air to breathe.

11. I need exercise.

12. I need a new car.

Name _____

Needs & Wants

Job Search

GOODS
Some people work to grow
or make the things we buy and use!
I am visiting those workers today.
Color my path RED.

SERVICES
Some people work
to do things for other people.
These things are called services.
I am visiting those workers today.
Color my path GREEN.

gardener

fire fighter

janitor

baker

auto salesperson

auto maker

piano teacher

banker

waiter

doctor

builder

cook

baseball player

librarian

artist

farmer

plumber

grocery store clerk

animal trainer

president

shoemaker

mayor

police officer

tent maker

Name _____

Everybody Is Good at Something

Do you know someone who can play a tuba or build a boat?

People have many different skills. Everybody is good at something!

Color the picture if you know someone who can do the skill it shows.

Then answer the questions below.

Do you know someone who can . . .

. . . play a violin?

. . . build a house?

. . . fix cars?

. . . paint?

. . . cook?

. . . sing well?

. . . listen well?

. . . tell a good story?

. . . grow a garden?

. . . ride a motorcycle?

Name _____

Money Can't Buy Everything

Layla has a purse full of money, and she wants to buy some things!
Even though she has a lot of money, she cannot buy everything.
Look for things that money can buy and that money cannot buy.
Color the things that money cannot buy.

Name _____

Where Does Our Money Go?

So many things cost money! How does a family afford everything they need?

Abby's family is wondering why their money disappears so fast!

They made a graph to show how the money was used last month.

The family earned $5,400 last month after they paid their taxes.

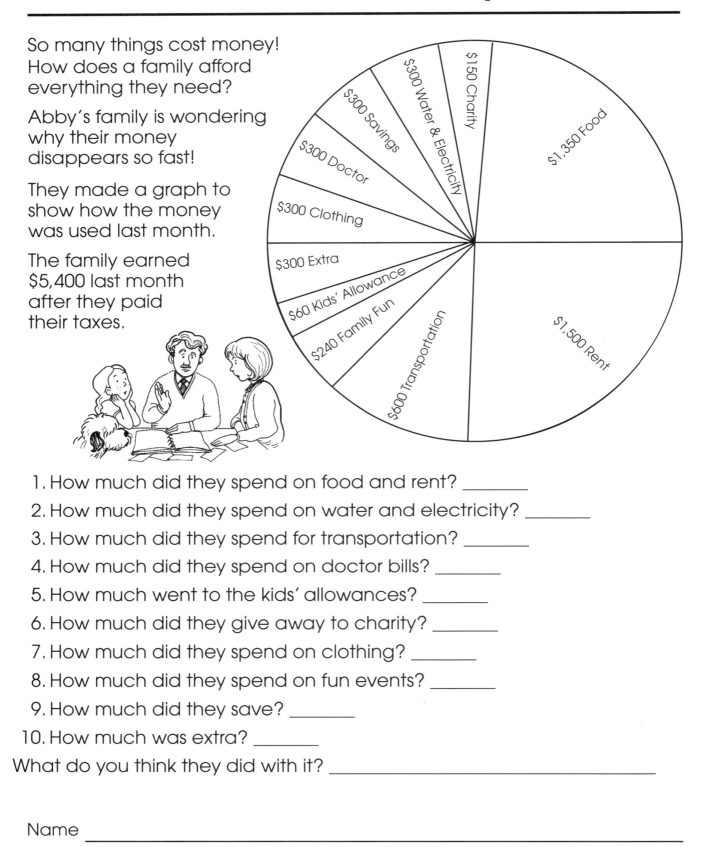

1. How much did they spend on food and rent? _____
2. How much did they spend on water and electricity? _____
3. How much did they spend for transportation? _____
4. How much did they spend on doctor bills? _____
5. How much went to the kids' allowances? _____
6. How much did they give away to charity? _____
7. How much did they spend on clothing? _____
8. How much did they spend on fun events? _____
9. How much did they save? _____
10. How much was extra? _____

What do you think they did with it? _____

Name _____

Where Did My Money Go?

Abby saved $40 from her allowance, birthday presents, and jobs.
She spent most of it. Now she is wondering where all her money went!
She's making a chart to see how she spent her money.
Color in the correct number of bars to show the amount she spent on each thing.

How I Spent My Money

		$1	$2	$3	$4	$5	$6	$7	$8	$9	$10
stickers	$2	▨	▨								
baseball cap	$10										
birthday present for Sasha	$5										
candy & ice cream	$4										
toy for dog	$3										
movie	$6										

1. What did she spend the most money on? _____

2. How much money does she have left over? _____

3. Below are some things she would like to buy. Can she get them all? _____

4. Circle one or more things she can afford to buy. The total cannot be more than $10.00.

cool poster	candy necklace	comic books	picture album
$4.00	**$1.00**	**$2.00**	**$5.00**

Name _____

Nature Gets Things Started

Things found in nature that people use are called **natural resources.** Many natural resources are used to make foods and other products.

Where does your orange juice really come from?

Where did your ice cream sundae begin?

Where did your peanut butter sandwich get started?

Many of the things we use, eat, wear, and enjoy come from nature.

Draw a line to connect each product (on the right) with the natural resource (on the left) that was used to produce it.

1.

2.

3.

4.

5.

6.

7.

8.

A.

B.

C.

D.

E.

F.

G.

H.

Name _____

Resources & Products

Getting Ice Cream From a Cow

How do you get ice cream from a cow? It takes some work!

Most of the foods and products we buy must be grown or made by machines or by hand.

Draw a path from each resource to the place where the product is made and then to the product.

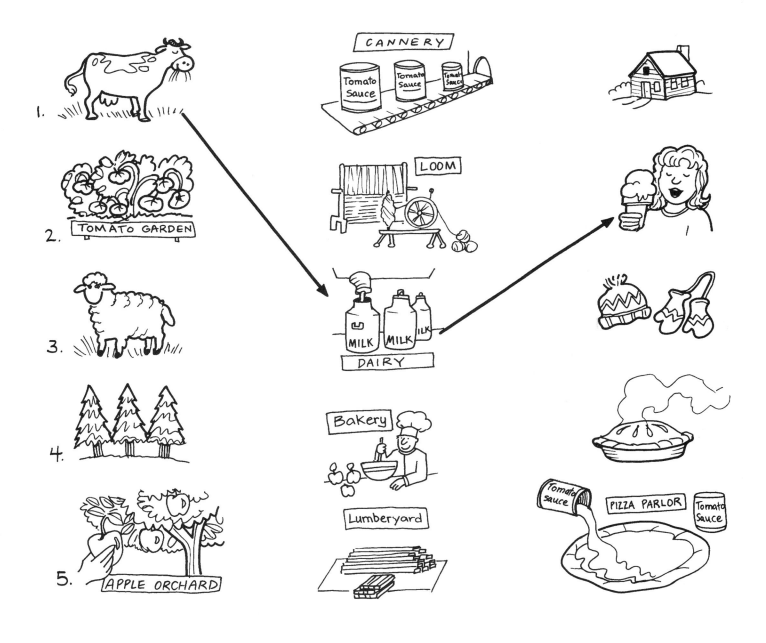

Once Upon a Table

It's not easy delivering ice cream to desert folks on a hot summer day.
Harry needs a big breakfast before starting his busy day.

A map is a flat picture of a real place.
Look carefully at the table. Then look at the maps of the table.

Which map matches Harry's table?
Color the map that is correct.

Now make a map of Harry's ice cream wagon.

See the picture on the next page (page 167).

Name _____

Harry's ice cream delivery wagon is loaded and ready to go.
Make a map of his wagon for him, so he will know where everything belongs!

Finish the map of Harry's wagon here.

Label each item.

Name _____

Use with page 166.

Define a Map • Make a Map

Digging for Treasure

Arvin's Airline is bringing treasure hunters to Skull Island to dig for treasure.
They have found an old treasure map.
Now they have to decide what it means.

Read about each part of the map. Follow the directions.

The **title** tells what the map is about.
Draw a red circle around it.
The **map key** explains symbols and pictures that
stand for things on the map. Color it yellow.
The **scale** tells about distances on the map.
Draw a green box around it.
The **compass** shows directions. Color it orange.
The **labels** tell what things on the map are.
Draw a purple circle around each label.

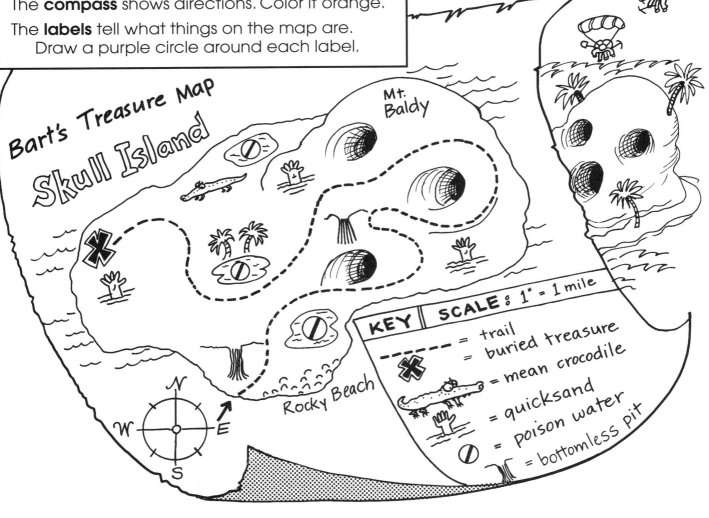

Bart's Treasure Map
Skull Island
Mt. Baldy
Rocky Beach

KEY   SCALE: 1" = 1 mile
- - - = trail
✗ = buried treasure
= mean crocodile
= quicksand
= poison water
= bottomless pit

Name _____

Parts of a Map

Map Mix-Up

Carl Crane has a package to deliver on Maple Street.
The titles have fallen off his maps, and he doesn't know which one to use.
Choose the best title for each map. Circle it.
Then color the map that Carl needs to make his delivery.

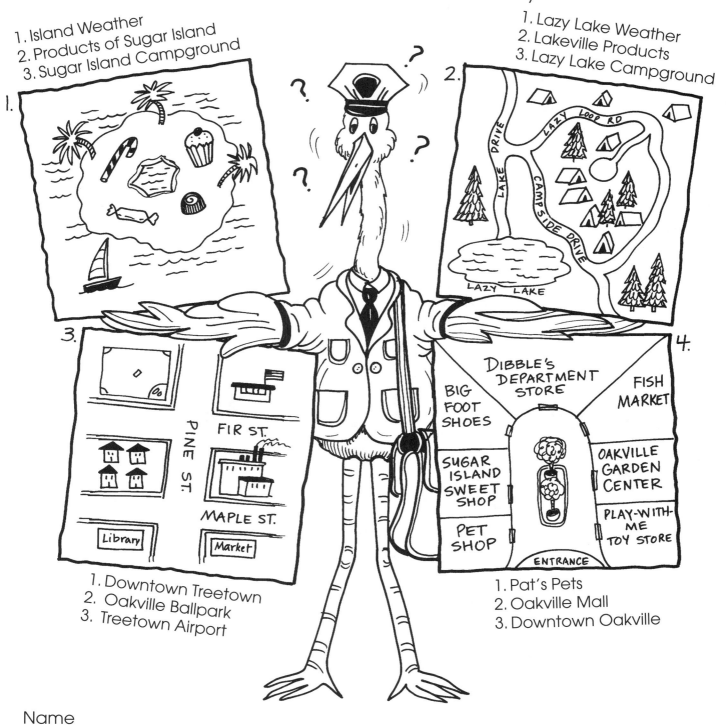

1. Island Weather
2. Products of Sugar Island
3. Sugar Island Campground

1. Lazy Lake Weather
2. Lakeville Products
3. Lazy Lake Campground

1. Downtown Treetown
2. Oakville Ballpark
3. Treetown Airport

1. Pat's Pets
2. Oakville Mall
3. Downtown Oakville

Name _____

Delivery for Bigfoot

Mail Carrier Millie has a delivery for Bigfoot. Help her follow the footsteps to Bigfoot's cave. Follow the directions.

Color a path along the footsteps as you go.

1. Walk 4 steps south.
2. Walk 2 steps west.
3. Walk 4 steps south.
4. Walk 6 steps east.
5. Walk 2 steps north.
6. Walk 5 steps east.
7. Walk 5 steps south.
8. Walk 1 step west.
9. Walk 2 steps south.
10. Walk 1 step east.

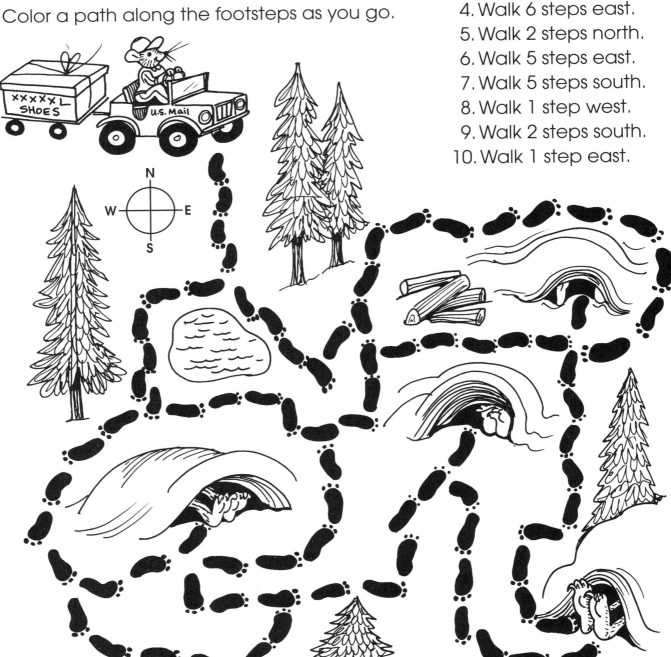

If you followed the directions correctly, you should be there!

Name _____

A Dangerous Delivery

Francie Frog always dreads bringing mail to the swamp.
She is very careful when she reaches out to a mailbox!
Today she has several packages to deliver.

Help her find the right
mailboxes.

Write **N, S, E, W,**
NE, SE, NW, or **SW** in each blank.

1. Turtle's box is _____ of Toad's.

2. Crayfish's box is _____ of Lizard's.

3. Toad's box is 1 box _____ of Pelican's.

4. Rat's box is _____ of Crocodile's.

5. Possum's box is _____ of Crayfish's.

Write the answer in each blank.

6. _____ box is just south of Toad's.

7. Crayfish's box is west of _____ .

8. _____ box is northwest of Crocodile's.

9. Is Pelican's north of Possum's? _____

10. Is Rat's box a little northeast of Lizard's? _____

11. Whose box is farthest north? _____

Name _____

Directions on a Map

Delivery by Dinosaur

Where is the manager of the Fossil Fun Park?
The mailman needs the manager's signature for a special package.
Follow the directions to help him find his way to the
manager's office. Draw a line to show the path he should take.

1. Go 3 steps south.
2. Go 10 steps east.
3. Go 6 steps south.
4. Go 8 steps southwest.
5. Go 6 steps east.
6. Go 1 step south.
7. Go 3 steps east.

MAIL POUCH

ENTER

Bucking Stegosaurus Ride

Fossil Hill

Pterodactyl Hop

See-saw-o-saurus Ride

Snack Bar

NW N NE
W   E
SW S SE

CLOSED- NAPTIME

MANAGER'S OFFICE

Name _____

Who Gets the Milk?

Here comes the milk truck to the Moptown Trailer Park!
Follow the directions to figure out who will get milk.

1. Only water is drunk in the trailer west of the milk truck. Color this trailer brown.
2. Milk is delivered to the trailer northeast of the truck. Color this trailer green.
3. Honey is the favorite drink in the trailer south of the truck. Color this trailer yellow.
4. The animal in the trailer southeast of the truck only drinks soda pop. Color this trailer orange.
5. The trailer north of the truck orders cactus juice. Draw a green box around it.
6. Milk is chosen by the animals to the northwest and southwest of the truck. Circle these two trailers, and then color them brown.

Name _____

Who Ordered the Pizza?

Poppie, the pizza delivery girl, is on her way to deliver a double cheese, double pepperoni pizza to some hungry pizza-lovers in Rivertown.

Help her find her way around the city!

> Many maps have symbols to show where things are.
> Symbols are small signs or pictures that stand for large things on the map.

Look at the symbols on the map key on the next page (page 175).

The words tell what the symbols mean.

Follow the directions and answer the questions.

You'll also find out who ordered the pizza!

1. Is the pencil factory on Speedway Blvd.? _____

2. Trace the nature trail in red.

3. Color the playground green.

4. Is the shoe store in the same block as the grocery store? _____

5. Is the post office in the same block as the airport? _____

6. Is the movie theater next to the gas station? _____

7. What is across Bridge St. from the school? _____

8. What street is Poppie's Pizza on? _____

9. The church is on the corner of Speedway and _____ Blvd.

10. If Poppie runs out of gas by the church, how many blocks will she have to walk to get to the gas station? _____

11. The pizza is delivered to workers at the building on the southwest corner of Speedway Blvd. and North Ave. Who ordered the pizza? _____

Name _____

KEY

 = airport
 = pencil factory
 = church
 = library
 = school
 = hospital
 = post office

 = grocery store
 = shoe store
 = playground
 = picnic area
 = gas station
 = movie theater
= Poppie's Pizza Palace

= street
= railroad track
= bridge
= nature trail

Map of Rivertown

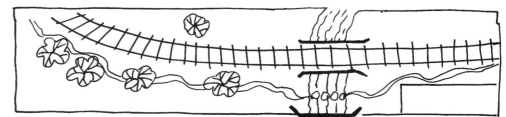

NORTH AVE.

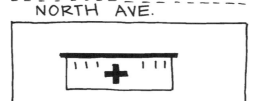

DOWNTOWN BLVD.

SPEEDWAY BLVD.

RIVER WAY

BRIDGE ST.

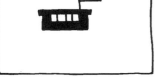

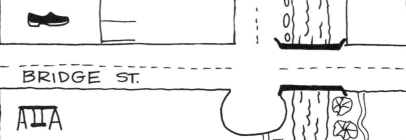

Name _____

Map Symbols

Map in a Candy Box

Curtis, the candy delivery guy, has a large box of candy for Miss Pansy.

Oops! He spilled all the candy!

Luckily, the lid of the candy box has a map key that tells where each kind of candy belongs.

Use the key to put the candy back in the box before Miss Pansy opens the door!

Draw and label the correct candy in each space in the box.

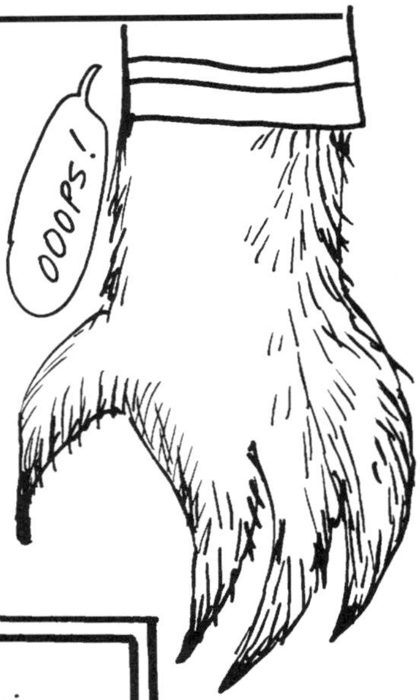

OOPS!

Vanilla Cream

Mint Cream

Orange Taffy

Chocolate Drop	Butter-nut	Cookie Stick
Lemon Taffy	Vanilla Cream	Mint Cream
Cherry Cream	Nut Cluster	Orange Taffy

Greamy-Dreamy Chocolates

Chocolate Drop

Lemon Taffy

Cookie Stick

Cherry Cream

Nut Cluster

Butter-nut

Name _____

A New Desert Route

Rod Roadrunner's mail route will take him across the desert every day.
Today is his first day of work, and he's learning to read his new map.
Help him get to know his map.

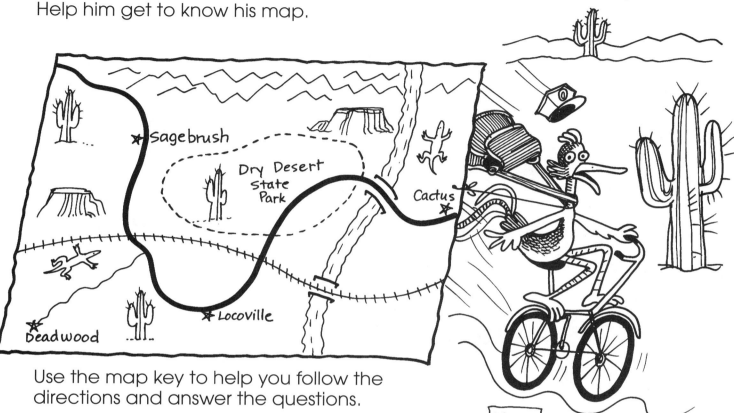

Use the map key to help you follow the
directions and answer the questions.

1. If Rod takes the highway,
   what is one city he will pass? _____

2. Color the mountains purple.

3. Color the cactuses green.

4. Color the dry riverbed brown.

5. How many lizard preserves are there? _____

6. How many plateaus will he see? _____
   Color them red.

7. How many times does his route
   cross the railroad? _____

8. What is the name of the park? _____

Key

∿∿∿	= mountains
🌵	= desert
⏟	= plateau
🦎	= lizard preserve
++++	= railroad
—	= highway
∼	= dirt road
═══	= dry riverbed
- - - -	= state park
★	= city

Name _____

Special Delivery

The stork has a special delivery for one of the families in the Critter Condos.

Follow the directions to find out where the new baby belongs.

Draw a line to follow the stork's path.

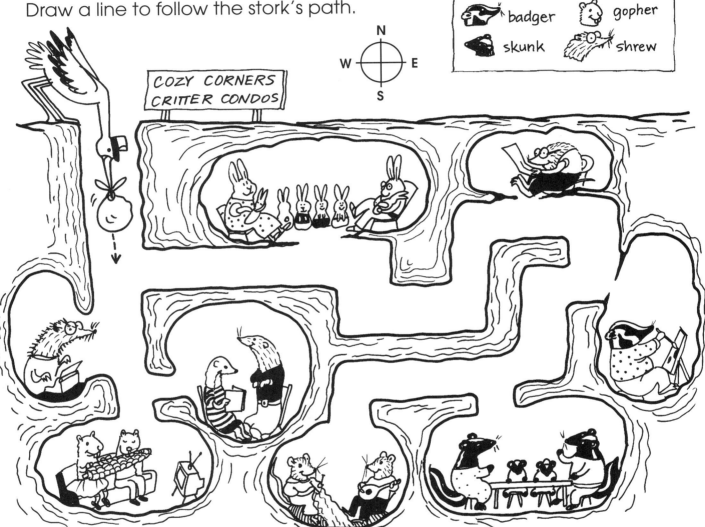

Follow the directions.

1. Go south to the first turn.
2. Go east past the rabbit home.
3. Follow the path past mole's home.
4. Turn south and pass badger's art studio.
5. Go west past the skunks' home.
6. Turn south into the first doorway past the skunks' home. This is the place for the special delivery!

Name _____

Toy Store Confusion

Felix has a huge delivery of toys for the toy store.

All the toys need to be put on the shelves, but he is not sure where to put them.

Draw a symbol in the key to match each word.

Draw each symbol on one of the boxes to show what is in the box.

This will make it easier for Felix to get the toys in the right places.

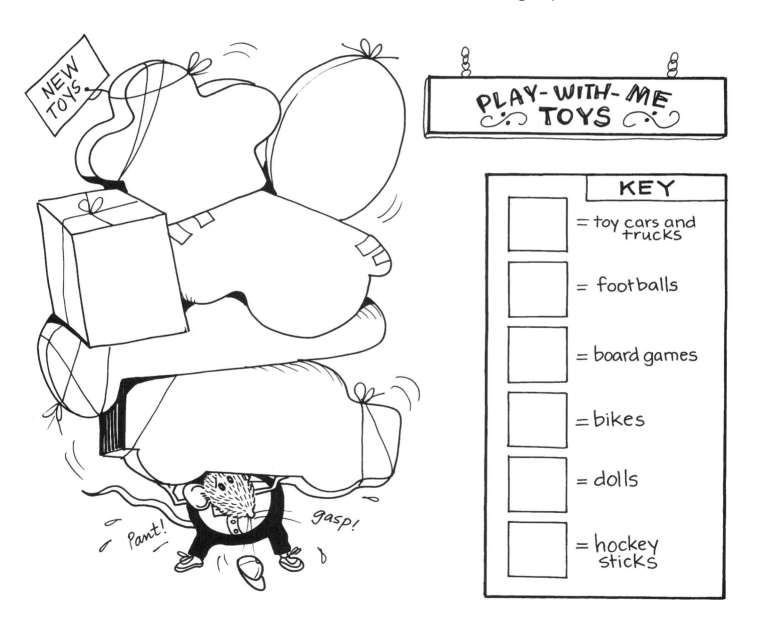

NEW TOYS

PLAY-WITH-ME TOYS

KEY

☐ = toy cars and trucks

☐ = footballs

☐ = board games

☐ = bikes

☐ = dolls

☐ = hockey sticks

Pant! gasp!

Name _____

Everybody Loves a Party

Birthday parties are such fun!
There are lots of treats at Eliza Bear's birthday party.
Look at the three maps of the party table.
Which map is correct?
Color the party and the correct map.

Recognize Maps

Eliza Bear's Room

After her party, Eliza's room was a mess!

She had better clean it up!

Draw a map of Eliza's cleaned-up room.

Use the pictures on the map key to help you draw the map.

Eliza's room

bed

lamp

TOYS
toy chest

chest of drawers

chair

desk

Name _____

Make Maps

Sara in a Hurry

It is the first day of school.

Sara Bearheart is in a big rush!

Look at the map of Sara's house.

Help her find the things she needs.

Circle the right answers.

1. What will Sara find in the living room?

2. What will Sara find in the bedroom?

3. Is a  on the stairs? **yes** **no**

4. Is the  in the kitchen? **yes** **no**

Name _____

Map Symbols

The First Day of School

Sometimes bears get lost in a new school.

Help Sara and Noah find their way around their new school.

Use the **map key** to help you read the map.

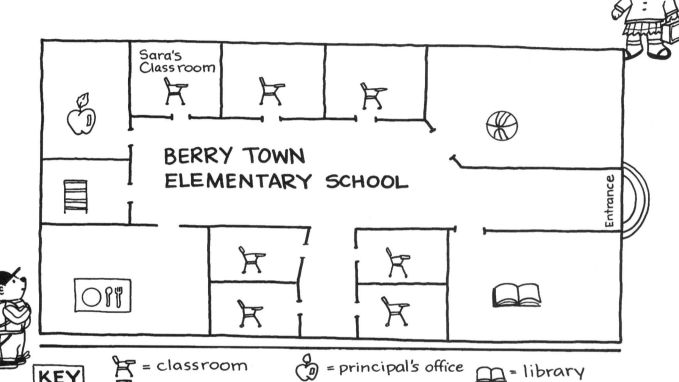

1. How many classrooms are in the school? _____

2. Is the principal's office next to the gym?   **yes**   **no**

3. Put an **X** in the room where Buddy will play basketball.

4. Color the library blue.

5. Color the lunchroom yellow.

6. Use a crayon to trace the path Sara will take to her classroom.

Name _____

Weekend Fun

Sometimes Noah and his friends go to Berry Town Fun Park.
They love the rides, the games, and the food!
Use the **map key** to answer the questions about the park.

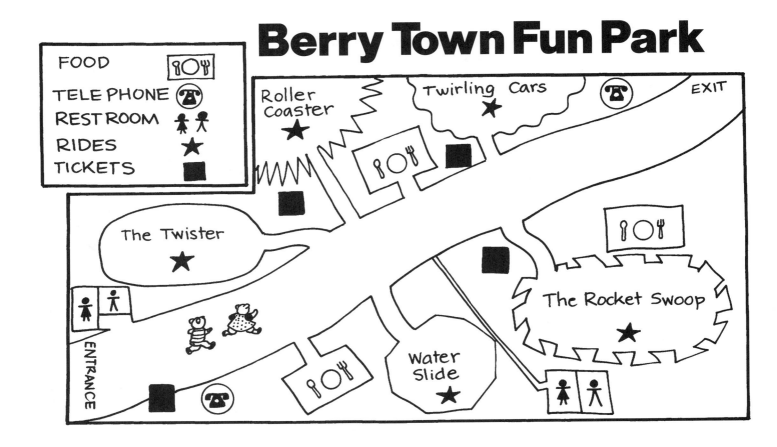

1. How many ticket booths are in the park?_____

2. Are there restrooms near the Water Slide?   **yes**   **no**

3. Is there a food booth near the Twirling Cars?   **yes**   **no**

4. How many phones are in the park?_____

5. How many different rides can Noah try?_____

Name _____

Follow the Parade!

Every year the circus comes to Berry Town.

Maybe the parade will pass by Noah's house.

Follow the route of the parade on the map.

Use the **map key** to answer the questions about the parade.

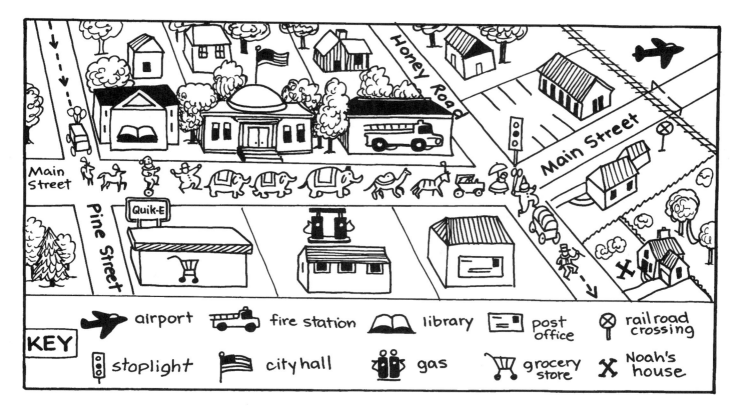

1. Will the parade pass the post office?   **yes**   **no**

2. How many stoplights will the parade pass? _____

3. Is the airport near the library?   **yes**   **no**

4. How many different streets will the parade be on? _____

5. Will the parade pass the airport?   **yes**   **no**

6. Will the parade pass Noah's house?   **yes**   **no**

Name _____

Wesley's Dream Plate

Cousin Wesley Bear is dreaming of his favorite dinner.

He made a map of his plate with his favorite foods.

Use the map key to help you make a map of your dream plate.

You may add foods that are not on the key, if you wish.

Wesley's Dream Plate

Your Dream Plate

KEY

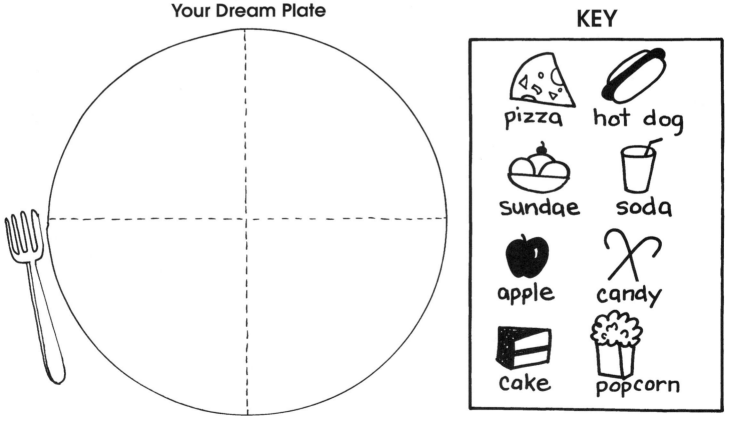

pizza   hot dog

sundae   soda

apple   candy

cake   popcorn

Name _____

Make a Map from a Key

Noah Goes North

These first-grade friends want to walk home from school.
They might get lost!
Give them some help with directions.

Noah's house is **north.** Color his path **blue.**

Sara's house is **south.** Color her path **green.**

Eliza's house is **east.** Color her path **yellow.**

Wesley's house is **west.** Color his path **red.**

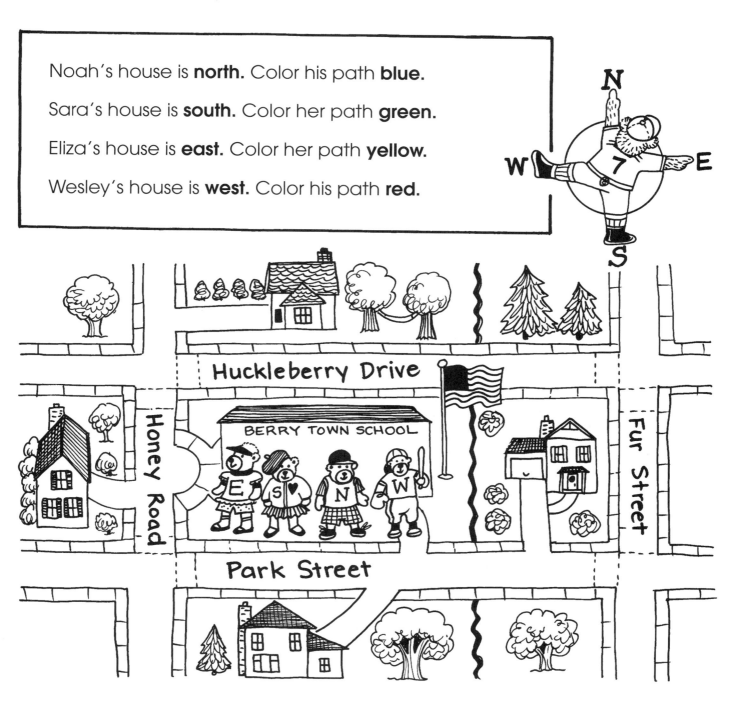

Name _____

Directions

A Jungle Trip

Noah and Sara visited a Jungle Fun Park.

They rode down the river in a boat.

Use the rulers to see how far apart things are in the jungle.

1 inch on the map = 10 feet in the jungle.

Answer the questions.

1. They rode the whole river. How far did they travel? _____ feet

2. How far is it from the snake to the gorilla? _____ feet

3. How far is it from the snake to the leopard? _____ feet

4. How far is it between the monkey's trees? _____ feet

5. How far is it from the leopard to the alligator? _____ feet

Name _____

Scale

An Underwater Puzzle

Wesley and Eliza are exploring a coral reef.

Use the grid to help them find wonderful things under the sea.

A grid helps you find where things are. The octopus is in row C across and row 4 down. Write C, 4.

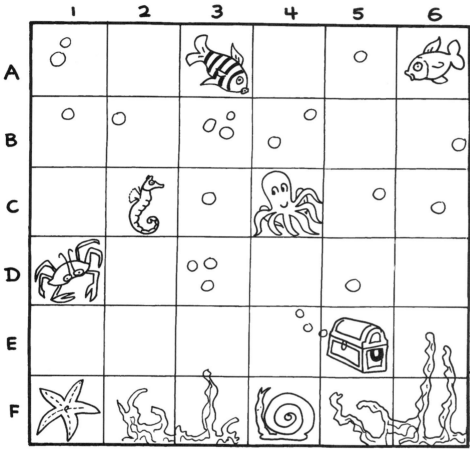

1. Where is the ? _____

2. Where is the ? _____

3. Where is the ? _____

4. Where is the ? _____

5. Is the in F, 5? **yes** **no**

6. Is the in D, 2? **yes** **no**

7. Is the in A, 6? **yes** **no**

8. Are  in B, 3? **yes** **no**

Name _____

Sara's Garden

It is so much work to grow a good garden!

Sara is ready to pick the vegetables.

Follow the directions to draw the vegetables in Sara's garden.

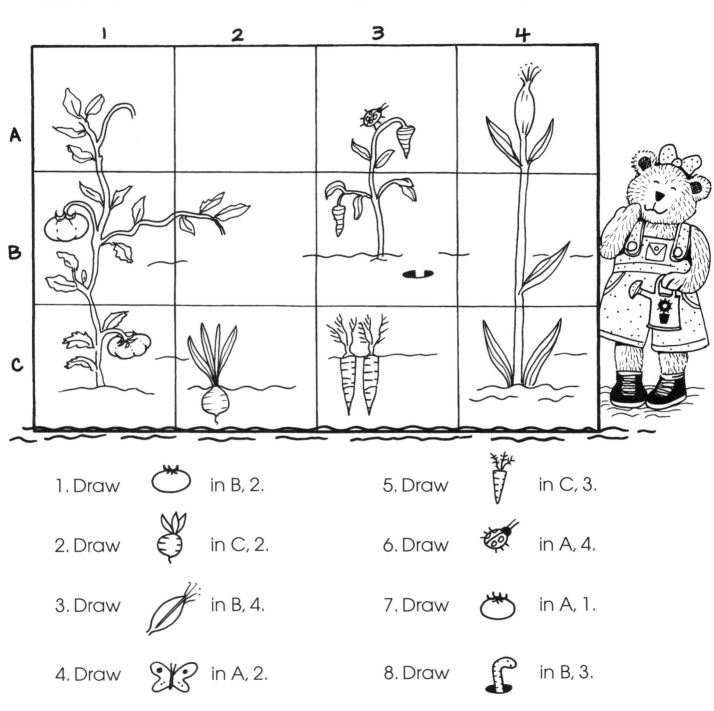

1. Draw ⬭ in B, 2.

2. Draw 🌰 in C, 2.

3. Draw 🌱 in B, 4.

4. Draw 🦋 in A, 2.

5. Draw 🥕 in C, 3.

6. Draw 🐞 in A, 4.

7. Draw 🍅 in A, 1.

8. Draw 🐛 in B, 3.

Name _____

Place Things on a Grid

Treasure Island

Noah found a map in Uncle Jack's attic.

Could it be a real treasure map?

Do you think it is real?   **yes**   **no**

Use the map to answer the questions.

1. Where is the ? _____

2. Where is the ? _____

3. Where is the ? _____

4. Where are the ? _____

5. Where is the ? _____

6. Where is the ? _____

7. Where is the  ? _____

8. Where is the  ? _____

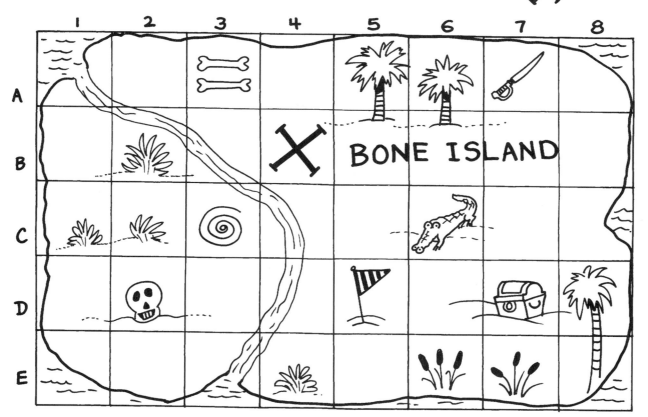

Name _____

Read a Map on a Grid

Round or Flat?

Miss Grizz is teaching about maps and globes.

Look at these maps along with her students.

Look at the globe and the flat map of the world.

Follow the directions to color both maps.

A globe is a model of Earth.

1. Color all the land green.

2. Color all the water blue.

3. Trace the equator with a red crayon.

4. Color the North Pole flags red.

5. Color the South Pole flags yellow.

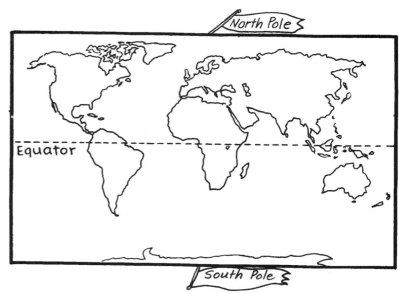

Name _____

Bear County Maps

Miss Grizz wants to visit Honeytown in Bear County.

Decide which map Miss Grizz needs to use.

Draw a line from each map to the box that describes it.

Put a ★ on the map Miss Grizz can use to get to Honeytown.

1.

2.

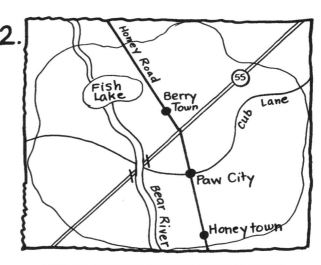

3.

A **weather map** shows the weather.

A **road map** shows where roads go.

A **topographic map** shows what the land is like.

Name _____

Kinds of Maps

Washington

Oregon

Idaho

Montana

North Dakota

South Dakota

Wyoming

Bear Creek

Bear Lake

Honeyville

Bear River City

Nebraska

Nevada

Utah

Colorado

Kansas

California

Arizona

oklahoma

Big Bear City

New Mexico

Texas

Honey Grove

Alaska

Hawaii

So Many Bear Places!

The Bear family wants to visit places with bear names. Look at how many places there are in the United States! Look at the map to see where the bears went. Follow the directions below.

1. Trace the Bears' trip with a red crayon.

2. Color your state green.

3. Color the states that touch your state blue.

4. Color the rest of the states yellow.

Name _____

Puzzle Time

Noah Bear and Sara Bearheart are puzzled.
Can you help them with their new jigsaw puzzle?
Draw a line to show where each piece belongs on the puzzle.

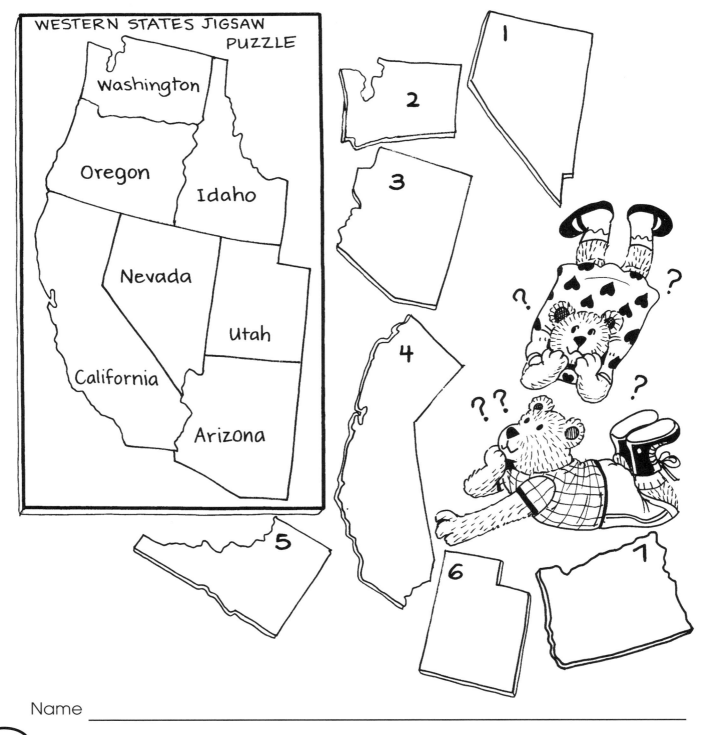

Name _____

The Great Lakes Are Great!

The Bears love to travel to the Great Lakes for their vacations.
They always take a good map.

Look at the map of the states around the
Great Lakes. Follow the directions!

5. Color Michigan pink.

6. Color Illinois orange.

1. Color the lakes blue.

7. Color New York brown.

2. Color Indiana green.

8. Color Pennsylvania purple.

3. Color Ohio red.

9. How many lakes are there? _____

4. Color Wisconsin yellow.

10. Does Lake Erie touch Ohio?
    yes   no

Name _____

Find Information on a Map

The Bus Ride to Camp

Grandpa Bear drives the bus to summer camp.

The bear kids sing camp songs in the back.

Grandpa never takes the short way to camp.

Everyone is having too much fun!

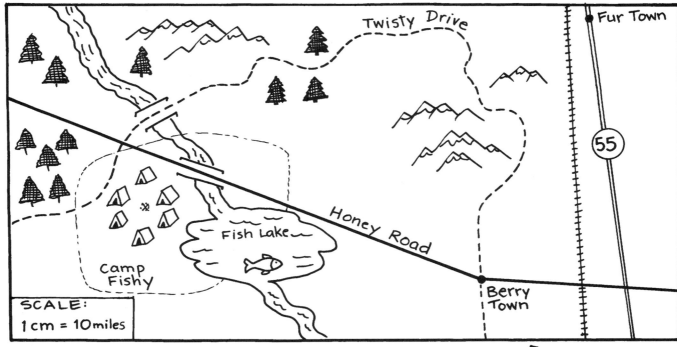

Answer these questions.

1. What route number is on the highway? ____

2. How many roads cross the river? ____

3. How many tents are in the campground? ____

4. How many roads go through Berry Town? ____

5. Is there a forest west of the river?   **yes**   **no**

6. Is Fish Lake north of Honey Road?   **yes**   **no**

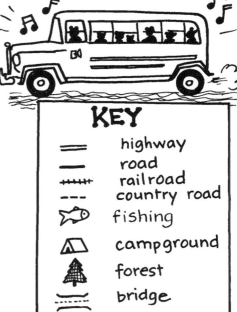

KEY

═══	highway
───	road
┼┼┼┼	railroad
---	country road
🐟	fishing
⛺	campground
🌲	forest
～～	bridge

Name _____

Find Information on a Map

Full Tents

Miss Grizz, the camp counselor, has her own tent.

Grandma Bear, the camp cook, has her own tent.

The other tents are for the campers.

Follow the directions to find out
who sleeps in each tent.

Grandma's tent is the farthest north. Color it blue.

The two girls' tents are west of the fire. Color them green.

The two boys' tents are east of the fire. Color them orange.

The only tent left belongs to Miss Grizz. Color it red.

Name _____

Find Information on a Map

First Prize Map

Wesley Bear won first prize for his map.

What did his map look like?

Follow the directions to find out!

1. Draw a 🚗 on the peninsula.

2. Draw a 🌴 on the island.

3. Draw a ⛵ in the bay.

4. Draw a 🐟 in the lake.

5. Draw some 🌲🌲 on the mountains.

6. Color the river blue.

7. Color the ocean green.

8. Color the plain brown.

Name _____

A Trip to the Farm

Noah wants to visit Grandma and Grandpa Bear on their new farm.

His family is taking a drive from Berry Town to Blue Bell Farm.

Noah is reading the map to help Papa find the way.

Help Noah read the map.

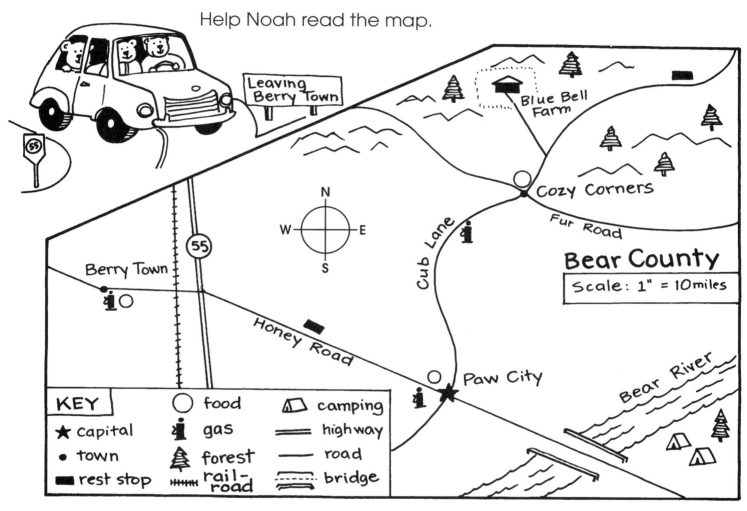

1. Trace the railroad with red.

2. Will they cross the river on the way to the farm?   **yes   no**

3. How many gas stations are shown on the map? _____

4. Is Berry Town a capital?   **yes   no**

5. How many rest stops are on Honey Road? _____

6. Can they get some food at Cozy Corners?   **yes   no**

Name _____

A Pen Pal in Japan

Benjy sent a jar of honey to his pen pal Miko in Japan.

Guess what Miko sent to Benjy? Raw fish!

They have lots of fish in Japan because Japan is made of islands.

Look at the map that shows some of Japan's products.

1. Is rice grown on the island of Hokkaido? **yes no**

2. Are fish found by all the islands? **yes no**

3. Do trees grow on all the islands? **yes no**

4. What symbol shows
   where ships are built? _____

5. What product is
   shown the most? _____

6. How many rice
   symbols are on the map? _____

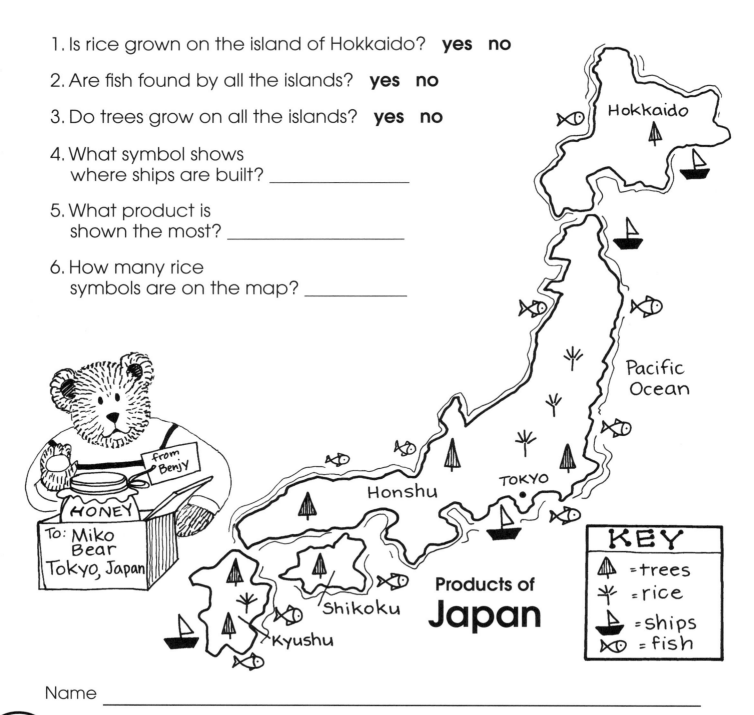

Products of **Japan**

KEY
⚲ = trees
�※ = rice
⛵ = ships
🐟 = fish

Name _____

Product Map

The Weather Reporter

Eliza Bear wants to be a weather reporter.
She listens to all the news about the weather.
Look at her weather map of Mexico.
Follow the directions to color the map.

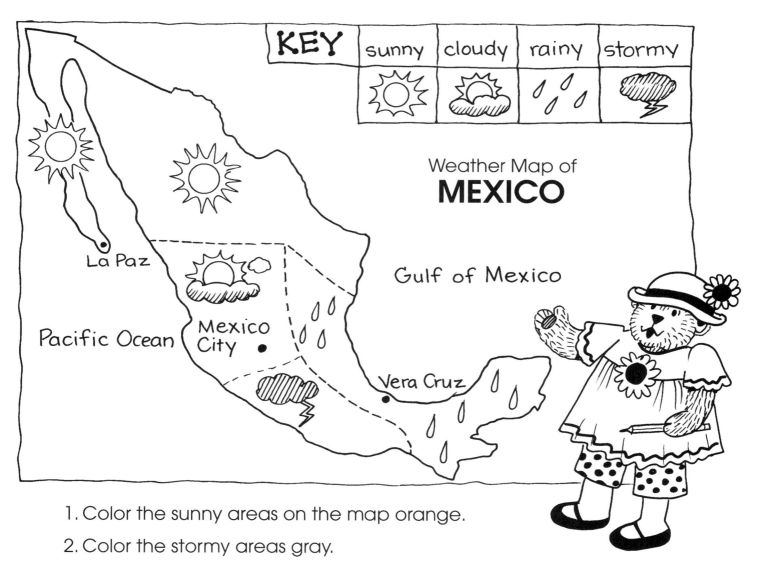

KEY | sunny | cloudy | rainy | stormy

Weather Map of
MEXICO

La Paz

Pacific Ocean

Mexico City

Gulf of Mexico

Vera Cruz

1. Color the sunny areas on the map orange.

2. Color the stormy areas gray.

3. Color the rainy areas blue.

4. Color the cloudy areas pink.

Name _____

Fishing Friends

Sara and Grandma love to fish.

This year they bought a fishing map at the Ranger Station.

The map tells them how many fish are in each lake or pond.

Now they know where to get the most fish!

Mountain Lakes

Read the map key.

See that 1 fish on the map means 10 fish in the lakes.

1. How many fish are in Trout Lake? _____

2. How many fish are in Minnow Pond? _____

3. How many fish are in Catfish Pond? _____

4. How many fish are in Salmon Lake? _____

5. Which place has the best fishing?

_____

- -

_____

Name _____

Population Map

What's for Dinner?

Grandma and Grandpa opened a restaurant in Cozy Corners.
They wanted to find out what bears love to eat most!
Noah, Eliza, Sara, and Wesley voted for their favorite foods.
Read the chart to find out what the bears like to eat.

Bears' Favorite Foods

Bear's Name	Pizza	Berries	Honey	Pancakes
Noah	X		X	
Eliza		X		X
Sara			X	X
Wesley	X			X

Answer each question.

1. Which food got the most votes?

_____

- -

2. Which food do Wesley and Noah both like?

_____

- -

3. Which food is Sara's favorite besides pancakes?

_____

- -

4. Which food got 1 vote?

_____

- -

5. Which foods got 2 votes?

_____

- -

_____

6. Which one of these foods is your favorite?

_____

- -

Name _____

Read a Chart

A Ride in a Hot-Air Balloon

Noah and Grandpa are off on another balloon ride.

They are going to stop at all their favorite places.

Some places are far away.

The chart tells how far it is to each place from Berry Town.

Favorite Places

Favorite Places	Miles from Home
Honeytown Mall	35 miles
Polar Bear Movies	15 miles
Grizzly Fun Park	100 miles
Beehive Village	45 miles
Choco-Hut Ice Cream Store	15 miles
Grandma's House	110 miles

1. Circle the place that is the farthest from Berry Town.

   Grandma's House   Grizzly Fun Park   Beehive Village

2. How far away is the Honeytown Mall? ____ miles

3. How far away is the Beehive Village? ____ miles

4. How far away is the Choco-Hut Ice Cream Store? ____ miles

5. Circle two places that are the same distance from Berry Town.

   Polar Bear Movies   Honeytown Mall

   Beehive Village   Choco-Hut Ice Cream Store

Name _____

Eliza's New Map

Eliza is ready to draw a new map of her favorite place.

Will it be a park? A secret fort? A tree house? A toy store?

It can be any place that you decide!

Choose a favorite place for Eliza and make a map of that place.

Give the map a title, a compass rose, and a key.

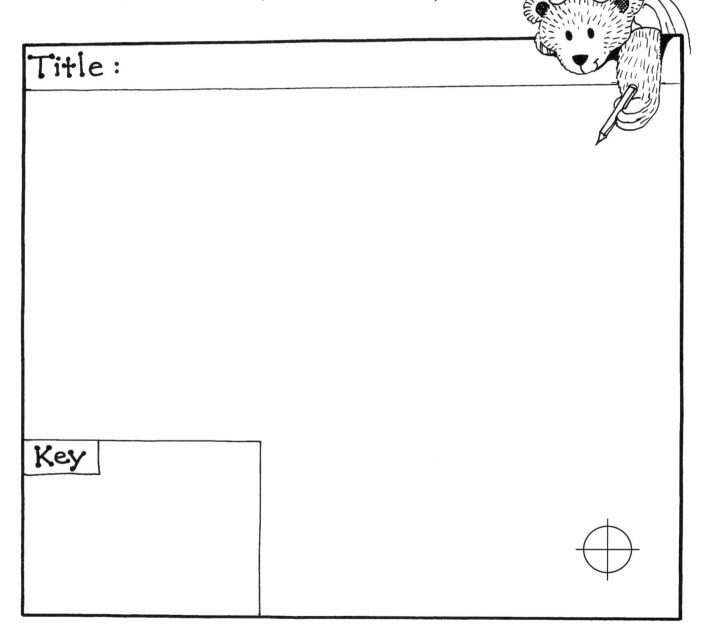

Title:

Key

Name _____

SCIENCE

Skills Exercises
Grade Two

astronomy

chemistry

biology

geology

anatomy

earth science

SKILLS CHECKLIST
SCIENCE

✔	SKILL	PAGE(S)
	Identify parts of some plants	211–215
	Examine the life cycle of seed plants	212
	Identify some characteristics and processes of plants	212, 215
	Identify parts of flowers and their functions	214
	Classify some animal groups	216, 217, 218–220
	Identify characteristics of some animal groups	216–221
	Match animals with their homes and habitats	222, 224, 225
	Describe some animal behaviors	223
	Identify and define some ecology concepts	226
	Describe ways organisms interact in their communities	227
	Identify some kinds of pollution and conservation	228, 229
	Describe the relationship of Earth, sun, and moon in space	230, 231
	Identify some planets and other objects in space	231, 232
	Identify some safety behaviors and skills	233
	Identify the effects of seasons and temperature changes	234, 235
	Name some of the body's parts	236–237
	Identify some features of the skeletal system	237
	Identify some dinosaurs	238
	Recognize fossils	239
	Describe some landforms on the Earth's surface	240, 241
	Describe some features of the Earth's oceans and waters	240, 241, 243, 244
	Identify some properties of air	242

Something's Missing

Abby is confused about these plants. They seem to be missing some parts. What's missing? Name the plant parts that are described below. Then decide which parts are missing from these plants, and draw them where they belong.

1. The ☐ hold the plant in the ground. They take in water and nutrients from the soil.

2. The ☐ holds up the leaves. It carries water and nutrients to the plant.

3. The ☐ use air, water, and sunlight to make food for the plant.

4. The ☐ is the place where fruits and seeds form.

5. The ☐ is where seeds form in plants like pine or fir trees.

Name _____

Circles Everywhere

Lots of things in life go around in circles. One of the most important circles is a life cycle. The life of a plant goes in a circle. A seed lives and grows. It becomes a plant. The plant makes more seeds. The seeds it makes give life to new plants.

Draw the pictures that show the life cycle of a pine tree.

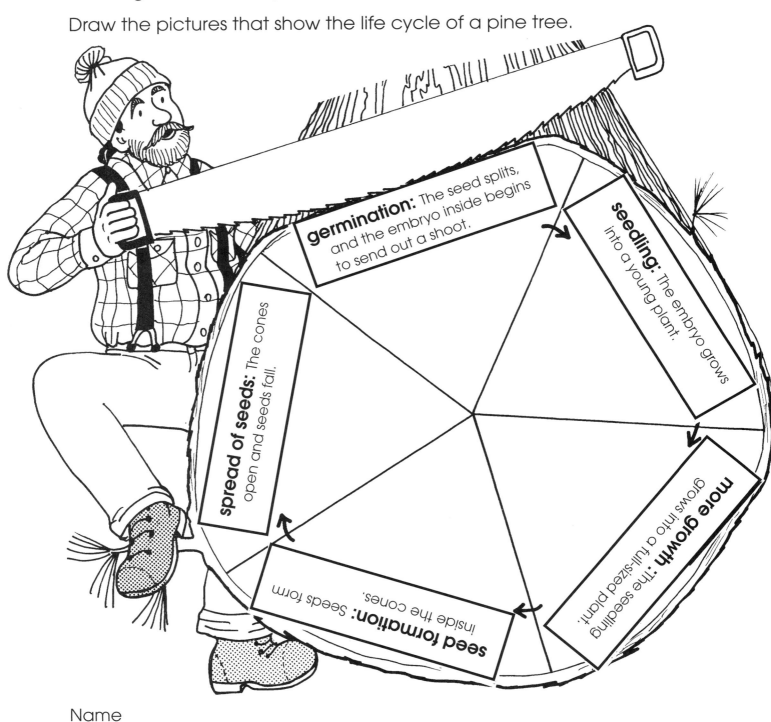

germination: The seed splits, and the embryo inside begins to send out a shoot.

seedling: The embryo grows into a young plant.

spread of seeds: The cones open and seeds fall.

more growth: The seedling grows into a full-sized plant.

seed formation: Seeds form inside the cones.

Name _____

Life Cycle of Seed Plants

What Do You Know About Trees?

Did you know that we look to trees
For food for birds, squirrels, and bees
For coffee, cocoa, and teas
For paper, pecans, and peaches
For pineapple and pear preserves
For floors, cabinets, and doors
For boats, boots,
and even books . . .

Wherever people
live, work, and play,
trees are very
important. Test your
knowledge of trees
by labeling the
parts of the
tree pictured
at the right.

Word Box
cambium layer
roots
crown
sapwood
outer bark
heartwood
trunk
inner bark
fruit

1. _____

2. _____

3. _____

4. _____

5. _____

6. _____

7. _____

8. _____

9. _____

Name _____

Identify Parts of Trees

What Do Bees Know?

Bees spend a lot of time around flowers. They know which part of a flower will supply food for them. Read about the flower parts. Then decide which bee is visiting each part. Write the letter of that bee on the line.

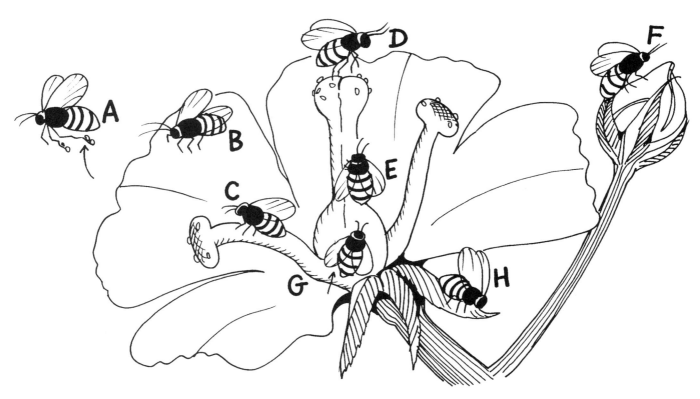

_____ 1. The **petals** protect the inside parts of the flower. They attract bees who bring pollen from other flowers.

_____ 2. A **bud** is a young flower that is not open yet.

_____ 3. The **sepals** cover and protect the flower bud before it opens.

_____ 4. The **pistil** in the center contains the ovary where seeds are made.

_____ 5. The **stigma** is the sticky top of the pistil. Pollen grains stick to it and send down tubes into the ovary to make seeds.

_____ 6. The **stamens** produce pollen.

_____ 7. The **ovary** is where seeds grow.

_____ 8. **Pollen grains** contain cells that join with egg cells in the ovary and produce new seeds.

Name _____

Photo-What?

Photosynthesis is a huge word about plants. Does it mean that plants know how to take photos? Not really!

Finish this puzzle with the words below to show that you know some things about how photosynthesis works.

Photosynthesis is the process in which plants use air, water, nutrients, and sunlight to make food.

Across

1. _____ dioxide is a part of air used by the plant to make food.
2. Plants need this to make food.
3. These tiny openings in leaves allow them to get air.
4. This gas is given off by the plant during photosynthesis.
5. Plants take air in through their _____.

Down

1. This makes the plant green and helps it make food.

leaves   chlorophyll   carbon   oxygen   sunlight   stomata

Name _____

Creeping Creatures

When Lucy opened her eyes this morning, she was shocked and surprised! A whole collection of creatures had gathered on her wall.

> Some of them were **insects.** Insects have 3 body sections, 6 legs, and 2 antennae. Draw a red circle around all the insects.
>
> Some of them were **arachnids** (spiders). Arachnids have 8 legs and no antennae. Draw a blue box around all the arachnids.

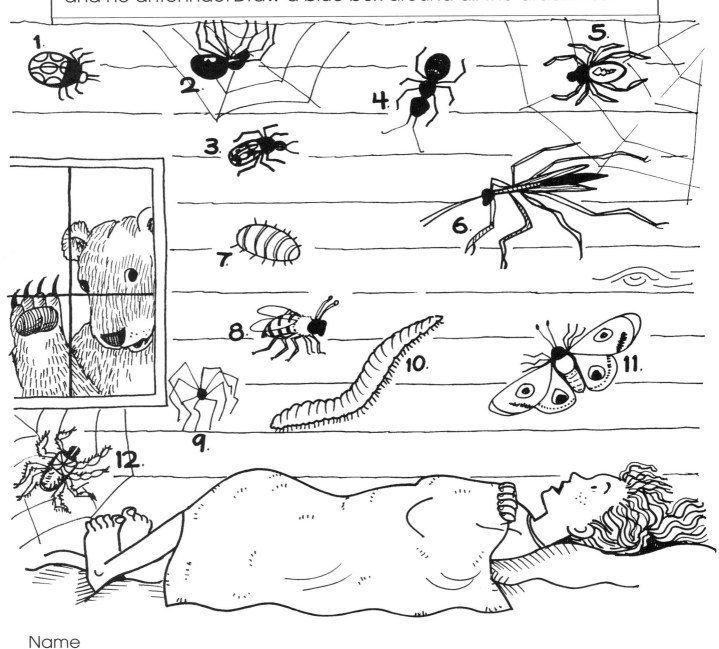

Name _____

Animal Classification

Animals With & Without

Nicholas has a pretty amazing collection of animals in his backyard. These animals can all be divided into two large groups: animals with backbones and animals without backbones.

Color all the vertebrates in the picture.

Animals with backbones are called **vertebrates.**
Animals **without** backbones are called **invertebrates.**

Name _____

Vertebrates on Wheels

Do you remember that vertebrates are animals with backbones? There are 5 different groups of vertebrates.

On these two pages, there is a wheel for each group. Some words or pictures are missing from the wheels. Look at the list. Write each word or draw each picture on the right wheel.

give milk to young
breathe only with gills
feathers
wings
fins
live on land or water
cold-blooded
smooth, moist skin
most fly
hair or fur
warm-blooded
scales
cold-blooded
babies grow inside mother
scaly, dry skin

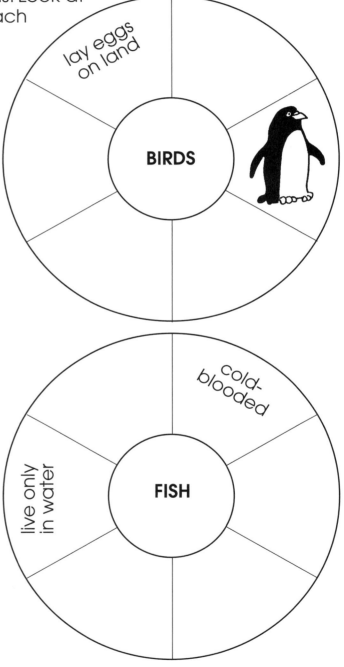

lay eggs on land

BIRDS

cold-blooded

FISH

live only in water

Name _____

Use with page 219.

Vertebrate Classification

Vertebrates on Wheels, cont.

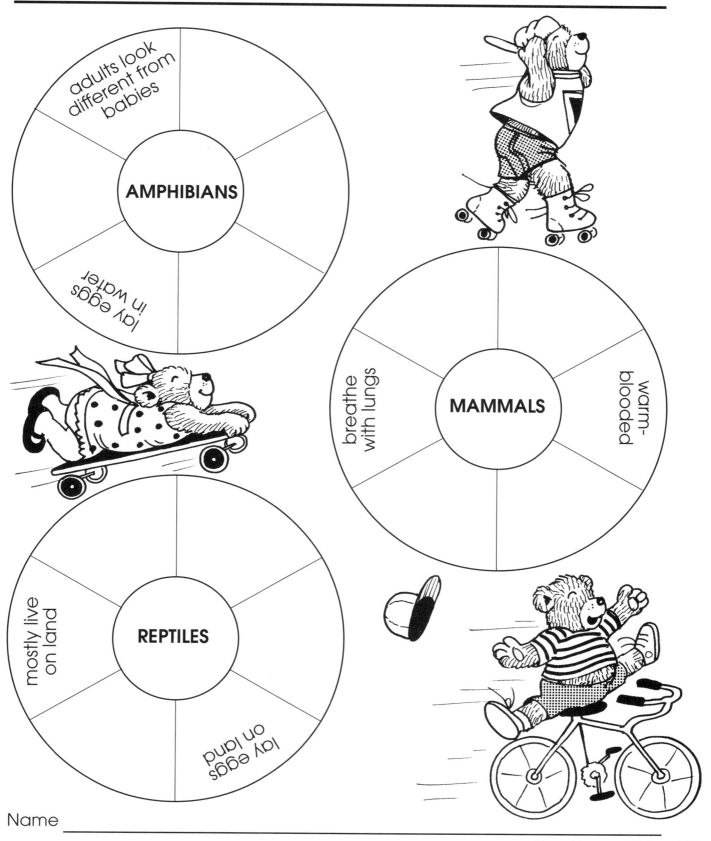

AMPHIBIANS

adults look different from babies

lay eggs in water

MAMMALS

breathe with lungs

warm-blooded

REPTILES

mostly live on land

lay eggs on land

Name

Use with page 218.

219

Copyright © 2016 World Book, Inc./
Incentive Publications, Chicago, IL

Vertebrate Classification

Mix-Up at the Zoo

Help! Some of the zoo animals got into the wrong homes.

Find the animal in each home that does not belong.
Draw an arrow from the animal to its correct home.

Name _____

Vertebrate Classification

Wormy Questions

There are millions of earthworms all over the world. But how much do you know about them? Does an earthworm have legs? Can you tell its head from its tail? How does it move?

Use the words down the side to finish these wormy statements. If you need some help, use your science book.

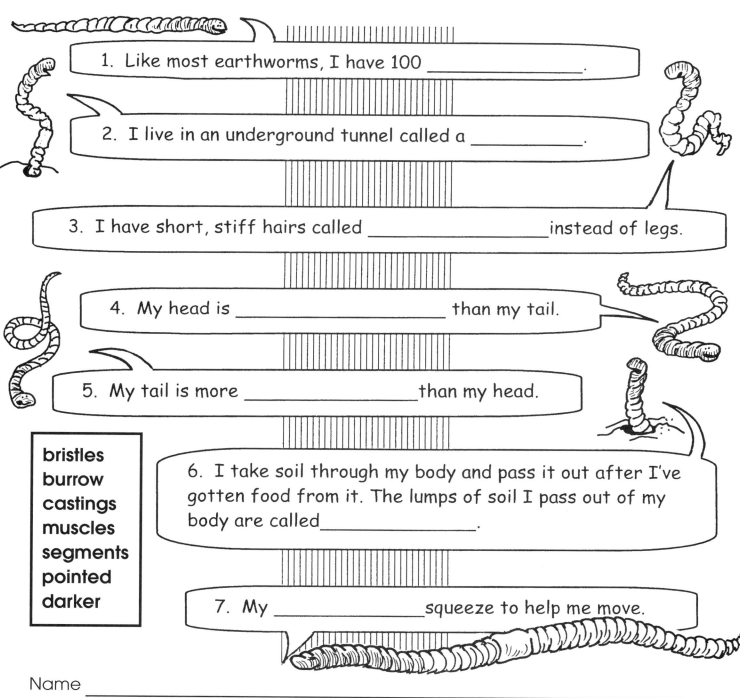

1. Like most earthworms, I have 100 _____.

2. I live in an underground tunnel called a _____.

3. I have short, stiff hairs called _____ instead of legs.

4. My head is _____ than my tail.

5. My tail is more _____ than my head.

6. I take soil through my body and pass it out after I've gotten food from it. The lumps of soil I pass out of my body are called _____.

7. My _____ squeeze to help me move.

bristles
burrow
castings
muscles
segments
pointed
darker

Name _____

Home, Sweet Home

This is home to one of these animals. But what is it? And which animal lives in this home? Follow the dots from 1 to 26 to find out what the home is. Color the home. Then circle the correct animal for the home. Color all the animals.

Name _____

Animal Homes

How Those Animals Behave!

Animals do some very strange and interesting things. What they do is called animal behavior. Here are some kinds of **animal behavior.**

C Animals **camouflage** themselves for protection. This means they blend in with things around them.

A Animals **adapt** to their environment. This means they develop body parts or behaviors that help them survive.

D Animals **defend** themselves when they are in danger.

H Animals **hibernate**, or sleep, for long periods of time to save energy.

M Animals **migrate**, or move, to other places for food or breeding.

Put the correct letter by each picture to tell what kind of behavior it shows.

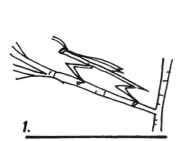

1. _____

2. _____

3. _____

4. _____

5. _____

6. _____

7. _____

8. _____

Name _____

Animal Behavior

Looking for Habitats

A **habitat** is a place where a living thing gets everything it needs — food, shelter, living space, the right temperature, and protection.

These plants and animals have wandered away from their habitats. Help them get back where they belong.

Look at the habitats on the next page (page 225). Draw each of the plants and animals below in the habitat where it belongs.

Name _____

Use with page 225.

Looking for Habitats, cont.

A **desert** has very little moisture.

On a **grassland,** most of the plants are grass.

A **coniferous forest** has trees with needles.

A **rain forest** is very hot and wet.

Ponds, lakes, swamps, and rivers are **fresh water** habitats.

An **ocean** is a **salt water** habitat.

Name _____

Use with page 224.

Habitats

Eco-Puzzle

Ecology is the study of the way plants and animals live together within their environment.

This puzzle is missing some ecology words. Write each of these words in the blank puzzle piece that is joined to the meaning of the word.

consumers   predator   food chain
scavenger   community   prey
decomposer   producers

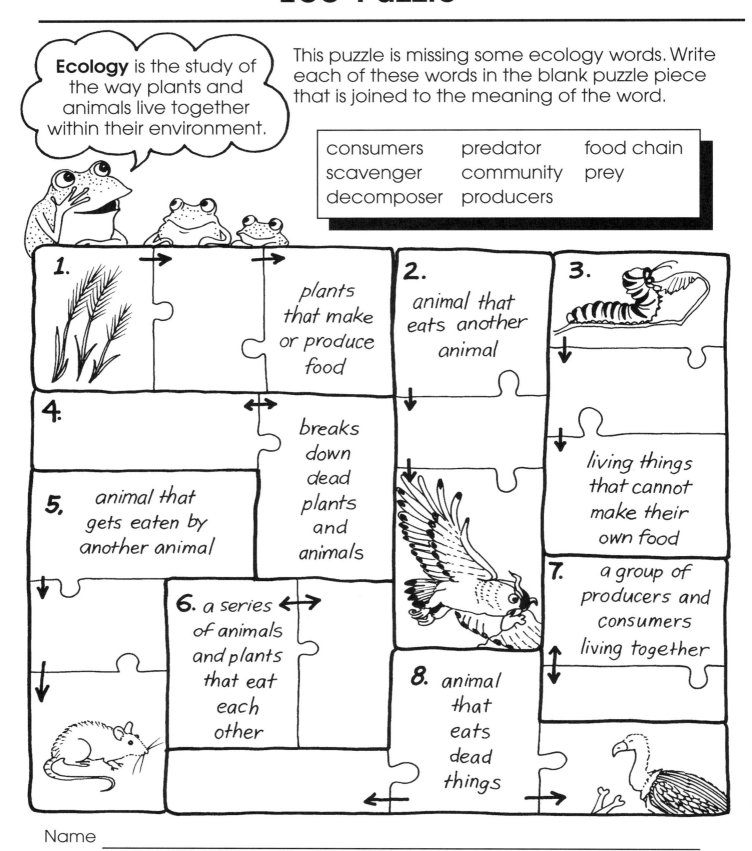

1.

plants that make or produce food

2. animal that eats another animal

3.

living things that cannot make their own food

4.

breaks down dead plants and animals

5. animal that gets eaten by another animal

6. a series of animals and plants that eat each other

7. a group of producers and consumers living together

8. animal that eats dead things

Name _____

Who's Who in the Community?

You know that people live in communities. So do plants and animals.

What is a **community?** It is a group of consumers and producers living together in an area.

A **producer** is a living thing that makes its own food.

A **consumer** is a living thing that cannot make its own food and must eat other living things.

Find the producers. Color them **green.**

Find the consumers. Color them **other colors.**

Circle any predators (animals that eat other animals) that you see.

Name _____

Too Much Pollution

Polly is surprised to see so much pollution.

Help her find all the different kinds of pollution shown in this picture. Put a large **X** on each example of pollution you see. How many did you find?

Name _____

Earth Care

The trash can is full of words that tell about pollution or ways to care for Earth. The sentences tell some things you need to know about how pollution can harm Earth or how you can help keep Earth clean.

One word in each sentence is scrambled. Unscramble it. (Use the words in the trash can for correct spelling.)

1. (noPilltou) _____ is a harmful thing that can damage the environment.

2. Be careful not to (etsaw) _____ water, paper, or other supplies.

3. If you (cryceel) _____ things, they can be used again.

4. Do not (rettil) _____ .
   Put waste in the
   (shrat) _____ can.

5. Sound that harms the environment is called (osine) _____ pollution.

6. Big ships sometimes spill (ilo) _____ in the ocean.

7. Toxic wastes are (noispo) _____ to the environment.

8. Cars, trucks, and machines put out (shaxute) _____ into the (ira) _____

9. (diAc) _____ rain contains chemicals from burning fuels.

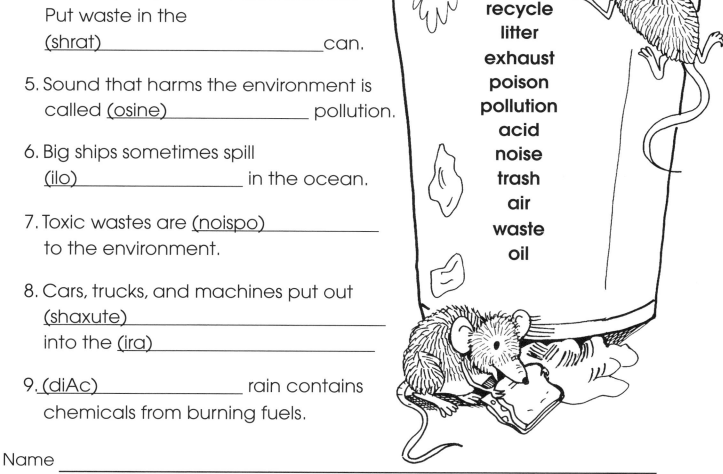

recycle
litter
exhaust
poison
pollution
acid
noise
trash
air
waste
oil

Name _____

Places in Space

Meg and Tom wish they could fly in a rocket and see planet Earth.
Planet Earth is like a big ball moving around the sun.

The sun is a star, and it gives off light.
It is much bigger than Earth.

The moon is not a planet or a star.
It is a smaller ball that moves around Earth.

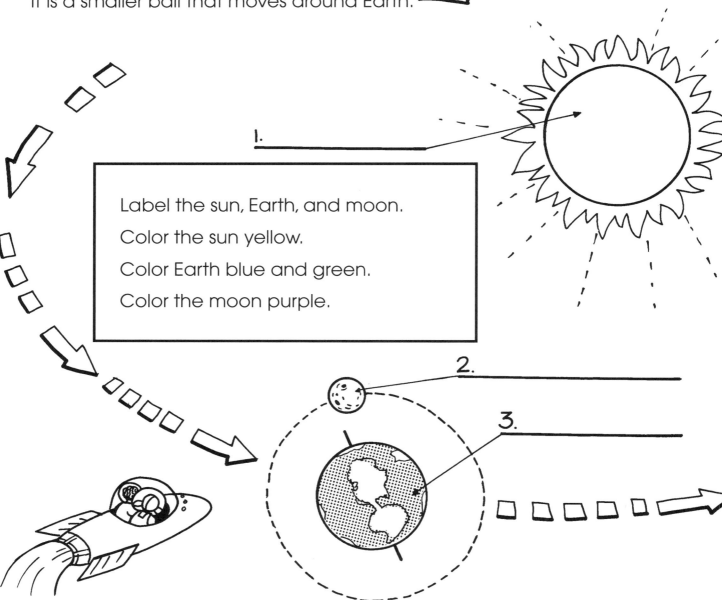

Label the sun, Earth, and moon.

Color the sun yellow.

Color Earth blue and green.

Color the moon purple.

1. _____

2. _____

3. _____

Name _____

Earth • Sun • Moon

The Spinning Earth

When it's dark, Meg looks at the sky through her telescope.

Do you know why darkness comes at the end of the day?

It is because Earth spins.

The sun is a star that gives off light that shines on the Earth.

Where the sunlight touches Earth, it is day.

For the half of Earth turned away from the sun, it is night.

A.

B.

Sun

1. Circle the letter that shows the person in the daytime.   **A** or **B**

2. Circle the letter that shows the person in the nighttime.   **A** or **B**

3. We have day and night because the Earth _____.

Name _____

Day and Night

What's Out There?

Imagine Tom and Meg exploring in a spaceship!

When they look out their window, they see some amazing things.

Look at the words below.

Put the number of the word on the correct picture in outer space.

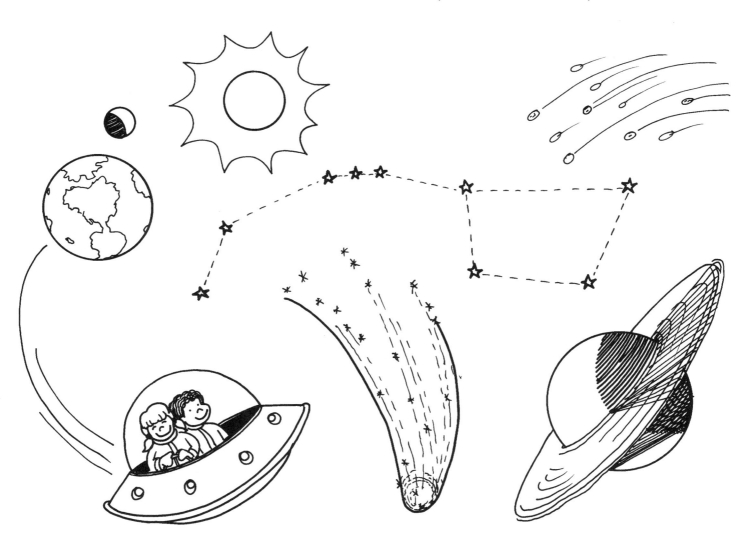

1. spaceship   **2. comet**   **3. sun**   **4. planet Earth**

5. the Big Dipper   **6. shooting stars**   **7. moon**   **8. planet Saturn**

Name _____

Unsafe!

Several things in this picture are not safe. Find them quickly, before anybody gets hurt! Circle any unsafe situations or actions you see.

Name _____

When Seasons Change

What happens to plants in winter?
What do animals do in spring?
What is the weather like in summer?

When the seasons change, some things are different.

Draw pictures on the seasons chart.

Show some things that happen in different seasons.

Season	What is the weather?	What do animals do?	What do plants do?	What do I do?
summer	(sun and clouds drawing)			
fall			(tree with falling leaves drawing)	
winter		(hibernating animal drawing)		
spring				(child flying kite drawing)

Name _____

Hot, Cold, or In-Between?

The great thing about seasons is that the temperature changes!
Meg and Tom get to do different things in different seasons.
A **thermometer** tells how hot or cold the temperature is.
Use a red crayon to color in the temperature on each thermometer.

1. The temperature is 90 °F.

2. The temperature is 60 °F.

3. The temperature is 30 °F.

4. The temperature is 70 °F.

Name _____

Seasons • Temperature

Body Parts You Can See

Meg and Tom are learning about body parts that they can see.

You can do the same thing!

Lie on a big piece of paper, and ask a friend to draw around your body.

Label each of these body parts
on your body drawing.

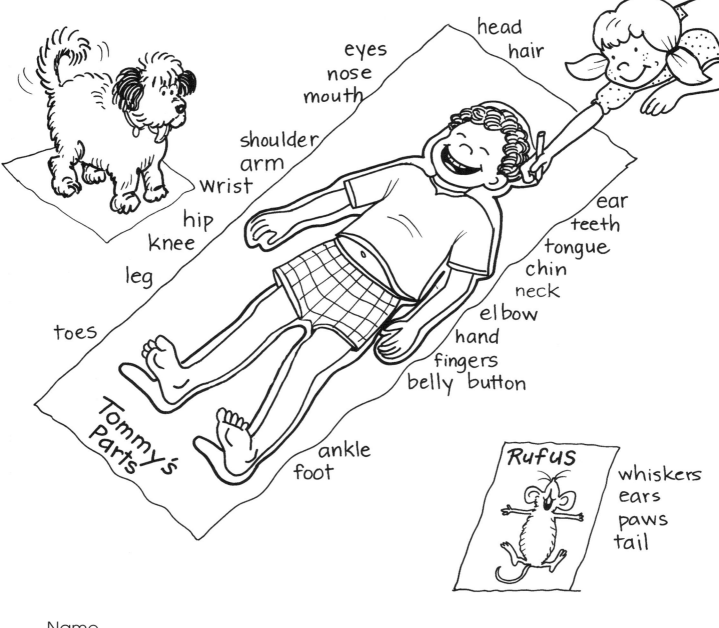

head
hair
eyes
nose
mouth
shoulder
arm
wrist
hip
knee
leg
toes
ear
teeth
tongue
chin
neck
elbow
hand
fingers
belly button
ankle
foot

Tommy's Parts

Rufus

whiskers
ears
paws
tail

Name _____

Body Parts

Body Parts You Can't See

Tom has learned that the bones in his body make a skeleton.

Skeletons hold the body up and help it move.

Look at all the bones on Tom's skeleton chart.

Draw an arrow from each bone to the matching word.

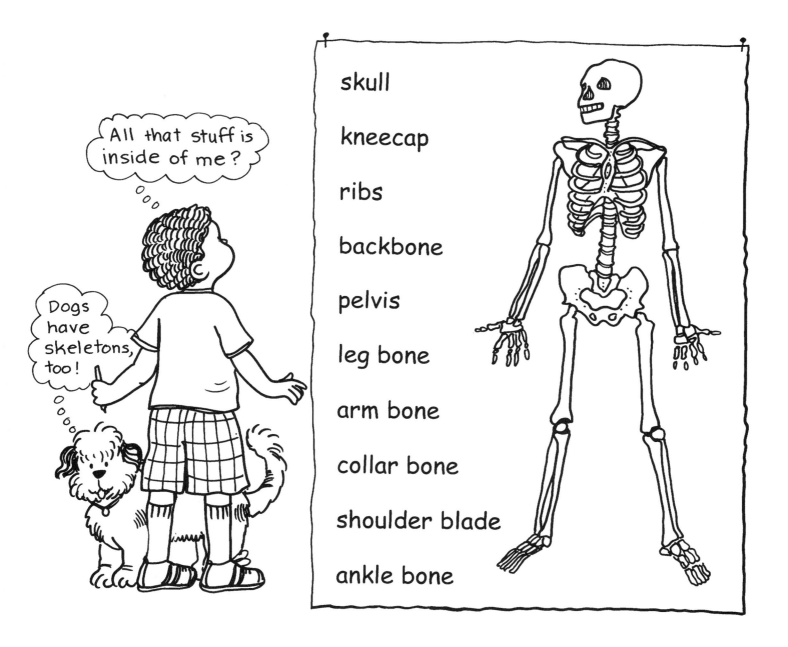

skull

kneecap

ribs

backbone

pelvis

leg bone

arm bone

collar bone

shoulder blade

ankle bone

Name _____

Disappearing Dinosaurs

Learning about dinosaurs is a favorite hobby of Tom's.
He likes the long names!

He knows that dinosaurs are extinct now, but a long time ago millions of them roamed the Earth.

Color each dinosaur the way you think it might have looked.

Triceratops
lived in a herd for protection

Troodon
the smartest dinosaur

Brachiosaurus
a long-necked dinosaur

Tyrannosaurus rex
a huge meat-eating dinosaur

Stegosaurus
had a spiky tail for protection

Name _____

Old Bones and Fossils

How do scientists know what dinosaurs looked like?

They study old bones and put them together.

These old bones are **fossils.**

Draw a line to match each fossil with the thing that made it.

A **fossil** is a print or a part of a plant or animal that lived long ago.

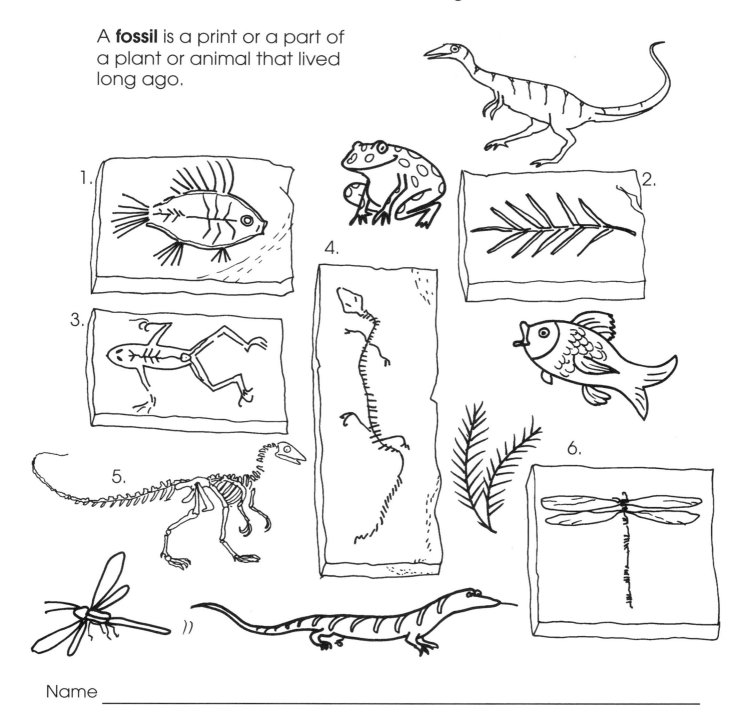

Name _____

A Fish on the Hook

Do you know the difference between a river and a lake?

If you do, find the lake and draw a fish on Tom's hook.

Show what you know about Earth's land and water.

Draw these pictures on the map.

...a fish on the hook.

...a raft on the river.

...alligator eyes in the swamp.

...a house on the hill.

Name _____

Use with page 241.
Land and Water

A Fish on the Hook, cont.

... a palm tree on the island.

... flowers on the plain.

... trees on the mountain.

... a ship in the ocean.

Name _____

Use with page 240.

Land and Water

How Much Air?

Air is made of different gases.
Air takes up space.
Air does not have its own
shape or size.

Which has more air. . .
a full tire or a flat tire?

In each row, color the thing that has the most air.

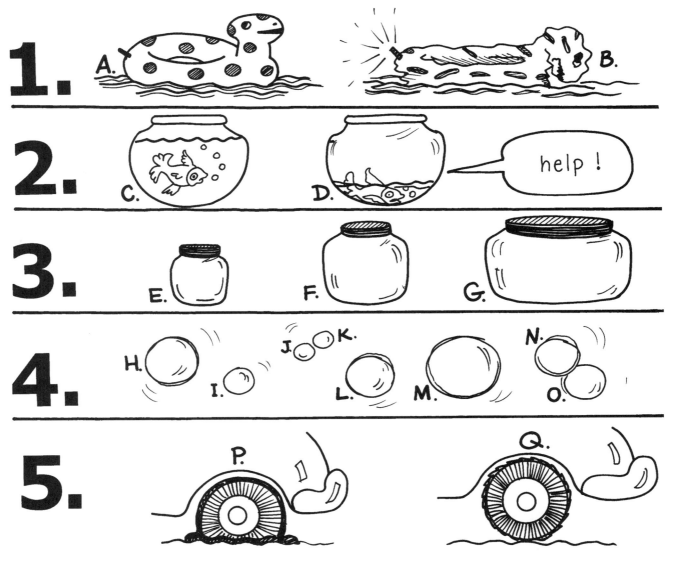

Air Properties

Name _____

What You See in the Sea

The ocean is full of plants, animals, and other interesting things.

Lucky Tom is exploring the ocean.

Help him name some of the things he sees.

Draw lines to match the words with the correct pictures.

waves	shells	beach	kelp
octopus	fish	crab	island
diver	jellyfish	starfish	dolphin

Name _____

Whales, Tales, and Other Mysteries of the Deep

Test your knowledge of ocean life by writing the letter of the correct definition beside each term.

___ 1. blubber

___ 2. dolphins

___ 3. flukes

___ 4. mackerel

___ 5. mammal

___ 6. Portuguese man-o-war

___ 7. sawfish

___ 8. sea cows

___ 9. sea otters

___ 10. species

___ 11. squids

___ 12. trilobite

A. the only ocean mammals that still have true hind legs with webbed toes

B. an edible fish of the North Atlantic with a greenish, blue-striped back and a silvery belly

C. ocean mammals that often play near passing ships and that communicate with each other through sharp chirps and squeaks

D. an animal that has hair, gives birth to young, is warm-blooded, and lives on its mother's milk as a baby

E. animals with the same characteristics that can mate and produce young

F. a marine predator that kills its victims by slashing them with a snout edged with sharp teeth

G. long, slender, fish-eating sea mollusks having ten arms

H. a warm-sea creature having a large, bladder-like sac which enables it to float on the water and long tentacles with powerful stinging cells

I. slow swimming sea mammals that eat kelp and sea grass

J. a sea floor scavenger that is now extinct

K. layer of fat under the skin of many marine mammals

L. two large fins at the end of a whale's tail

Name _____

Science Words to Know

adaptation—a characteristic that helps a living thing survive in its environment

allergy—a reaction of the body to something, such as pollen

air—layer of gases around Earth

amphibian—a cold-blooded animal with a backbone that can live both on land and in water

arachnid—an 8-legged animal with no antennae

atmosphere—the air around Earth

behavior—any response an animal makes to its environment

bird—a warm-blooded animal with a backbone, feathers, and a beak

bristles—short, stiff hair that helps worms move

bruise—blood vessels broken by an injury to a muscle

burrows—underground tunnels that are homes to some animals

camouflage—a way that an animal blends into its environment

castings—lumps of dirt that have passed through an earthworm's body

clouds—groups of tiny drops of ice or water that hang together in the air

community—a group of plants and animals that live together in an area

condense—to change from a gas to a liquid

consumer—an animal that eats plants or animals to live

continental shelf—the slope of land underneath the water of the ocean

crest—the highest point on a wave

crust—the outer layer of Earth

disease—a sickness

earthquake—a sudden movement of the rock near Earth's surface

energy—being able to work

environment—everything around you

evaporate—to change from a liquid to a gas

fault—a crack in Earth's surface

fish—a cold-blooded animal with a backbone that lives in water, breathes with gills, and is covered with scales

force—the push or pull that moves an object

fossil—a print or part of an animal that lived long ago

freeze—to change from a liquid to a solid by becoming colder

fracture—a break in a bone

fuel—something that is burned to make heat

gas—a form of matter that has no definite size or shape

germination—the beginning growth of a seed into a plant

glacier—a large body of ice that moves

habitat—the place where an animal or plant lives

hibernate—to sleep for a long period of time to save energy

insect—an animal with 3 body segments, 6 legs, and 2 antennae

invertebrate—an animal that has no backbone

kelp—brown seaweed

landform—shapes of land on the surface of the Earth

lava—melted rock that flows out of a volcano

liquid—a form of matter that has a definite size but no definite shape

litter—trash scattered around the environment

mammal—a warm-blooded animal with a backbone that is covered with fur or hair

melt—to change from a solid to a liquid by becoming warmer

migrate—to move to another place for food or breeding

noise—a sound that is not pleasant

nutrition—the foods needed for a living thing to survive

orbit—the path a planet follows around the sun

peninsula—a narrow piece of land with water on all sides but one

petal—the outer, protective part of a flower

photosynthesis—the process in which plants use sunlight to make food

pistil—the part of a flower that contains the ovary where fruit grows

pitch—the highness or lowness of a sound

plain—the bottom of the ocean

planet—a body in space that orbits around the sun

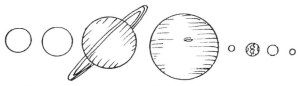

pollutant—something that is harmful to the environment

predator—an animal that eats other animals

prey—an animal that is eaten by another animal

producer—living thing that makes its own food

recycle—to use things again so they are not wasted

reptile—a cold-blooded animal with a backbone and dry, scaly skin

sepal—the outside part of the flower that protects the bud

skeleton—the bones inside a living thing

skin—the outer covering of the body

solar system—the sun and the planets that revolve around it

scavenger—an animal that eats dead things

solid—a form of matter that has a definite size and shape

sprain—when a joint is twisted too far

stamen—the part of the flower that produces pollen

strain—when a muscle is stretched too far

stomata—tiny openings in a leaf that allow air to get in

temperature—a measurement of how warm something is

trench—the deepest part of the ocean floor

trough—the space between the crests of waves

vertebrate—an animal that has a backbone

vibrate—to move back and forth

volcano—a mountain formed by melted rock that comes from inside Earth

weather—the conditions of the air outside

wind—moving air

work—happens whenever an object is moved

Science Words to Know

MATH

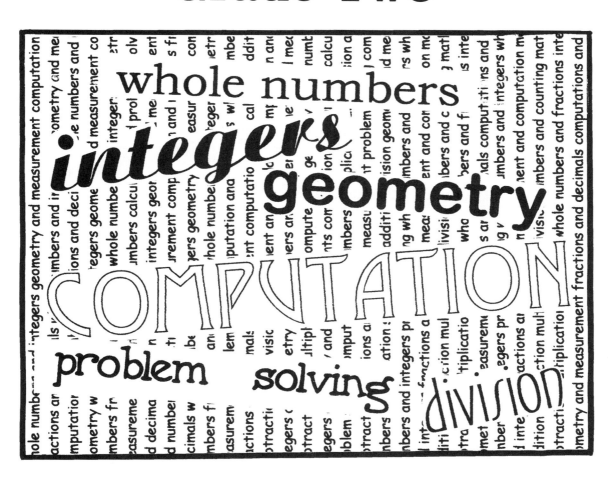

Skills Exercises
Grade Two

SKILLS CHECKLIST
NUMBER CONCEPTS & RELATIONSHIPS

✔	SKILL	PAGE(S)
	Order whole numbers	253, 266
	Compare amounts using comparison words	254, 261
	Compare whole numbers using < and >	254–257
	Identify place value through hundreds	258, 259
	Read and write numbers in expanded form	258, 259
	Count money	260
	Identify values of coins	260
	Write and compare amounts of money	261
	Read and use ordinals	262, 263
	Match numerals to whole number word names	264, 265
	Read and write whole numerals	264, 265
	Estimate amounts	267
	Round numbers to the nearest place through hundreds and thousands	268
	Recognize and extend number patterns and sequences	269
	Describe relationships between numbers	270

SKILLS CHECKLIST
MATH COMPUTATION & PROBLEM SOLVING

✔	SKILL	PAGE(S)
	Add whole numbers with and without renaming	272, 273
	Add columns of 3 or more addends	273
	Subtract whole numbers with and without renaming	274-275
	Use multiplication for computations	276
	Do simple division computations	277
	Choose the correct operation for a problem	278, 279
	Solve problems with money	278, 279
	Solve word problems, including multi-step problems	278, 279
	Write, compare, and estimate amounts of money	278, 279, 284
	Solve problems using illustrations	278, 280, 281
	Read and write fractions	280, 281
	Identify and write mixed numerals	281
	Complete a variety of time-telling tasks; work with dates	282, 283
	Solve problems using maps, charts, and tables	282, 283
	Read and write whole numbers	285
	Identify place value to 6 places	285

SKILLS CHECKLIST
GEOMETRY, MEASUREMENT, & GRAPHING

✔	SKILL	PAGE(S)
	Identify and draw points and lines	287
	Compare geometric figures	287–291
	Identify and draw plane geometric figures	287–291
	Distinguish among different kinds of triangles	288, 289
	Distinguish among different kinds of quadrilaterals	288–290
	Identify and draw different kinds of angles	290
	Identify solid geometric figures	291
	Identify congruent figures	292
	Identify and find length	293–296
	Do a variety of measurement tasks	293–302, 304
	Compare measurements and units of measure	297
	Identify and find units for measuring liquid capacity	297
	Count money and make change	298, 299
	Create and solve problems with money	298, 299
	Write, compare, and estimate amounts of money	298, 299
	Solve problems with measurements	298, 299, 300–301
	Find information on a calendar	300–301
	Solve problems with time	300–301
	Perform a variety of time-telling tasks	300–301, 304
	Solve problems with temperature	302
	Answer questions from data on graphs and charts	303

Critters in Canoes

In the canoe race, the Beetle Bug Team is trying to row faster than the Ant Mania Team.

Look at the numbers on the canoe paddles.

On each paddle, one number is out of order. Figure out which one it is.

A. Circle the number that is out of order, going from smallest to largest.

1.
47
57
37
67
77

2.
500
700
800
900
600
1,000

3.
130
131
132
134
133
135

4.
100
101
102
104
105
103

5.
250
300
350
400
500
450

B. Circle the number that is out of order, going from largest to smallest.

6.
28
27
25
24
23
26

7.
100
95
90
80
75
85
70
65

8.
240
239
234
238
237
236
235

9.
164
154
144
134
114
104
124

10.
565
563
562
561
560
564

Name _____

Goofy Golfing Gophers

Golfers count the number of times they hit the ball for each hole.
The golfer with the lowest number of hits is the winner.

Count the number of hits each golfer takes
to get the ball into this hole. Write the numbers
on the scorecard.

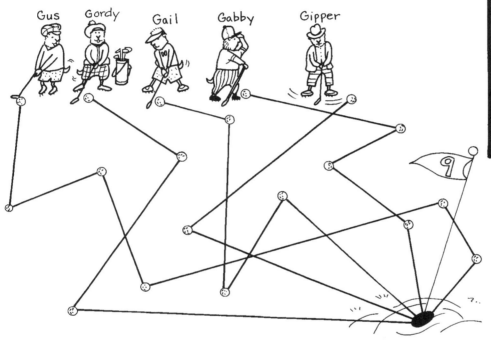

SCORECARD

Gus	
Gordy	
Gail	
Gabby	
Gipper	

1. Who took more hits than Gabby? _____

2. Who took fewer hits than Gordy? _____

3. Who took the most hits on this hole? _____

4. Who is the winner at this hole? _____

Color the golfers.

Name _____

Use with page 255.

Comparing Numbers

Goofy Golfing Gophers, cont.

At the end of the day, the goofy gophers added up all their scores. Look at the scorecard to compare their scores.

< means **less than**
> means **greater than**

SCORECARD	
Gus	50
Gabby	68
Gail	104
Gordy	42
Gipper	66
Greta	114

Then write < or > in each box.

1. Gordy ☐ Gus

2. Gail ☐ Gordy

3. Gabby ☐ Gus

4. Gordy ☐ Greta

5. Gail ☐ Gipper

6. Gus ☐ Gail

7. Gipper ☐ Gabby

8. Greta ☐ Gabby

9. Gipper ☐ Gus

10. Gordy ☐ Gabby

Color the golfers.

Name _____

Use with page 254.

Comparing Numbers

On the Shelves

Mr. Stork has to count all the equipment in his store every year.
It's a big job. He needs your help.
Count each group, and write the number on the next page (page 257).

Color all the things on the store shelves.

Name _____

Use with page 257.

Comparing Numbers

On the Shelves, cont.

Write the number of each kind of thing you counted.

    < means **less than**

    > means **greater than**

    = means **equal to**

Put **<** or **>** in each box.

1.
2.
3.
4.
5.
6.
7.
8.
9.
10.
11.

Look at the shelves on page 256. Count the sports stuff.

a. _____ ?
b. _____ ?
c. _____ ?
d. _____ ?
e. _____ ?
f. _____ ?
g. _____ ?
h. _____ ?
i. _____ ?
j. _____ ?
k. _____ ?
l. _____ ?
m. _____ ?

Name _____

Use with page 256.

Comparing Numbers

Full Tents

This is the best camping trip of the year.

The tents are full of campers.

The number on each tent tells how many are inside.

Write the tent number that means the same as each of these.

1. 20 + 3 = ☐   2. 80 + 8 = ☐   3. 40 + 7 = ☐

4. 20 + 6 = ☐   5. 10 + 6 = ☐   6. 30 + 0 = ☐

7. Which number has the most tens? ☐

8. Which number has the fewest tens? ☐

9. Which number has the most ones? ☐

10. Which number has the fewest ones? ☐

Color the picture.

Name _____

Place Value

A Wild Tennis Game

This tennis game has gotten very wild.
There are tennis balls everywhere!
Look at the numbers on the balls.
Follow the directions to color the balls.

Find the ball that means the same as each of these, and color it.

30 + 2 . . . . . . red	10 + 1 . . . . . . blue	40 + 5 . . . . pink
10 + 4 . . . . . blue	80 + 4 . . . . . . green	100 + 20 + 3 . . . . red
90 + 0 . . . . . purple	50 + 0 . . . . . . green	20 + 9 . . . . orange
60 + 6 . . . . . brown	70 + 6 . . . . . . yellow	100 + 10 + 1 . . . . purple

Name _____

Place Value • Expanded Notation

Under the Bleachers

The friends found money under the bleachers at the ball game.
Circle the correct names of the coins they found.
Count the money, and write the amount on the line.

1.

Max found 2

pennies

dimes

quarters

_____ ¢

2.

Tracy found 6

dimes

pennies

nickels

_____ ¢

3.

Ollie found 1

quarter

dime

penny

_____ ¢

4.

Ben found 4

nickels

dimes

quarters

$_____ . ___

5.

Annie found 1

dime
quarter
penny
and 1
nickel
penny
quarter

_____ ¢

6.

Ellen found 2

dimes

nickels

pennies

_____ ¢

Color the friends.
Who found the most money?

_____

- -

_____

Name _____

Counting Money

Snacks at the Ball Game

Simon Skunk sells snacks at softball games.
Look at all the yummy snacks in his tray.

Soda   75¢

Popcorn   50¢

Cotton Candy $1.50

Peanuts
25¢

Circle **more**
or **less.**

Hot Dog $1.00

1. popcorn costs **more**   **less** than soda
_____
2. hot dog costs **more**   **less** than cotton candy
_____
3. soda costs **more**   **less** than hot dog
_____
4. cotton candy costs **more**   **less** than hot dog
_____
5. peanuts costs **more**   **less** than popcorn
_____
6. hot dog costs **more**   **less** than soda

Color Simon and his snacks.

Name _____

Comparing Money

Welcome to the Swamp

The critters who live in the Hokee Penokee Swamp are lining up for tickets to the big Swamp Sports Meet. Patrick Pelican is lucky to be the first one in line.

Write words (such as **first** or **eleventh**) to answer these questions about the line-up.

1. Pokey Porcupine is third in line. Where is Sammy Snake? _____

2. Is Boscoe Bear second, tenth, or fifteenth in line? _____

3. The critter hanging upside down is _____ in line.

4. The froggy kids in the wagon are _____ and _____ in line.

5. Who is fourteenth in line? (Circle the answer.)

  bat   turtle   bird   alligator   bug

6. Sylvia Swamp Serpent is the tallest. What place is she in line? _____

7. Which critters are wearing skirts? the _____ and _____ in line.

8. Are there spots on the twelfth critter in line? _____

9. The critter with the baseball glove is _____ in line.

10. The critter with the dots on his tie is _____ in line.

Name _____

Use with page 263.
Ordinals

Follow the directions below.

They will tell you how to add some things to the drawing.

11. Flossy is fifth in line. Color her clothes red.

12. Color the ninth creature yellow.

13. Color the first creature blue.

14. Color the shoes of the tenth and fifteenth critters.

15. Draw a bumblebee on the nose of the twelfth critter.

16. Draw a flower between the fifteenth and sixteenth critters in line.

17. Color Finn's shirt bright orange. He is fourth in line.

18. Draw a hat on the eighth critter in line.

19. Color the seventeenth critter pink.

20. Draw a butterfly flying between the ninth and tenth creatures.

Name _____

Use with page 262.

Ordinals

Ball Team Hang-Ups

It's time to wash the Swamp Ball Team uniforms.

Jake is hanging the shirts out to dry.

Find the right shirt for each player.

Write the correct numeral to match the words from the chart.

TEAM LIST

Name	Number
Slurpy	ninety-five
Bog	four hundred forty five
Muck	five hundred forty
Quirk	nine hundred fifty
Grunt	five thousand
Muppy	nine hundred five
Biff	forty five
Oozy	four hundred twenty
Dip	fifty four
Sloppy	five hundred ninety
Flossie	four thousand
Finn	five hundred nine

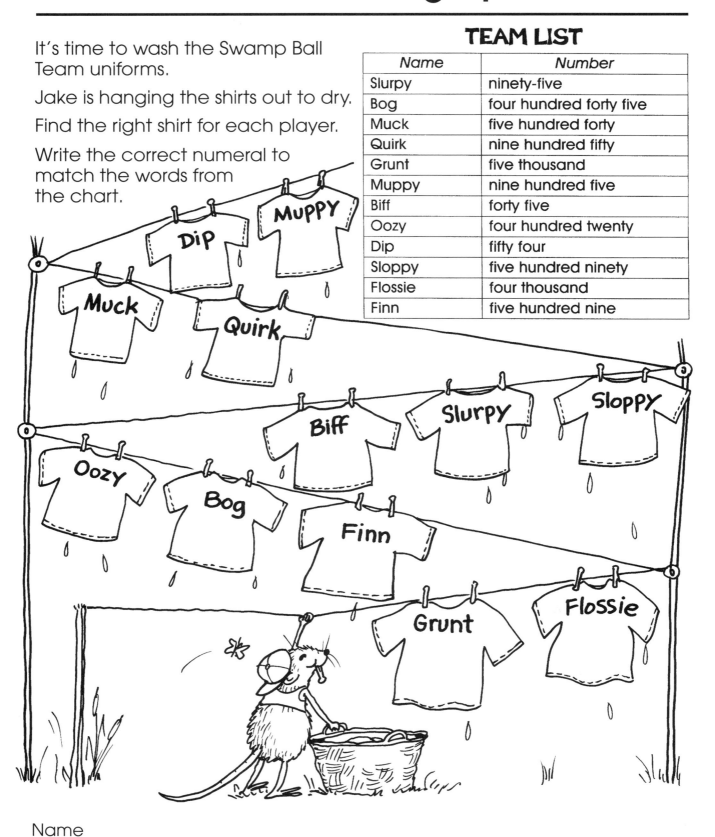

Name _____

Read & Write Whole Numbers;
Match Numerals to Word Names

Trouble Underwater

Big Daddy Catfish swims laps around the swamp every day.
Today, the swamp is full of bubbles, which he must dodge.
Quick! Draw a line from each word name to the matching bubble
before Daddy Catfish swims away.

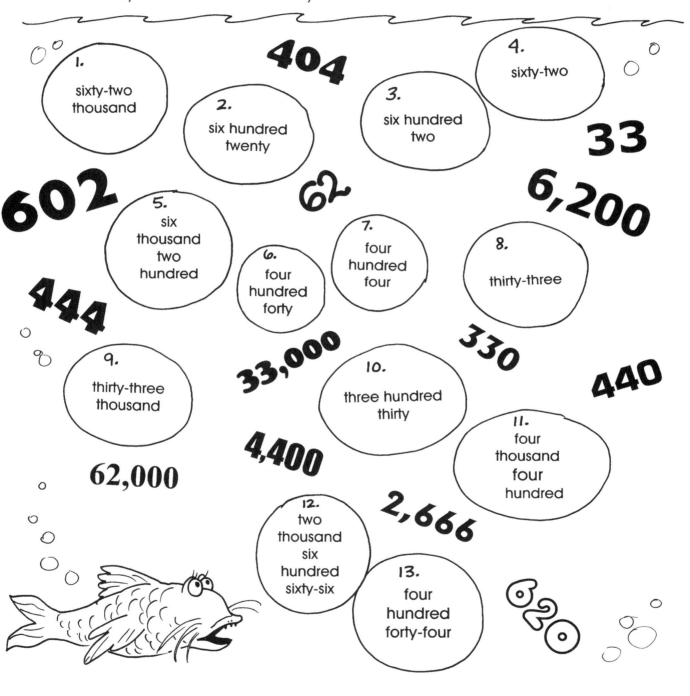

404

1. sixty-two thousand

2. six hundred twenty

3. six hundred two

4. sixty-two

33

602

62

6,200

5. six thousand two hundred

6. four hundred forty

7. four hundred four

8. thirty-three

444

9. thirty-three thousand

33,000

10. three hundred thirty

330

440

11. four thousand four hundred

62,000

4,400

2,666

12. two thousand six hundred sixty-six

13. four hundred forty-four

620

Name _____

**Read & Write Whole Numbers;
Match Numerals to Word Names**

Ant Antics

The Ant family is having a food race at the Swamptown picnic.

They are racing to see who is the fastest at getting food across the finish line.

Follow the trail of each ant.

Draw a line that connects the numbers from smallest to largest.

Which ant did not end up across the finish line?

Go! Go! Go!

#1 Apple Annie	#2 Chester Cheese	#3 Robby Radish	#4 Betty Banana	#5 Gary Grape

#1 Apple Annie: 16, 45, 50, 22, 27, 54

#2 Chester Cheese: 604, 699, 644, 696, 640, 694, 649, 700

#3 Robby Radish: seventeen, twenty-three, fifty, eighteen, fifty-one

#4 Betty Banana: 40, 64, 49, 72, 44, 76, 90

#5 Gary Grape: 322, 214, 232, 226, 240, 294, 288

FINISH LINE

Order Whole Numbers

Name

Summer Swamp Supplies

The swamp critters keep some supplies handy for their summer activities.

Each item has a label that tells how much it costs.

Answer these questions about them.

1. About how many cans of bug spray can Finn buy for $5.00? _____

2. Which item costs a little more than $5? _____

3. Which item costs about $4? _____

4. How many pieces of licorice can Finn buy for a quarter? _____

5. Can he buy a beach ball and a sand pail & shovel for under $5? _____

6. Which item costs about $8 less than the beach towel? _____

7. Could Finn buy 3 beach chairs for $20? _____

8. Which item costs about $2? _____

9. Which item costs about $4 less than the beach chair? _____

10. Which would cost more: 3 hats or 4 beach balls? _____

11. Could Finn buy a float and a towel for about $15? _____

12. Which two different items together cost closest to $20?

_____ and _____

Name _____

Estimate Amounts

A "Weighty" Round-Up

Wrestling is a popular sport in the Hokee Penokee Swamp.
The wrestlers always get weighed before every wrestling match.
Round the weight for each wrestler to the nearest TEN.

Write the rounded weight
under each animal's name.

Bout No. 2:
Slippery Sheila   vs. Dinah the Destroyer
3._____   4._____

Bout No. 1:
Maniac Mouse   vs. Big Al
1._____   2._____

277 oz.

51 lb.

3,555 lb.

3,403 lb.

Bout No. 3:
Beetle Brain vs. Bug Eyes
5._____   6._____

65 oz.

97 oz.

Bout No. 4:
Ferocious Flamingo vs. Perilous Polly
7._____   8._____

514 oz.

276 oz.

Bout No. 5:
Big Bad Bosco vs. Sam the Squeeze
9._____   10._____

1,025 lb.

987 lb.

Name _____

Rounding Whole Numbers

Derby Warm-Up

When Darla Dragonfly gets ready for the Draggin' Fly Derby, she follows a very regular pattern.

She does exactly the same thing before every race. Here's what she does.

Look for the pattern in her chart.

Fill in the missing numbers.

Darla's Derby Warm-Up

	ACTIVITY	TIME
1	Wing Stretches	2 minutes
2	Tail Lifts	3 minutes
3	Leg Stretches	5 minutes
4	Leg Lifts	8 minutes
5	Abdomen Stretches	12 minutes
6	Abdomen Lifts	
7	Rest	

Here are some other patterns. These are number patterns.

Look at each one. Then fill in the missing pieces to continue each pattern.

A.
$$10 + 8 = 18 \qquad 9 + 9 = 18 \qquad 8 + 10 = 18 \qquad 7 + 11 = 18 \qquad 6 + 12 = 18 \qquad \boxed{}$$

B. $50 + 9 = 59 \qquad 51 + 8 = 59 \qquad 52 + 7 = 59 \qquad \boxed{} \qquad 54 + 5 = 59$

C. $20 - 7 = 13 \qquad 21 - 8 = 13 \qquad 22 - 9 = 13 \qquad 23 - 10 = 13 \qquad \boxed{}$

D. $\boxed{} \qquad 25 + 25 = 50 \qquad 35 + 35 = 70 \qquad 45 + 45 = 90$

E. $12 + 10 = 22 \qquad 13 + 20 = 33 \qquad 14 + 30 = 44 \qquad \boxed{} \qquad 16 + 50 = 66$

F. $12 + 21 = 33 \qquad 23 + 32 = 55 \qquad 34 + 43 = 77 \qquad \boxed{}$

Name _____

A Bad Fit

At the Swamptown Gym, there is a huge box of lost shoes.

Henrietta Heron just can't find her running shoes.

All the other shoes are the wrong size. They just do not fit her feet.

In each of these groups of numbers, there is one number that does not fit. All the other numbers have something in common.

Find the number in each group that doesn't fit. Draw a big X on it.

A.

B. 52   82   402   12   62   8,302

C. $5\frac{1}{2}$ $22\frac{1}{4}$ $19\frac{1}{2}$ $64\frac{3}{4}$ 26.8 $101\frac{1}{2}$

D. 38.5   10.3   0.5   5,333   7.7   100.4

E. 30   3,300   33,003   330   303   3,033

F.
$17 - 6 = 11$
$22 - 11 = 11$
$20 - 9 = 11$
$88 - 77 = 11$
$1,122 - 1,111 = 11$

G.
$6 + 6 = 12$
$9 + 9 = 18$
$42 + 42 = 84$
$17 + 17 = 34$
$23 + 23 = 46$

Name _____

Relationships Between Numbers

Number Concepts & Relationships Words to Know

decimal—a number that uses a decimal point to show tenths and hundredths, such as *.2* or *.02*.

decimal point—the dot in a decimal number.

denominator—the bottom number in a fraction. It tells how many in all. In the fraction $\frac{4}{5}$, *5* is the denominator.

digit—the symbol *0, 1, 2, 3, 4, 5, 6, 7, 8,* or *9*.

estimate—an answer that is not exact.

even number—a number that has *0, 2, 4, 6,* or *8* in the ones place. *6, 20, 132,* and *450* are even numbers.

expanded notation—a number sentence that shows the place value of the digits in a numeral. *457 = 400 + 50 + 7*

factor—a number that is multiplied by another number.

fraction—a number such as $\frac{1}{2}$, $\frac{3}{4}$, or $\frac{7}{8}$.

mixed fractional number—a whole number plus a fraction, such as $1\frac{1}{2}$.

number line—a line along which numbers can be pictured.

number sentence—a sentence that shows how numbers are related. *5 + 4 = 9* is a number sentence.

numerator—the top number in a fraction. It tells how many parts of the whole thing you're talking about. In the fraction $\frac{2}{3}$, *2* is the numerator.

odd number—a number that has *1, 3, 5, 7,* or *9* in the ones place. *5, 767, 33,* and *91* are odd numbers.

ordinals—the word names written to describe the order of things. *First, second,* and *third* are ordinals.

patterns—characteristics of numbers or pictures that repeat.

place value—the value a digit has in a number, such as *one, ten, hundred, thousand,* or *ten thousand*. In the number *437, 4* is in the hundreds place, so it has a value of four hundred.

probability—the chance that an event is likely to occur.

rounding—changing a number so that it is an estimate to the nearest tens place, hundreds place, thousands place, or other place. *567* rounded to the nearest ten is *570. 2,111* rounded to the nearest hundred is *2,100.*

sequences—numbers or patterns that repeat in a certain order.

skip count—to count following a pattern that skips certain numbers (for instance, to count by *5, 10,* or *50*).

Math Words to Know

Lost in the Weeds

Michael has lost his sports equipment in the weeds. What is it?
Solve each addition problem. Find the answer in the code box.
Color each section with the color that matches the answer.

Code

36 = blue	84 = yellow
99 = green	62 = orange
70 = brown	100 = red
179 = purple	

Name _____

Addition

Throw Three!

In this dart game, Ramon gets to throw 3 darts in each game.

Add up his score for each game.
Which game is his best?

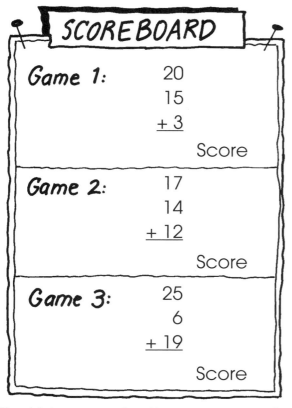

SCOREBOARD

Game 1:
20
15
+ 3
_____
Score

Game 2:
17
14
+ 12
_____
Score

Game 3:
25
6
+ 19
_____
Score

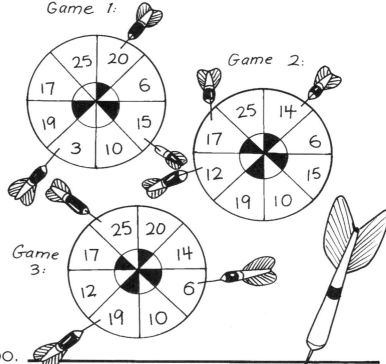

Find his score for these games, too.

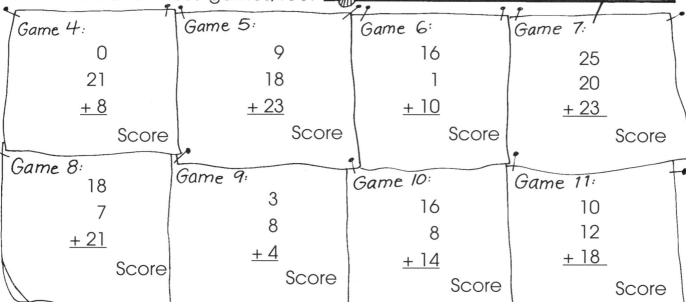

Game 4:
0
21
+ 8
_____
Score

Game 5:
9
18
+ 23
_____
Score

Game 6:
16
1
+ 10
_____
Score

Game 7:
25
20
+ 23
_____
Score

Game 8:
18
7
+ 21
_____
Score

Game 9:
3
8
+ 4
_____
Score

Game 10:
16
8
+ 14
_____
Score

Game 11:
10
12
+ 18
_____
Score

Name _____

Column Addition

Different Sails

A **difference** is the answer in a subtraction problem.

Each sail has a different difference!
Solve the subtraction problems on each sail.
Then follow the directions for coloring the sails
in the box at the bottom.

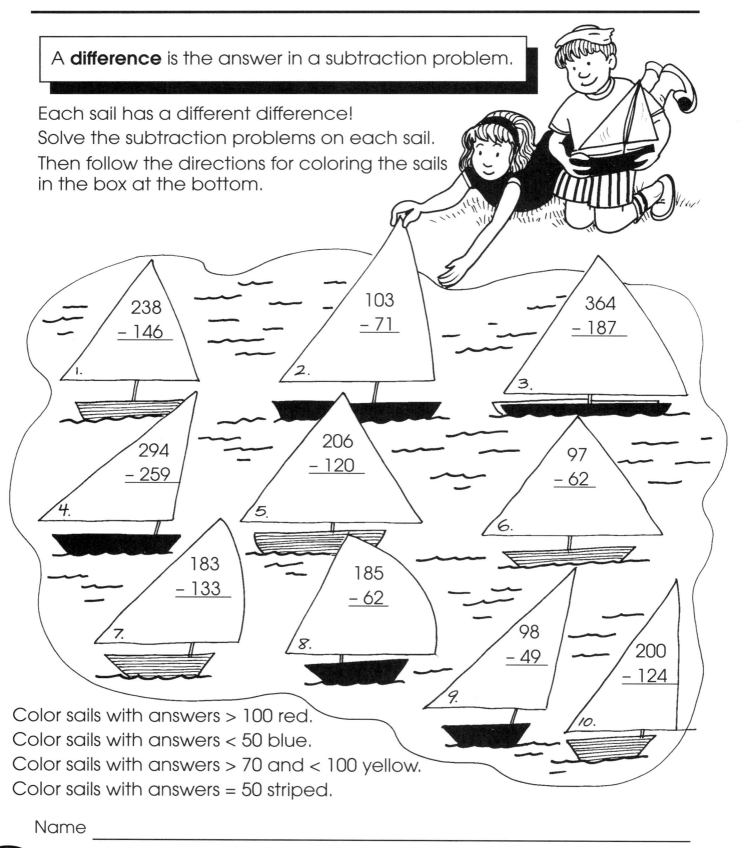

1. 238
   − 146

2. 103
   − 71

3. 364
   − 187

4. 294
   − 259

5. 206
   − 120

6. 97
   − 62

7. 183
   − 133

8. 185
   − 62

9. 98
   − 49

10. 200
    − 124

Color sails with answers > 100 red.
Color sails with answers < 50 blue.
Color sails with answers > 70 and < 100 yellow.
Color sails with answers = 50 striped.

Name _____

Subtraction

Subtracting Snowballs

Every time one of the teams throws a
snowball, they have to subtract it from
their stack.

1. Sal has thrown 17 of her snowballs.
   She started with 85. How many
   does she have left?

   _____

2. Skip made 99 snowballs. He has
   45 left. How many did he throw?

   _____

Solve the rest of the snowball
subtraction problems.

3.   271 snowballs
      − 44 thrown
           left

4.   116 snowballs
      − 10 left
           thrown

5.   312 snowballs
      − 24 left
           thrown

6.   138 snowballs
      − 109 thrown
           left

7.   233 snowballs
      − 61 left
           thrown

8.   98 snowballs
      − 19 thrown
           left

9.   952 snowballs
      − 64 left
           thrown

10.   55 snowballs
      − 33 thrown
           left

Name _____

Subtraction

Mystery Athlete

Who is the mystery athlete? Solve the problems to find out!
Use the Key to find the letters that match each answer.
Write the letters in the spaces at the bottom of the page.

1. 668
    x 2

2. 334
    x 4

3. 156
    x 7

4. 109
    x 9

5. 361
    x 6

6. 816
    x 2

7. 501
    x 3

8. 238
    x 4

9. 246
    x 4

10. 467
    x 2

KEY

952 = T
1,336 = R
1,632 = C
984 = U
1,503 = P
1,092 = S
981 = Y
2,166 = E
934 = H

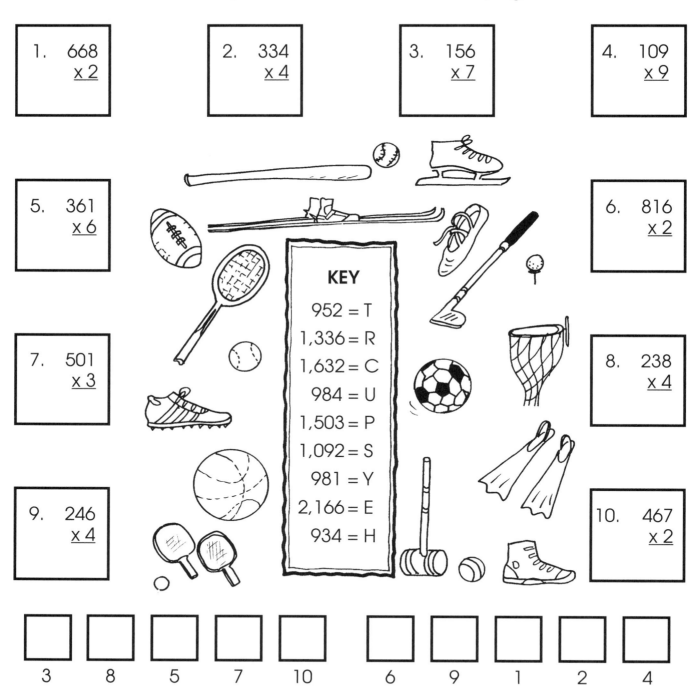

3	8	5	7	10	6	9	1	2	4

Name _____

How Many Jumps?

This hurdler jumps 9 spaces with each jump.

He starts at the beginning of the number line and finishes 45 spaces later at the finish line.

He must jump 5 times to get the end.

> We can write this problem.
>
> 45 spaces ÷ 5 jumps = 9 spaces per jump

Practice these facts.

1. $56 ÷ 7 = \boxed{}$ per jump

2. $72 ÷ 8$ jumps $= \boxed{}$ per jump

3. $\boxed{} ÷ 3$ jumps $= 9$ per jump

4. $\boxed{} ÷ 4$ jumps $= 4$ per jump

5. $81 ÷ \boxed{}$ jumps $= 9$ per jump

6. $40 ÷ \boxed{}$ jumps $= 5$ per jump

7. $20 ÷ 5$ jumps $= \boxed{}$ per jump

8. $27 ÷ 3$ jumps $= \boxed{}$ per jump

9. $64 ÷ \boxed{}$ jumps $= 8$ per jump

10. $15 ÷ \boxed{}$ jumps $= 3$ per jump

11. $\boxed{} ÷ 3$ jumps $= 4$ per jump

12. $\boxed{} ÷ 7$ jumps $= 7$ per jump

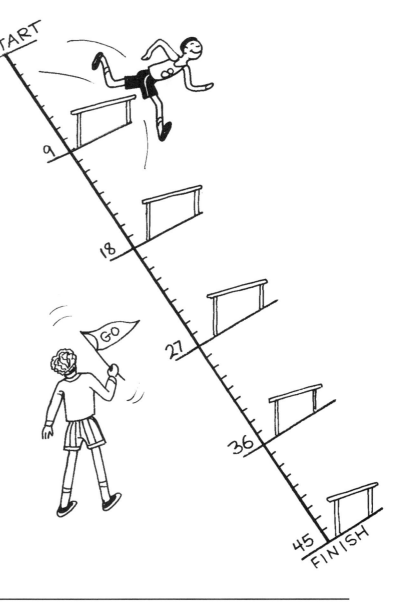

Name _____

Icy Problems

Hannah and Harvey can't get on the ice to play hockey until they have all the right equipment.

Here are the costs of some of the things they need for their sport.

Use this picture to help you solve the problems on the next page (page 279).

Name _____

Icy Problems, cont.

Use the picture on page 278 to solve the problems.

1. How much did Hannah spend on her skates and her stick?
$200.00
+ 48.83

2. Harvey had $100.00. He bought a helmet. How much change did he get?
$100.00
− 59.95

3. Which costs less, a jersey or a stick?

_____

How much less?

_____

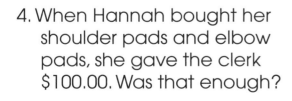

4. When Hannah bought her shoulder pads and elbow pads, she gave the clerk $100.00. Was that enough?

_____

5. How much would 2 jerseys cost?

_____

6. Which is more: elbow pads and a stick or knee guards?

_____

7. $200.00 skates
+ 59.95 helmet

8. $55.00 jersey
+ 48.83 stick

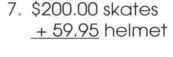

9. $69.98 pants
+ 59.95 helmet

10. $56.49 knee guards
− 29.99 elbow pads

Name _____

Use with page 278.

Copyright © 2016 World Book, Inc./
Incentive Publications, Chicago, IL

Problems with Money

Swimmer's Line-Up

The top number is the **numerator.** It answers the question.
The bottom number is the **denominator.** It tells how many in all.

The swim team is ready for the big race. Let's take a look at all their equipment!

$\frac{6}{6}$ of the team is ready to go!

Write a fraction to answer each question.

1. How many swimmers have goggles?

2. How many feet have on fins?

3. How many swimmers are wearing suits with stripes?

4. How many swimmers are still wet?

5. How many swimmers are wearing bathing caps?

6. How many feet have aqua socks?

7. How many swimmers are wearing a float?

8. How many swimmers have suits with NO dots?

9. How many noses have a nose plug?

10. How many swimmers have black suits?

Name _____

Pizza Party

A **mixed numeral** is a number that shows a whole number and a fraction.

The football players were really hungry after their games.
They all ate a lot of pizza. Who ate the most?
Write mixed numerals to show how much each player ate.

Rocky ate _____   Ernest ate _____   Bruiser ate _____

1.   2.   3.

4.   5.   6.

Jess ate _____   Kujo ate _____   Bud ate _____

Who ate the most? _____ Who left the most? _____

Name _____

Mixed Numerals

A Busy Baseball Season

Nick's days get very busy during baseball season.
Here is his calendar for June.

Use the calendar to answer the questions on the next page (page 283).

> What a month

JUNE

Sunday	Monday	Tuesday	Wednesday	Thursday	Friday	Saturday
	1 trumpet lesson	2 baseball practice 3:30 PM	3	4	5 baseball practice 3:30 PM	6 first game (we won!)
7	8	9	10 Big Math Test Killer	11	12 Last Day of School	13 game 2:00 (lost)
14	15 Ellie's swim party 1–4 PM	16	17 overnight at Frank's (oh boy!)	18 Practice 3:30	19	20 game 10:30 (won)
21 Aunt Ruby's visit!	22 trumpet lesson	23 practice 3:30	24	25 scooter goes to Vet	26 Frank's Birthday party !!!	27 game — noon (won)
28 Waterslide Party !! 4–8 PM	29	30 Oh, no! Dentist 10:45 am practice 3:30				

Name _____

A Busy Baseball Season, cont.

1. What things does Nick have to do on June 30?

   _____ and

   _____

2. On which two dates will Nick be at Frank's?

   _____ and _____

3. How long after school gets out is Nick's dentist appointment?

   _____ weeks and _____ days

4. If Nick goes on a trip from June 18–20, what will he miss?

   _____ and

   _____

5. What is Nick looking forward to on June 15?

   _____

6. When is Aunt Ruby's visit? _____

7. What happens every Saturday in June? _____

8. Which day will he have to get Scooter into the car?

   _____

9. How many Tuesdays in June does he have practice? _____

10. How many parties will Nick go to in June? _____

11. How long is it between his trumpet lessons? _____

12. How many Mondays are there in June? _____

13. What day and date is his big math test? _____

14. How long before Frank's birthday is Ellie's party? _____

15. In which week does Nick have 2 baseball practices? _____

Only 5 more minutes.....

Name _____

Use with page 282.

Time • Calendar

Hula Hoop Numbers

How long can each of these kids spin the hula hoop without dropping it?

The numbers in the box show the number of spins.

Write the number to match each clue next to the hoop.

0	409	254	156	621
43	311	80	7	4010

Jan
Odd number with 3 digits and a 3

June
a number = 400 + 200 – 600

Julie
a number = 106 + 100 – 50

Jamie
Even number > 78 and < 82

Janet
> 400 with a 0 in the tens place

James
a number that has 6 in the hundreds place

Jerri
a 1-digit number that is not found in any other hula hoops

Jenny
a number = 200 + 54

John
8 more than 7 x 5

Justin
2 places have 0

Name _____

Problem Solving

The Great Bug Race

Every year these bugs run a big race.
While you watch them run, look at the numbers on their shirts.
Answer the questions below about place value.

806   1,137   41,446   62,520   15,047   1,612   2,014   310,923

1. Color the body of the bug with 6 in the hundreds place purple.
2. Color the body of the bug with 5 in the thousands place green.
3. Put red spots on the bug with the 0 in the tens place.
4. Put yellow stripes on the bug with the 4 in the ones place.
5. Color the bug with 3 in the hundred thousands place brown.
6. Draw feelers on the bug with the 4 in the ten thousands place.
7. Color the bug with 3 in the tens place orange.
8. Find the bug with the 0 in the ones place. Color it black.
9. Color the shoes red on the bug with the 4 in the hundreds place.
10. Find the bug with the 7 in the ones place. Color her shoes yellow.

Name _____

Place Value

Math Computation & Problem Solving Words to Know

addend—a number added to another number. In the number sentence $3 + 2 = 5$, 3 and 2 are addends.

difference—the answer in subtraction.

equivalent fraction—fractions that have the same value. $\frac{2}{6}$ and $\frac{1}{3}$ are equivalent fractions.

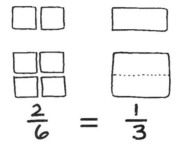

$$\frac{2}{6} = \frac{1}{3}$$

fact family—a group of facts with the same numbers, such as: $2 + 4 = 6, 4 + 2 = 6, 6 - 2 = 4,$ $6 - 4 = 2.$

mixed number—a whole number plus a fraction, such as $1\frac{1}{2}$.

product—the answer in multiplication. In the number sentence $6 \times 7 = 42$, the product is 42.

quotient—the answer in division. In the number sentence $50 \div 10 = 5$, the quotient is 5.

remainder—the number left over when a division is complete. The solution for $27 \div 5$ is 5, with a remainder of 2.

sum—the answer in addition. In the number sentence $4 + 9 = 13$, the sum is 13.

zero—the word name for the digit 0, which means none.

Line Up for Cheers

Lines are everywhere!

Look all around Sadie to find line segments.

Answer the questions below.

You'll need to do a lot of counting!

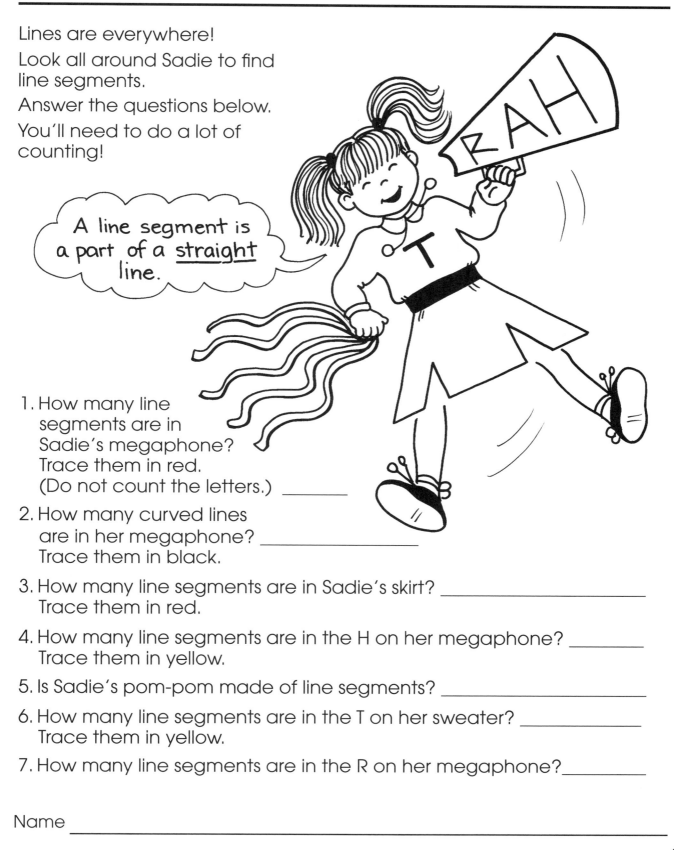

A line segment is a part of a <u>straight</u> line.

1. How many line segments are in Sadie's megaphone? Trace them in red. (Do not count the letters.) _____

2. How many curved lines are in her megaphone? _____ Trace them in black.

3. How many line segments are in Sadie's skirt? _____ Trace them in red.

4. How many line segments are in the H on her megaphone? _____ Trace them in yellow.

5. Is Sadie's pom-pom made of line segments? _____

6. How many line segments are in the T on her sweater? _____ Trace them in yellow.

7. How many line segments are in the R on her megaphone?_____

Name _____

High-Flying Geometry

Kites would be boring without geometry.

Decorate the kites to show that you know the names of geometric figures.

Color all the hexagons ⬡ blue.

Color all the squares ☐ green.

Color all the triangles △ red or purple.

Color all the rectangles ▭ yellow.

Color all the circles ◯ pink.

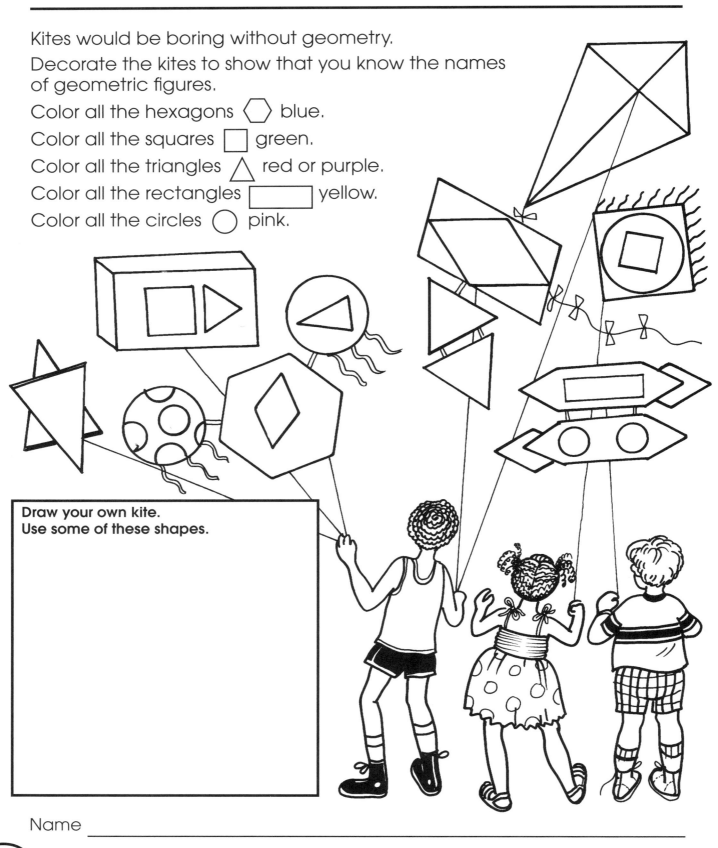

Draw your own kite.
Use some of these shapes.

Name _____

Plane Figures

Pool Bottom Geometry

The painter has just finished painting a new design on the bottom of the pool.

It is full of different shapes.

Follow the directions to color the pool bottom.

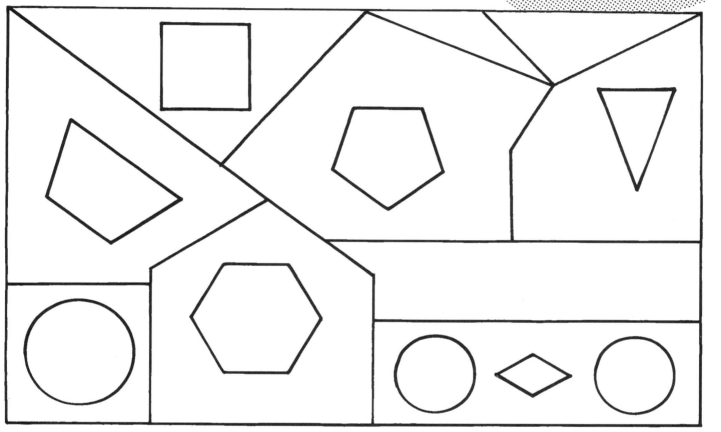

1. Triangles have 3 sides. Color them green. How many did you find? _____

2. Squares have 4 equal sides. Color them blue.
   How many did you find? _____

3. Circles are round. Color them with stripes. How many did you find? _____

4. Pentagons have 5 sides. Color them purple.
   How many did you find? _____

5. Hexagons have 6 sides. Color them red. How many did you find?_____

Name _____

Plane Figures

Flags Everywhere!

Sporting events usually have lots of flags—for countries, states, or teams.
Get a ruler, a compass, and some crayons or markers.
Help Joe, Jana, Joy, and Jon make their flags.
Read the directions to see what to put on each flag.

1.	2.	3.	4.
1 circle 3 triangles 1 rectangle	3 circles 2 line segments	2 angles 4 squares 2 curved lines	6 triangles 1 rectangle 1 circle

Color the flags!

Name _____

Inside the Gym Bag

Look at all the mixed-up stuff inside Trisha's gym bag! These things are all space figures. They include spheres, cones, rectangular prisms, cylinders, a cube, and a pyramid.

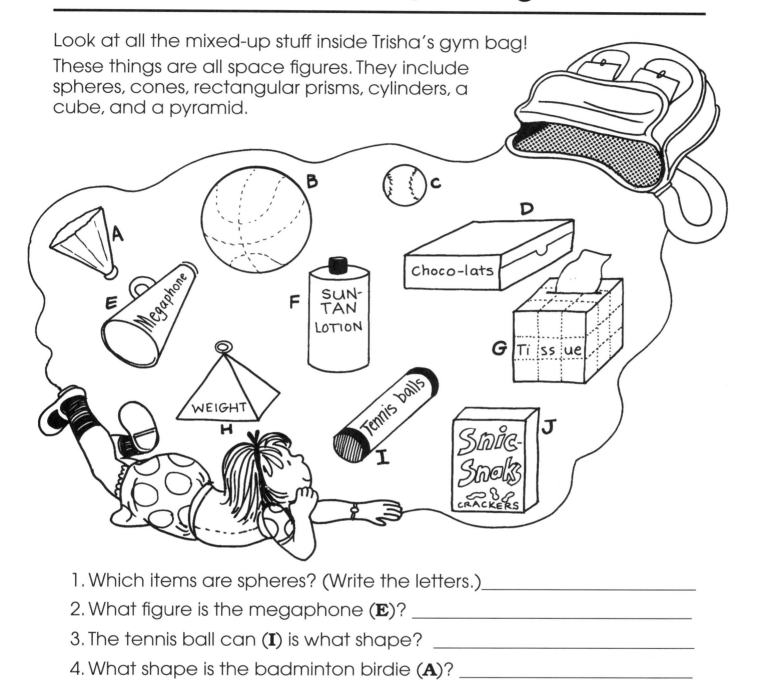

1. Which items are spheres? (Write the letters.) _____

2. What figure is the megaphone (**E**)? _____

3. The tennis ball can (**I**) is what shape? _____

4. What shape is the badminton birdie (**A**)? _____

5. Which one is a cube? (Write the letter.) _____

6. What things are rectangular prisms? (Write the letters.) _____

7. What shape is the bottle of suntan lotion (**F**)? _____

8. Is the weight (**H**) a pyramid? _____

Name _____

Solid Geometric Figures

The Topic Is T-Shirts

Congruent figures are exactly the same size and shape. The soccer team has hung T-shirts on the clothesline to dry.

I like this one!

Some of the shirts have figures that are congruent to the figures on other T-shirts.

Find the T-shirts with congruent figures and draw a line to connect them. One shirt does not match another shirt.

Color the shirts!

Name _____

Congruent Figures

The Great Spaghetti Marathon

These weight lifters eat loads of spaghetti to give them energy.
Whose string of spaghetti is the longest?

Have a friend help you measure the spaghetti strings. Get some string
and lay it on each piece of spaghetti. Mark the string to match
the length of the spaghetti, and then straighten it.

Measure the string with a centimeter ruler. Write the
measurement to the nearest centimeter.

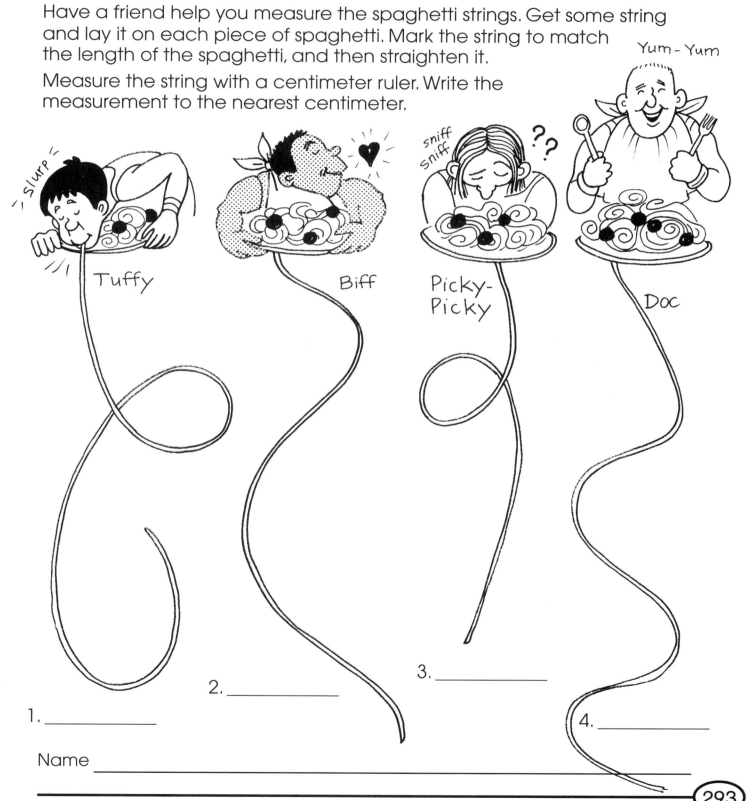

Tuffy

Biff

Picky-Picky

Doc

Yum - Yum

slurp

sniff sniff

??

1. _____

2. _____

3. _____

4. _____

Name _____

Measuring Length: Metric

Sticks & Stuff

Melissa's stilts are taller than she is.

There are lots of sticks and poles and other long, narrow things in sports.

Measure the pictures of each of these pieces of long sports equipment.

Use a centimeter ruler, and write the measurement to the nearest centimeter.

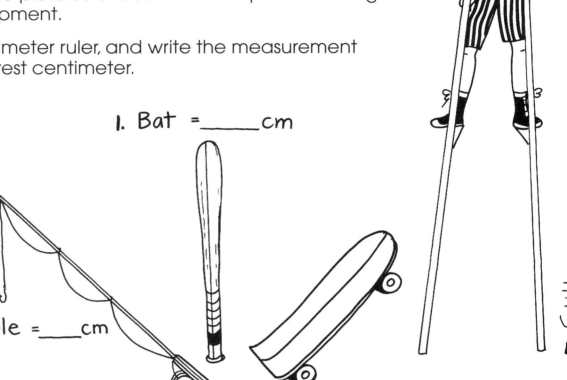

1. Bat = _____ cm

2. Fishing pole = _____ cm

3. Golf club = _____ cm

4. Hockey stick = _____ cm

5. Ski = _____ cm

6. Skateboard = _____ cm

7. Stilts _____ cm

Name _____

Measuring Length: Metric

The Big Bug Race

The bugs are at it again! Every year they have a race to find out who can crawl or hop the farthest.

Measure the path for each bug from the end near the hand to the tip of the arrow. Use an inch ruler to measure each path. Write the number of inches each bug traveled. (Round to the nearest **fourth** of an inch.)

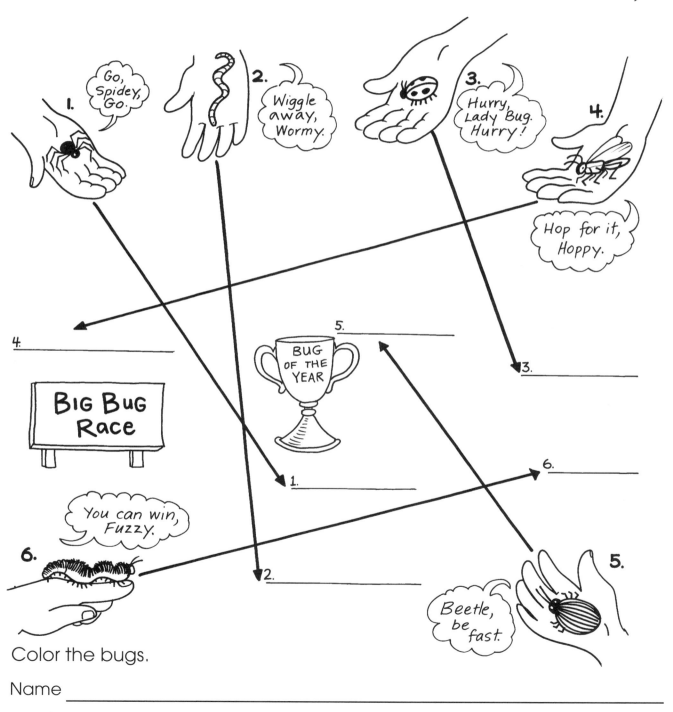

Color the bugs.

Name _____

Measuring Length: U.S.

Can't Stop Measuring!

Harriet can't stop measuring things!

She measures the distances she can jump. She also measures everyone's houses, pets, and even their noses and toes. She thinks it's fun.

Join her in the fun.
Use a ruler and a yardstick with inches and feet.
Measure as many of these things as you can find.
Label your measurements with inches or feet.

_____ 1. a nose

_____ 2. length of your foot

_____ 3. from your elbow to the tip of your thumb

_____ 4. the width of your bedroom or classroom

_____ 5. the height of a toaster

_____ 6. length of your pillow

_____ 7. length of an eyebrow

_____ 8. length of your bathtub or shower

_____ 9. size of a sandwich

_____ 10. length of a book

_____ 11. length of your shoelace

_____ 12. height of a desk or table

_____ 13. height of your mom, dad, or teacher

_____ 14. height of your best friend

_____ 15. length of your friend's hand

_____ 16. length of someone's hair

Name _____

Measuring Length: U.S.

Taking the Plunge

These critters always head for water on hot days.

Try to decide how much water is in each container before they take the plunge into the water!

A liter is about the size of a quart.

Write L to mean liter.

Circle the measurement that is the best estimate for the amount of water in each container.

1. $\frac{1}{2}$ L   10 L

2. 100 L   1 L

3. 200 L   20 L

4. 2 L   300 L

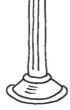 
5. 7 L   7,000 L

6. 10 L   10,000 L

7. 30,000 L   300 L

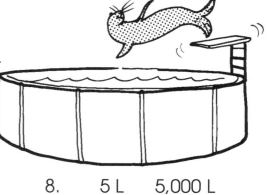 
8.   5 L   5,000 L

Color the pictures.

Name _____

Choosing Units of Liquid Capacity: Metric

Who Has the Most Money?

The Frogman Diving Club members are headed for the Snack Bar after the swim meet.

Help them count their money. Tell how much money each frogman has.

SNACK BAR

1. **Fred**
   2 nickels
   1 dime
   1 quarter
   How much?
   _____

2. **Happy**
   3 dimes
   1 quarter
   How much?
   _____

3. **Wart**
   4 pennies
   2 dimes
   3 quarters
   How much?
   _____

4. **Toady**
   5 pennies
   2 quarters
   How much?
   _____

5. **Rikki**
   3 pennies
   1 nickel
   2 dimes
   How much?
   _____

6. **Legs**
   4 quarters
   How much?
   _____

Color the diver with the most money.

Name _____

Counting Money

Don't Miss the Sale!

Help Tara and Todd shop for some sports equipment.

Something's wrong.....

TABLE TENNIS BALL SALE
3 for 30¢
what a deal!

SALE

DON'T MISS OUR SOCCER SPECIAL! JERSEYS were $14.00 Now — ½ off!

"Glow-in-the-Dark" TENNIS BALLS (1 CAN)
WERE: $3.75
NOW: $2.50
save $2.25 !!

all bikes sale priced!
regularly $60 – $50 – $40
now $10.⁰⁰ off
(bikes in stock only)

Read the signs carefully. Answer the questions.

1. Todd wants a bike that was $60.00. How much will he pay on sale? _____

2. How much will a soccer jersey cost? _____

3. If Tara gives $10.00 for a jersey, how much change will she get? _____

4. Todd notices something wrong with the sale price of a can of tennis balls. What is wrong? _____
_____

5. Tara has a quarter. Can she buy 3 table tennis balls? _____
If no, how much more does she need? _____

6. Todd wants 6 table tennis balls. How much change will he get from $1.00? _____

Name _____

Problems with Money

One Very Busy Family

Members of the Wilder Family can't sit still for one second. They are all busy doing sports.

Look at their busy calendar! (See page 301.)

Use the calendar to help you answer the questions below.

1. How long after Seth's birthday are soccer tryouts?
   _____ week(s) and _____ day(s)

2. Which day of the week is the family picnic?
   _____

3. Will Tim and Mom go hiking before or after the beach trip?
   _____

4. What is happening on Friday, June 5?
   _____

5. How long before Granny's water skiing is her bungee jumping?
   _____

6. What is the date of Dad's and Tammy's tennis game?
   _____

7. How long after the tennis game is the picnic?
   _____ week(s) and _____ day(s)

8. How many days are there between Steve's swim classes?
   _____

9. How long after Steve's first swim class is the meet?
   _____ week(s) and _____ day(s)

10. How many nights will the canoe trip last? _____

Name _____

Use with page 301.

Time • Calendar

Use the calendar to answer the questions on page 300 about the busy Wilder family.

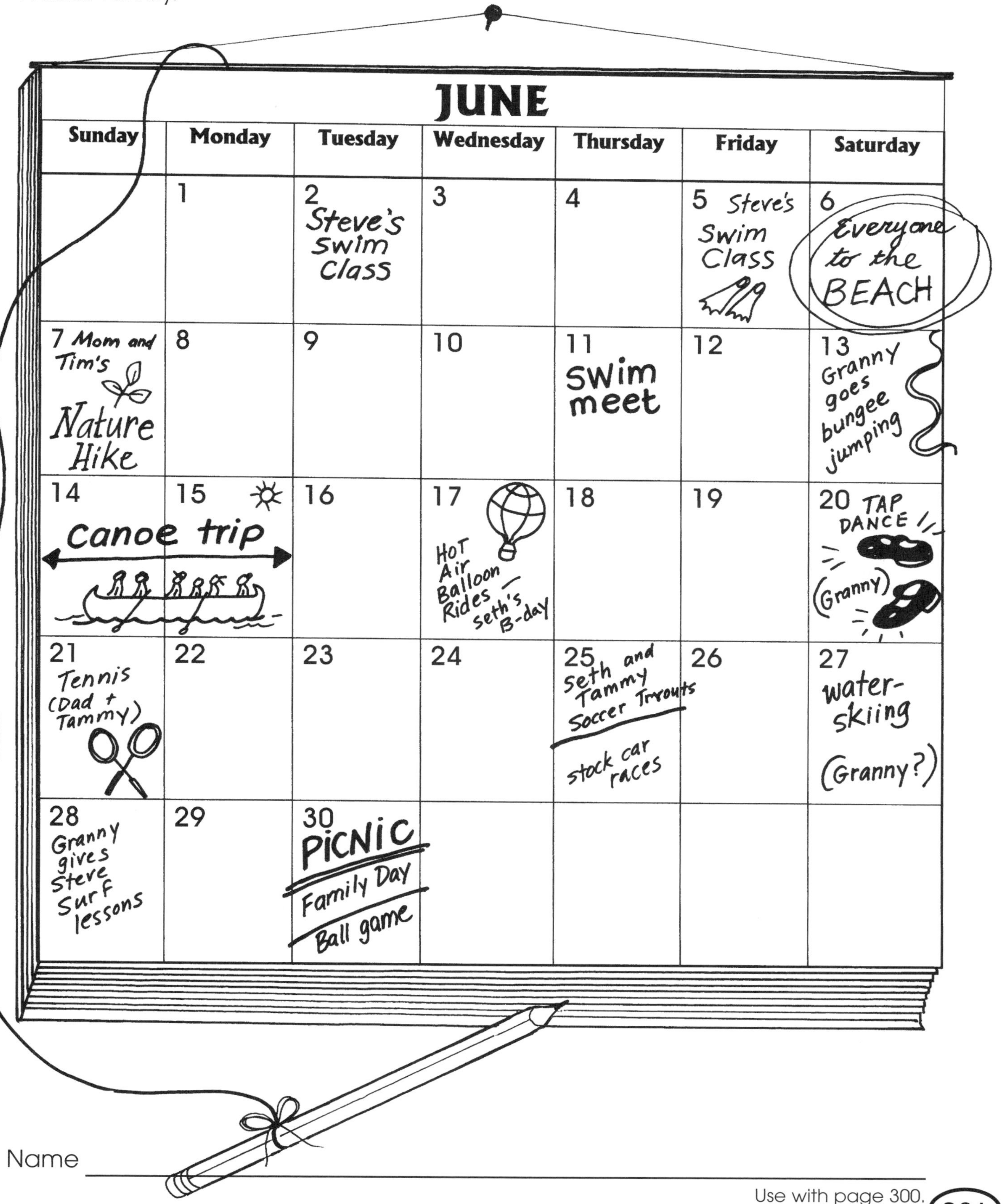

JUNE

Sunday	Monday	Tuesday	Wednesday	Thursday	Friday	Saturday
	1	2 Steve's Swim Class	3	4	5 Steve's Swim Class	6 Everyone to the BEACH
7 Mom and Tim's Nature Hike	8	9	10	11 swim meet	12	13 Granny goes bungee jumping
14 Canoe trip	15 ☀	16	17 Hot Air Balloon Rides — Seth's B-day	18	19	20 TAP DANCE (Granny)
21 Tennis (Dad + Tammy)	22	23	24	25 Seth and Tammy Soccer Tryouts stock car races	26	27 water-skiing (Granny?)
28 Granny gives Steve Surf lessons	29	30 PICNIC Family Day Ball game				

Name _____

Time • Calendar

Hot, Cold, or Just Right?

Athletes pay a lot of attention to the weather and the temperature.
Some sports are just right for hot weather.
Some are just right for cold weather.

Answer these questions about
the temperatures shown.

1. Is the temperature at point D right for
the ice where Sandy skates? _____

2. Which would the runner probably
choose for running a race: temperature
D or C? _____

3. Would surfer Suzanne be more
comfortable on a day that is at
temperature F or C? _____

4. At which temperature would a
snowball fight probably happen?

_____

5. Would the biker take a bath in
water at temperature A? _____

6. Would the diver probably be
diving in water at the
temperature of B? _____

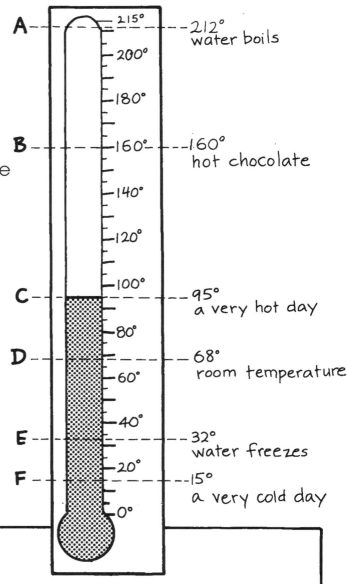

A — 215° — 212° water boils
200°
180°
B — 160° — 160° hot chocolate
140°
120°
100°
C — 95° a very hot day
80°
D — 68° room temperature
60°
40°
E — 32° water freezes
20°
F — 15° a very cold day
0°

**What is a good temperature
for a hot drink?
Color the thermometer red
to show that temperature.**

Name _____

Big Gulpers

This pogo jumping team gets very thirsty.

The graph shows how much they drink during a contest.
It also shows which drinks they choose at the sports drink stand.

Use a different color of crayon to color each row
of drinks. Then read the graph to answer the questions.

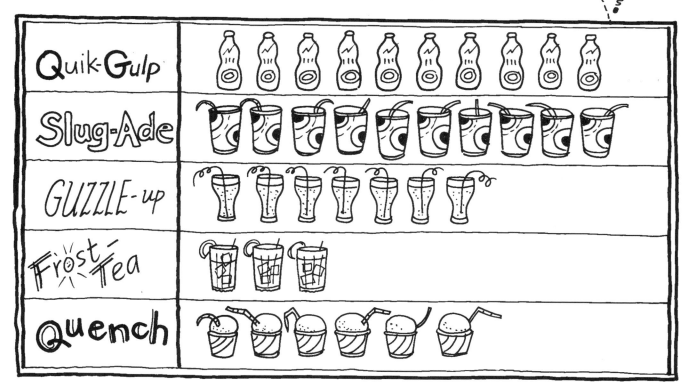

1. Which drink sold the least? _____

2. How many Slug-Ades and Frost Teas were drunk? _____

3. How many more Quik-Gulps than Guzzle-ups were sold? _____

4. How many more Guzzle-ups than Quenches were sold? _____

5. Which 2 drinks sold the same? _____ and _____

6. Pat drank 2 Frost Teas. How many were drunk by someone else? ____

7. Pam drank 4 Slug-Ades. How many more were sold? _____

8. Which was more popular, Quench or Slug-Ade? _____

Name _____

Reading a Picture Graph

Jungle Time

These runners have new jungle watches. Help them figure out the right time on their watches.

Write the time shown on each watch. Then color the watches.

1. _____

3. _____

2. _____

4. _____

5. Put the hands on these jungle clocks! Make them show the right time. Then color the clocks.

9:40   2:55   11:20

Name _____

Telling Time

Geometry, Measurement, & Graphing
Words to Know

area—the number of square units that will fit inside a figure. *The area of this figure is 4.*

bar graph—a picture that uses bars to show information.

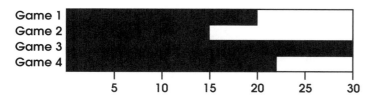

Grizzly Points

centimeter (cm)—a standard metric unit for measuring length. 100 cm = 1 meter (m)

circle—a flat, round figure.

cone—a space figure that looks like this:

congruent—having exactly the same size and shape. These 2 figures are congruent.

cube—a space figure with six sides, all of the squares the same size.

cubic unit—a unit used for measuring volume.

cup (c)—a U.S. Customary unit of capacity. 2 c = 1 pt

cylinder—a space figure that looks like this:

degree (°)—a standard unit for measuring temperature.

foot (ft)—a U.S. Customary unit for measuring length. 1 ft = 12 in.

gallon (gal)—a U.S. Customary unit for measuring capacity. 1 gal = 4 qt

gram (g)—a standard metric unit used to measure the mass of light objects. 1000 g = 1 kg

hour—a unit of time equal to 60 minutes.

inch (in.)—a U.S. Customary unit for measuring length. 12 in. = 1 ft

kilogram (kg)—a standard metric unit for measuring mass. 1 kg = 1000 g

kilometer—a standard metric unit for measuring length. 1 km = 1000 m

line graph—a picture that uses line segments to show changes in information.

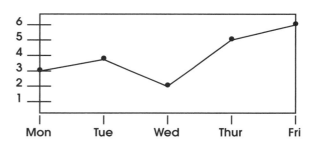

Joe's Miles Run

liter (L)—a standard metric unit for measuring capacity.

meter (m)—a standard metric unit for measuring length. 1 m = 100 cm

mile (mi)—a U.S. Customary unit for measuring long distances. 1 mi = 1760 yds or 5280 ft

minute—a unit of time. There are 60 minutes in an hour.

number pair—two numbers whose order shows a location on a grid. The B is at (3, 2)— 3 over and 2 up.

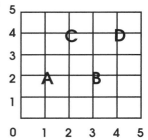

ounce (oz)—a U.S. Customary unit for measuring weight. 16 oz = 1 lb

perimeter—the distance around a figure. The perimeter of this figure is 7 $\frac{1}{2}$.

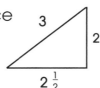

pictograph—a graph in which pictures stand for objects.

pint (pt)—a U.S. Customary unit of capacity. 1 pt = 2 c

polygon—a figure formed by joining 3 or more segments.

pound (lb)—a U.S. Customary unit measuring weight. 1 lb = 16 oz

pyramid—a space figure that looks like this:

quart (qt)—a U.S. Customary unit for measuring capacity. 1 qt = 2 pt

rectangle—a figure with 4 sides and 4 right angles.

rectangular prism—a space figure with 6 sides, all of which are rectangles.

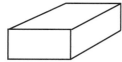

segment—part of a line with a starting point and an ending point.

sides—the segments that make a polygon.

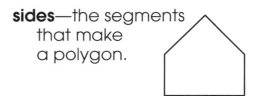

This polygon has 5 sides.

sphere—a round space figure.

square—a figure with 4 sides, all the same length, and 4 right angles.

square unit—a unit used for measuring area.

This figure has an area of 6 square units.

temperature—the measure in degrees (°) of how hot or cold something is.

triangle—a figure with three sides.

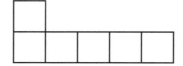

volume—the amount of space a figure takes up.

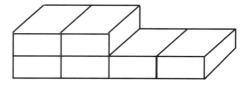

This figure has a volume of 6 cubic units.

yard (yd)—a U.S. Customary unit for measuring length. 1 yd = 3 ft or 36 in.

APPENDIX

CONTENTS

Language Arts Skills Test 308

Social Studies Skills Test 321

Science Skills Test 328

Math Skills Test 332

Skills Test Answer Key 342

Skills Exercises Answer Key 344

Language Arts Skills Test

PART ONE: PHONICS & WORD RECOGNITION

Write the consonants that are missing from the beginning, middle, and end of each of these words.

1. __ a __ e __

3. __ i __ ar __

5. __ i __ e __

2. __ a __ o __

4. __ a __ __ e __

Write the missing consonant blend at the beginning of each word.

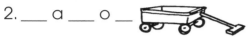

6. _____easure ____est

7. _____agon

8. ___aceship

Write the missing consonant blend at the end of each word.

9. du____

11. bu_____

13. sta_____

10. swi____

12. bran____

14. Circle the double consonants in each of these words.

yellow   rabbit   middle   mess   balloon

15. Circle the words that have a silent letter.

thumb   plum   comb   wrong   win   ghost

16. Circle the words where **y** is a consonant.

yes   funny   lady   yolk   yodel   monkey

17. Circle the words where **y** is a vowel.

yelled   silly   myself   you   Monday   money

Name _____

18. Number these words in alphabetical order:

___ bat

___ boat

___ bite

___ black

___ butter

19. Number these words in alphabetical order:

___ snorkel

___ rhinoceros

___ dinosaur

___ iceberg

___ treasure

___ lion

Write the missing vowels in the spaces.

20.

t _ r n _ d _

21.

v _ l c _ n _

22.

f _ r _

23.

b _ _ t

24. Circle the words with short vowel sounds.

throat   witch   shut   smile   whistle   thunder

25. Circle the words with long vowel sounds.

trouble   groan   right   wrinkle   starve   late

26. Circle the words that have the same vowel sound as **ow** in **clown.**

frown   cloud   flow   growth   mouth   loud

Put the missing ending on each word. Use ing **or** ed.

27. We paddl____ our canoe between the icebergs.

28. It was fun try_____ to find Bigfoot.

29. We should have been watch_____ the dragon more carefully!

30. It's a good thing the helicopter land____ safely in the hurricane.

31. Circle the prefix in each word.

rewrite   disappointment   unhappiness   mistake   impossible

Name _____

Language Arts Skills Test

32. Circle the suffix in each word.

unfriendly   dangerous   homeless   drinkable   excitement

Write the root word for each of these words.

_____ 33. happiness   _____ 36. hopeless

_____ 34. strangest   _____ 37. disappear

_____ 35. undrinkable

38. Circle the pictures whose names have a long vowel sound.

39. Circle the pictures whose names have a short vowel sound.

40. Circle the pictures whose names have a long vowel sound with a **silent e** at the end.

41. Write the number of syllables next to each word.

____ iceberg   ____ alligator   ____ elephant   ____ hurricane

____ rhinoceros   ____ crocodile   ____ tornado   ____ helicopter

42. Draw a line to match each pair of synonyms.

chilly   easy   mad   awful   difficult

terrible   angry   hard   simple   frosty

Name _____

43. The pictures show three different meanings of one word.

Write the word.   tr_____

44. The pictures show two different meanings of one word.

Write the word.   b_____

45. The pictures show two different meanings of one word.

Write the word.   b_____

46. Draw a line to match the antonyms (opposites).

beginning	always
late	happy
interesting	full empty
boring never	early
grumpy	ending

47. Add a word to make each noun into a compound word.

_____fly   camp_____

school_____   _____ball

48. Add **s** or **es** to make each noun plural.

box_____   elephant_____   bush_____

lunch_____   scorpion_____   glass_____

49. Add **'s** to show that each animal owns something.

the gorilla_____ teeth   Bigfoot_____ footprints   the giraffe_____ spots

50. Circle the words that are proper nouns. Underline the letters that should be capitalized.

texas   september   school   halloween

tuesday   grandmother   red   monkey

Name _____

Language Arts Skills Test

PART TWO: READING

Read the following poem, and then answer the questions.

Ernie stepped in quicksand
Even though the sign was there.
He walked right into the middle
Though the sign told him, "Beware!"

The sand was filled with water,
Which turned it into muck
All wet and thick and gooey,
Poor Ernie was out of luck!

His feet sank in up to the knees
He tried to run on through.
He grabbed and pulled and hollered,
But the quicksand was like glue.

We all went out to find him.
Poor Ernie was up to his ears.
We threw him a rope and dragged
   him out,
And he's lived for years and years!

51. What would be a good title for this poem?
   a. Ernie's Walk
   b. Foolish Ernie
   c. All About Sand

52. Where did Ernie step into the quicksand?
   a. the edge
   b. the river bottom
   c. the middle

53. How many people went to look for Ernie?
   a. no one
   b. one person
   c. many people

54. What word in stanza #3 is a synonym for **yelled?** _____

55. What did the sign tell Ernie? _____

_____

56. What did Ernie do after he sank into the quicksand? _____

_____

Name _____

57. Write three words the poem used to describe the quicksand.

_____   _____

_____

58. What kind of a person do you think Ernie was?

_____

59. This limerick is mixed-up!
Number the lines in the correct order.
_____ So why was he giggling
_____ A certain young man from France
_____ And shaking and wiggling?
_____ It's because he was covered with ants!
_____ Was always too bashful to dance.

Read the paragraph, and answer the questions.

Frannie started up the helicopter motor. She shouted to Felix, "Are you ready?" "Yes!" he hollered. "Let's take off!" And off they went, flying over the bridge. Then Felix had an idea. "Let's try flying under the bridge!" he shouted.

60. What do you think will happen next?

_____

_____

61. Find a pair of synonyms in the story. _____ , _____

62. Find a pair of opposites. _____ , _____

63. What did Frannie start? _____

Name _____

Language Arts Skills Test

Read the passage and answer the questions.

A long time ago in the jungle, a big, fierce lion caught a tiny mouse for a snack. Just as the lion was about to gobble up the mouse, the mouse cried, "Oh please! Please! Don't eat me! If you let me go, I promise to come back and help you some day!" Now the lion thought that was pretty funny that such a tiny thing could help him, the king of the jungle! While he was laughing, the mouse escaped and ran away.

Yum

Many days later, the big, powerful lion, was caught in a tricky trap set by some lion hunters. The mouse was far away, but he heard the lion's painful roar. He ran quickly through the jungle and found the trapped lion. "Here I am to help you!" cried the mouse. This time, the lion did not laugh. He needed all the help he could get! The tiny mouse gnawed the ropes off the lion. In no time at all, the lion was loose again. From that day on, the lion and the mouse were best friends.

64. How did the mouse escape from the lion? _____

65. When did this story take place? _____

66. What word describes the trap? _____

67. What word describes the lion's roar? _____

68. What word means the same as **mighty?** _____

69. What title would you give to this? _____

70. This story is a fable. A fable teaches a lesson. What lesson does this teach?

_____

_____

_____

_____

Name _____

Read the passage and answer the questions.

In 1980, Mt. St. Helens, in Washington, erupted three times in two months. The first blast was 500 times as powerful as an atom bomb. The volcano caused 60 deaths. It caused three billion dollars in damage.

A volcano is an opening in the surface of Earth. Gases and melted rock erupt through the opening. There are hundreds of active volcanoes in the world today. Some volcanoes are slow and quiet, but many are very violent. The big explosions do a lot of damage. Here is an example of the harm a volcano can do. A volcano on an island in Indonesia killed 2,000 people in 1883. The next day, the mountain collapsed. This killed 3,000 more people. The collapse of the mountain caused a huge tidal wave in the ocean. That wave crashed onto other countries and killed another 31,000 people.

71. When did Mt. St. Helens erupt? _____

72. How many active volcanoes are there in the world today? _____

73. Is it true that all volcanoes erupt violently? _____

74. What was the cost of the eruption at Mt. St. Helens?

_____ people and _____ dollars

75. How many deaths were caused by the tidal wave? _____

76. What is the main idea of this passage? _____

_____

_____

77. What do you think the author's purpose was in writing this passage?

_____

_____

_____

Name _____

Language Arts Skills Test

PART THREE: SPELLING

Find the correct words in each row. Circle them.

78. dolar   zipper   hugging   gost
79. puddle   garadge   million   laugh
80. afraid   lemmon   appear   sumer
81. graph   quizes   cotton   friend

Circle the correct spelling.

82. absent   abcent   84. sise   size
83. krayon   crayon   85. jiraffe   giraffe

Write ie or ei in each blank to spell the word correctly.

86. fr _____ nd   88. bel _____ ve
87. w _____ gh   89. p _____ ce

Choose a pair of vowels from the hat to spell each word correctly.

ai   ou   e^e   ia   oo   oi   oa   ea   ui

90. m _____ ntain
91. r _____ ster
92. r _____ son
93. g _____ nt
94. sp _____ ch
95. motorb _____ t
96. r _____ se
97. b _____ ldings
98. n _____ se

Write the plural form of each of these words. Write the whole word.

99. candy _____
100. box _____
101. donkey _____
102. mouse _____
103. tooth _____
104. family _____
105. goose _____

Name _____

106. **Circle the words on the trash can that are spelled correctly.**

garbige   judge
brige   cabbege
fudge   hedge
ridge   garadge
ledge

107. **Circle the words on the rock that are spelled correctly.**

tryed   wishd
caught   rubed
worryed   slipped
grabbed   getted
keeped   enjoyed

Choose a prefix from the poster to add to each word. Write the whole word.

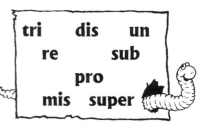

tri   dis   un   re   sub   pro   mis   super

108. angle _____
109. write _____
110. tie _____
111. marine _____
112. take _____

113. **Which of the bee's words are correct? Circle them.**

none   once   choclat
people   forty   ocean
wheather   opin   voice
trubble

114. Mimi chose some wrong words when she wrote her story. **Circle the wrong words.**

Polly road along on an old hoarse threw the woulds. The hoarse tripped and lost a shoo in the creak. Polly fell off. Did she brake her tow?

Circle the word in each group that is spelled wrong.

115. moter   doctor   cotton
      mystery   double   tomato

116. chocolate   around   vegetable
      different   Lincoln   memary

117. squirrel   squeak   quake
      questun   Africa   quietly

- **tomatoe sause**
- **suger cookies**
- **cheese pissa**
- **lettice salid**
- **bannanna pie**
- **hamburglers**

The menu has some wrong spellings. **Write each food again. This time, spell it right.**

118. _____
119. _____
120. _____
121. _____
122. _____
123. _____

Find the word that is spelled wrong. Write it correctly.

124. Cassie's friends were quiet mad at her. _____

125. Felix can't remember witch path to take. _____

126. Bruno already tired to open that door. _____

127. **Circle the animal names that are spelled correctly.**

giraffe   ant   eagel

turtel   goose   monky

rooster   parrot   raccoon

Write these numbers in words.

128. 500 _____
129. 55 _____
130. 38 _____
131. 3rd _____
132. 19 _____

Write each word correctly.

133. shood _____
134. Wensday _____
135. evry _____
136. brocken _____
137. littel _____
138. befour _____
139. pepel _____
140. Febuary _____

Write each headline again below it. Spell all the words right.

141.
Forest News, July 5
Fourty Millon Dollers Found in Garbidge

142.
Forest News, July 6
Ladder Falls on Anamal Docter

_____
_____
_____
_____

Name _____

143. **Circle the words that can be nouns.**

friendly	Mrs. Clown
afternoon	suddenly
trick	gobbled
Friday	laughter
merry-go-round	

144. **Circle the words that are proper nouns and should be capitalized.**

easter	mexico
teacher	boston
thursday	school
texas	

145. **Circle the words in the magician's hat that can be verbs.**

swing   leaping   roar
clown   laugh
magic   tricks
flying   tricked
    music
grabbed   slowly

146. **Underline the sentence below that is a statement.**

Put a box around the sentence that is a question.

Put a check mark in front of the sentence that is an exclamation.

a. Can you ride a unicycle?

b. Never put your hand in the tiger's cage!

c. It is a good idea to be friendly to the gorillas.

Circle the numbers of the sentences that have correct punctuation.

147. Don't look down!

148. Which bear is good at dancing.

149. Did you try the giant hot dogs with grilled onions?

150. The juggler dropped a toaster on his head yesterday.

151. That is not a very good idea?

152. **Circle the subject of the sentence.**

Two brave clowns jumped on the pirate ship this morning.

153. **Circle the subject of the sentence.**

A nervous Gino put his head in the lion's mouth.

154. **Circle the predicate of the sentence.**

The monkeys climbed all over their barrel.

155. **Circle the predicate of the sentence.**

Chester, grab those balloons before they float away!

156. **Circle the letters in Allie's envelope that should be capitalized.**
Add the missing punctuation.

allie clown
112 fun street
central city iowa

abby apricot
2222 laughter lane
cow's ear illinois 60001

Name _____

Language Arts Skills Test

157. Circle the letters in Allie's letter that should be capitalized.

Add the missing punctuation.

dear abby

you won't believe the news   the carnival came
to our town last Thursday molly and i rode the
roller coaster seven times   we bought cotton
candy four times guess what happened when
I went to see the circus acts   they invited me to
be in the show   they gave me the job of fire-eater
it isn't all that hard—just a little hot

love

allie

Make a contraction from each of these pairs of words.

158. we will _____

159. they are _____

160. will not _____

161. Circle the letters on the poster that should be capitalized.

Add the missing punctuation.

don't miss the carnival

see the most amazing things

we have clowns acrobats and jugglers

eat delicious treats

you can play lots of fun games

there are 25 great rides

thursday october 20 2015

central city iowa

Name _____

162. **Draw a line through the idea in this story that is not necessary.**

You won't believe what happened on the Pirate Ride today! Four visitors fell overboard! Three pirates had to walk the plank, and the mechanical shark sank. Everything was going wrong. Just then the circus show started. The sails fell down, too. Luckily, all the visitors thought these things were part of the ride. They laughed and laughed and said, "This is the best ride we've taken yet!"

163. **Circle the title that would be best for the above story.**
   a. Time to Walk the Plank
   b. The Mechanical Shark
   c. Trouble on the Pirate Ride
   d. Trouble at the Carnival

164. **Choose one clown. Circle the one you chose.** Imagine what this clown is like and what he or she might do, wear, or say!

Give the clown a name. _____

Write 6 words that describe what you imagine this clown to be like.

   1. _____   4. _____
   2. _____   5. _____
   3. _____   6. _____

Write a sentence telling something the clown might do.

_____

_____

_____

Name _____

Language Arts Skills Test

Social Studies Skills Test

PART ONE: SOCIAL STUDIES

Circle the correct answer.

1. A place where people live and play and work is a
   neighborhood   government   history

2. A behavior that must be followed by everyone in a community is a
   rule   law   need   want

3. A place to go in a community to get a car fixed is a
   cleaners   bank   service station   hospital

4. A place to call to report a stolen bike is a
   recycling center   park   school   police station

5. A way to go from one place to another is called
   community   transportation   government

Choose the words that tell the meaning of each sign. Write the letter.

A   B   C   D   E

_____ 6. first aid   _____ 8. no smoking   _____ 10. rest rooms

_____ 7. stop   _____ 9. handicapped access

Circle the correct answer.

11. The head of a city or town government is a
    congressman   senator   mayor   council member

12. The group that makes rules and decisions for a community is a
    city or town council   congress   doctor's office

13. Something that city taxes would probably not be used for is
    schools   streets & roads   groceries   city parks

Name _____

14. Circle the sign that shows a law.

A   B   C   D   E

15. A special way that a family or other group does something is a

     law   custom   constitution   need

16. Things that people must have to survive are called

     wants   laws   needs   customs

17. Circle the pictures that are not needs.

A   B   C   D

18. Money paid each month to live in a place that you do not own is called

     taxes   rent   charity   savings

Draw a line from each natural resource to a product that is made from it.

19.

20.

21.

22.

Name _____

Circle the correct answer.

23. Which country is not a neighbor of the United States?

    Mexico   Canada   India   Costa Rica   Haiti

24. Which country is in South America?

    Canada   Russia   Bolivia   Germany

25. Which country is in Europe?

    France   Panama   China   Australia

26. Which country is in North America?

    Japan   United States   Ireland

27. Which part of the U.S. government makes the laws?

    the president   the Supreme Court   the Congress

28. Which happened first?

    the first airplane was flown   the first person stepped on the moon

29. Which happened last?

    Washington   Kennedy   Lincoln
    was president   was president   was president

30. Which building is not in Washington, DC?

    the Statue of Liberty   the Capitol Building   the Lincoln Memorial

Look at the grid. Write the location of each American symbol or monument.

_____ 31. flag

_____ 32. Statue of Liberty

_____ 33. eagle

_____ 34. White House

_____ 35. pilgrim

_____ 36. fireworks

_____ 37. Liberty Bell

_____ 38. Washington Monument

Name _____

Social Studies Skills Test

39. Circle the workers who are working to make or grow something.

A B C D

40. Circle the workers who are doing a service for someone.

A B C D

Use the map to answer the questions.

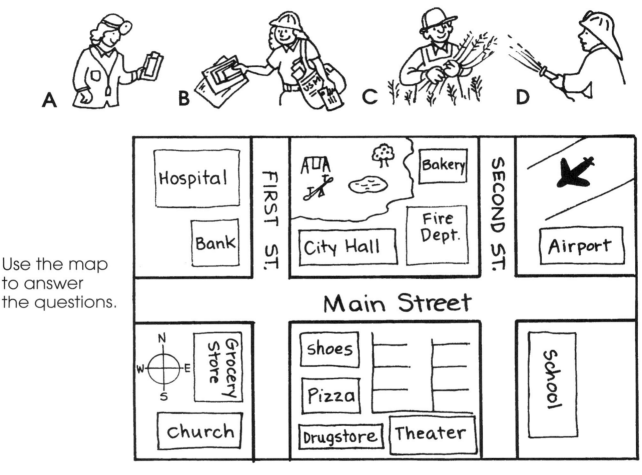

41. What direction is the park from the airport? _____

42. Is the school on First Street? _____

43. Which one is not on Main Street?   bank   drugstore   parking lot

44. How many blocks is it from the hospital to the airport? _____

45. What store is west of the shoe store?

grocery store   pizza shop   drugstore   bakery

Name _____

PART TWO: MAP SKILLS & GEOGRAPHY

Look for these parts of the map. Write the letter for each one next to its name.

_____ 46. title

_____ 47. key

_____ 48. scale

_____ 49. compass

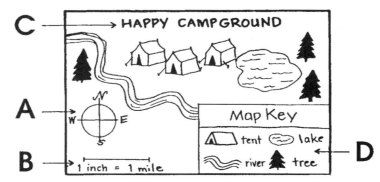

50. Which one is the map that correctly shows the things on the table?

Circle the letter of the correct map.

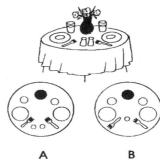

Use the map to answer the questions. Write N, S, E, or W in each blank.

51. The town is _____ of the airport.

52. The river is _____ of the town.

53. The lake is _____ of the river.

54. The town is _____ of the lake.

55. The airport is _____ of the lake.

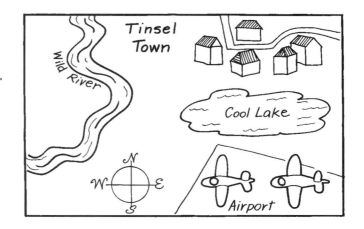

Use the map key to match the words to the symbols.

Write the correct letter next to the word for each symbol.

_____ 56. river

_____ 57. house

_____ 58. railroad track

_____ 59. airport

_____ 60. forest

_____ 61. bridge

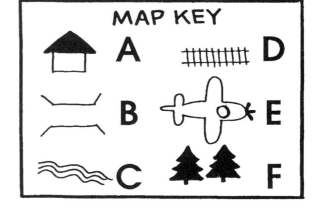

Name _____

**Use the maps to find the hemispheres for these continents and oceans.
Write E for Eastern, W for Western, and B for both.**

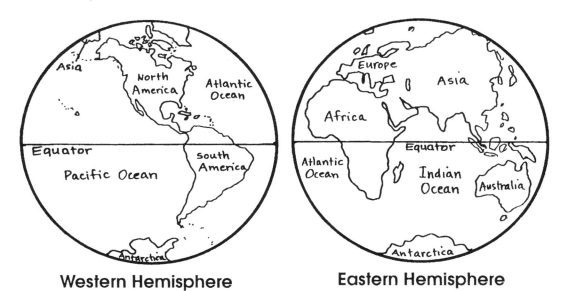

Western Hemisphere   **Eastern Hemisphere**

_____ 62. Africa   _____ 63. The Atlantic Ocean   _____ 65. Europe

          _____ 64. South America   _____ 66. Asia

67. Circle the word that is NOT a continent.

Asia   Africa   Texas   North America   Australia

68. Circle the word that is NOT a city.

Dallas   Chicago   San Francisco   Europe   Seattle

69. Circle the word that is NOT a state.

Iowa   Pennsylvania   Kansas   Boston   Georgia

70. Circle the word that is NOT a country.

France   India   Chicago   Mexico   Canada

71. Circle the country that is on the northern border of the United States.

Alaska   Germany   Canada   Montana   Mexico

72. Circle the country that is a neighbor to the south of the United States.

Japan   Mexico   Canada   China   Russia

Name _____

Use the grid to help you find things on the picnic table.

_____ 73. Where is the 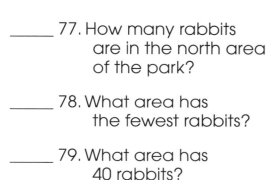 ?

_____ 74. Where is the 🐜 ?

_____ 75. Where is the 🧁 ?

_____ 76. Where is the 🥪 ?

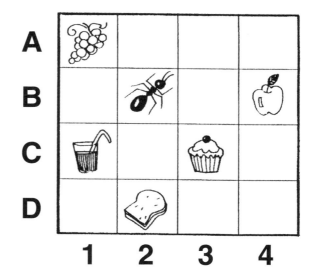

Use the map to answer the questions.

_____ 77. How many rabbits are in the north area of the park?

_____ 78. What area has the fewest rabbits?

_____ 79. What area has 40 rabbits?

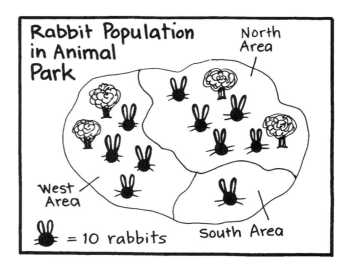

Write the word that matches the definition.

_____ 80. tells distances on a map   west

_____ 81. land surrounded by water   continent

_____ 82. opposite of east   ocean

_____ 83. a large body of land   scale

_____ 84. a large body of water   title

_____ 85. tells what a map is about   compass

_____ 86. tells directions on a map   island

Name _____

Science Skills Test

Write the letter of the word that matches each definition.

1. _____ process where plants use sunlight to make food
2. _____ plant part that holds plants in the ground
3. _____ parts of the flower that produce pollen
4. _____ part of the plant that makes seeds
5. _____ tiny openings in leaves that take in air

a. flower
b. stomata
c. roots
d. stamens
e. photosynthesis

Write the letter of the word that matches each definition.

6. _____ animal with a backbone
7. _____ animal with 8 legs and no antennae
8. _____ animal with 6 legs and 2 antennae
9. _____ animal with no backbone
10. _____ animal with many segments and bristles

f. vertebrate
g. invertebrate
h. arachnid
i. insect
j. earthworm

Circle the correct answer or answers.

11. Which plant part makes food?

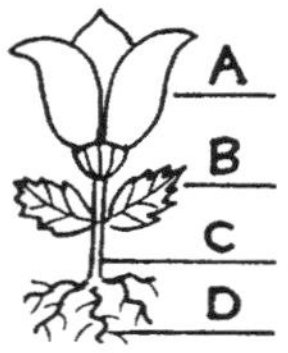

12. Which things are part of the circulatory system?

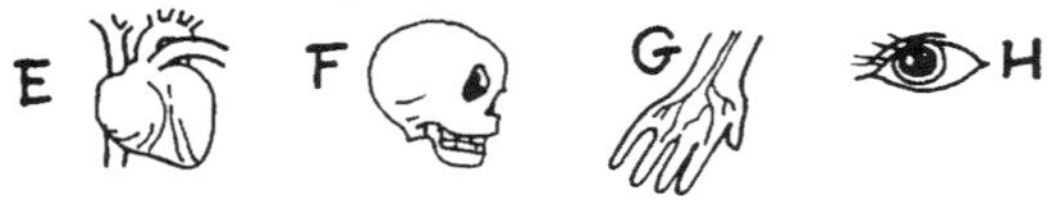

13. Which thing is NOT alive?

14. Which animal belongs in a grassland habitat?

15. Which picture shows germination?

Write the letter of the word that matches each definition.

16. _____ has gills and scales
17. _____ covered with feathers
18. _____ covered with dry scales
19. _____ covered with fur or hair
20. _____ can breathe on land or in water

a. mammals
b. birds
c. amphibians
d. fish
e. reptiles

Name _____

Circle the correct answer or answers.

21. Which of these living things are producers?

A   B   C   D

22. Which of these are consumers?

23. Which one of these is a predator?

E   F   G

A   B

24. Which plant part is a petal?

25. Which animal is a vertebrate?

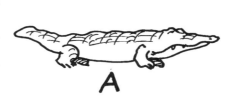

A

B

C

D

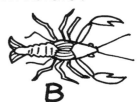

A   B

Write the letter of the word that matches each definition.

26. _____ sleep to save energy

27. _____ fight back to protect itself

28. _____ move somewhere else for a while

29. _____ change to survive in the environment

30. _____ blend into the environment

a. camouflage

b. hibernate

c. migrate

d. defend

e. adapt

Circle the correct answer or answers.

31. Which animal is an insect?

A   B   C

32. Which animal is an arachnid?

D   E   F

33. Which end of this earthworm is the tail?

A   B

34. Which animal is NOT a reptile?

C   D   E

35. Which animal is NOT a mammal?

A   B   C   D

Name _____

Circle the correct answer or answers.

36. Which animals are cold-blooded?

37. Which animals are warm-blooded?

38. Which animal can live both on land and in water?

39. Which picture shows an animal hibernating?

40. Which picture shows rib bones?

41. Which shows the molecules in a gas?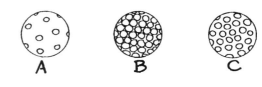

42. Which swimmer is on the crest of the wave?

43. Which does this picture show?  A. freezing   B. evaporation   C. melting

44. An animal that eats dead animals is

    A. prey   B. a producer   C. a scavenger

45. An animal that eats another animal is called the

    D. predator   E. decomposer   F. producer

46. The radius, ulna, and humerus are bones in the

    A. arm   B. leg   C. back

Name _____

47. The tibia, fibula, and femur are bones in the

　　D. ankle　　　　E. arm　　　　　　F. leg

48. Which one of these is caused by germs?

　　A. a bruise　　　B. an infection　　C. a fracture

49. Which cloud is a cumulonimbus?

50. Which machine is an inclined plane?

51. Which machine is a pulley?

52. Which one of these is an island?

53. Which boat is at the mouth of the river?

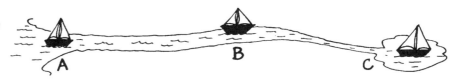

Write the letter of the matching word.

54. _____ a push or a pull　　　　　　　　　　a. vibrate

55. _____ to move back and forth　　　　　　　b. pitch

56. _____ the way sound travels　　　　　　　c. melt

57. _____ a change from a solid to a liquid　　　d. waves

58. _____ the highness or lowness of a sound　　e. force

Name _____

Math Skills Test

PART ONE: NUMBER CONCEPTS & RELATIONSHIPS

Look at this picture to answer the questions below.

Circle the correct answer.

1. The snake is _____ in the line.

   fourth   first   third   second   fifth

2. Is the bird fourth in line?

   yes   no

3. Which is second in line?

   snake   rat   turtle   frog   bird

Write the numeral for each number.

_____ 4. forty-seven

_____ 5. three hundred twenty-six

_____ 6. six hundred ten

_____ 7. seven thousand two hundred sixteen

For problems 8-10, circle the answers.

8. Which words match this numeral? **440**
   a. four hundred fourteen
   b. four hundred forty-four
   c. four hundred four
   d. four hundred forty
   e. four thousand, four hundred

9. Which words match this number? **6,207**
   a. six hundred twenty-seven
   b. six thousand, two hundred, seventy
   c. six thousand, two hundred, seven
   d. six thousand, twenty-seven

10. Which number is **two million**?
    a. 20,000
    b. 200,000
    c. 2,000
    d. 2,000,000
    e. 20,000,000
    f. 2,000,000,000

11. Write this number in words. **59**

    _____

12. Write these numbers in order from smallest to largest:
    237 333 273 193 103

    ____ ____ ____ ____ ____

13. Write these numbers in order from largest to smallest:
    72 67 39 36 94

    ____ ____ ____ ____ ____

Write these numbers:

_____ 14. 9 ones and 7 tens

_____ 15. 4 hundreds, 3 tens, 9 ones

_____ 16. 8 hundreds and 6 ones

_____ 17. 2 thousands and 5 hundreds

Name _____

Use this picture for questions 18-21.

48   102
93    $4.50   27
66    $17.75 $8.15

_____ 18. Which number is about 50?

_____ 19. Which number is about 100?

_____ 20. Which number is about $18?

_____ 21. Which number is 7 < 100?

22. Look at the beaver's sign.

_____ Which number is in the hundreds place?

_____ Which number is in the tens place?

7 2 0 3

Round these to the nearest 10.

_____ 23. 77

_____ 24. 232

_____ 25. 885

Round these to the nearest 100.

_____ 26. 521

_____ 27. 759

In 28-30, finish each pattern. Write or draw what will come next.

28.  _____

29. 2, 5, 8, 11, 14, _____

30. AB, BC, CD, _____

_____ 31. Write a fractional number to show how much pizza has NOT been eaten.

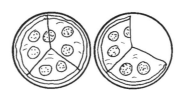

32. Circle the words that match this number: $10 \frac{3}{7}$
   a. thirteen sevenths   c. ten thirds
   b. ten and seven thirds   d. ten and three sevenths

33. Does this make sense? (Circle your answer.)
   A frog hopped 4,786 miles in one day.   Yes   No

Name _____

Math Skills Test

34. Does this make sense?
(Circle your answer.)
A family of four crickets ate 300 giant swamp burgers at one meal.
Yes   No

35. Allie practices tennis every day.

On Monday, she hit 325 balls.
On Tuesday, she hit 412 balls.
On Wednesday, she hit 352 balls.

Which day did she hit the least number of balls?
Write your answer.

_____

36. Does this make sense?
(Circle your answer.)
A thirsty runner drank 5 glasses of water after a big race.
Yes   No

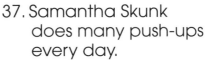

37. Samantha Skunk does many push-ups every day.
The number she did today has these digits in it: 4   8   2
The largest number is in the ones place. The smallest number is in the tens place.
What is the number?

Write your answer. _____

PART TWO: MATH COMPUTATION & PROBLEM SOLVING

38. **Circle all the even numbers.**

    7   21   10   100   14   47

Write the answers.

_____ 39. In the number 473, which number is in the tens place?

_____ 40. In the number 115, which number is in the ones place?

_____ 41. In the number 716, which number is in the hundreds place?

_____ 42. In the number 2816, which number is in the hundreds place?

_____ 43. Round 56 to the nearest ten.

_____ 44. Round 73 to the nearest ten.

_____ 45. Round 228 to the nearest ten.

_____ 46. Round 472 to the nearest hundred.

47. What number sentence matches the picture? Circle the answer.

A. 3 + 5 = 8   B. 3 x 5 = 15

48. What number sentence matches the picture? Circle the answer.

A. 7 – 5 = 2   B. 12 – 7 = 5

49. What number sentence matches the picture? Circle the answer.

A. 4 + 9 = 13   B. 4 x 9 = 36

Name _____

50. What does this picture show?
Circle the answer.

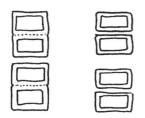

A. $\frac{1}{2} = \frac{1}{4}$ B. $\frac{1}{2} = \frac{2}{4}$

51. What does this picture show?
Circle the answer.

A. $\frac{1}{3} = \frac{2}{6}$ B. $\frac{2}{3} = \frac{1}{6}$

Solve the problems.

52. 403
    +192

53. 6911
    +1044

54. 295
     - 62

_____ 55. Write a fraction that tells what part is checkered.

_____ 56. Write a fraction that tells what part is checkered.

_____ 57. Write a fraction that tells what part is striped.

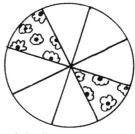

_____ 58. Write a fraction that tells what part has flowers.

_____ 59. Write a fraction that tells what part is checkered.

Write the missing numbers in the number sentences.

60. 3 x 6 = _____   63. 9 x 3 = _____

61. 4 x _____ = 20   64. 4 x 8 = _____

62. _____ x 6 = 42   65. 6 x _____ = 36

_____¢ 66. Count the coins. Write how much money is shown.

_____¢ 67. Count the coins. Write how much money is shown.

Name _____

Math Skills Test

68. Circle the number that is the largest.

111   101   10   110

69. Circle the number that is the largest.

4.5   4   1.4

Solve the problems.

70.   17
       29
    +12

71.   101
       75
    +11

SOCCER SCORES	
TEAM	GOALS
Grizzlies	7
Eagles	2
Lions	5
Panthers	9
Cougars	6

72. Which team has the lowest score?
    A. Cougars
    B. Eagles
    C. Lions

73. Which team scored more than the Grizzlies?
    A. Lions
    B. Cougars
    C. Panthers

Write in the missing numbers in the number sentences.

74. $28 \div 4 =$ ⬜

75. $18 \div 9 =$ ⬜

76. $40 \div 8 =$ ⬜

77. $21 \div 3 =$ ⬜

78. $36 \div 4 =$ ⬜

79. $35 \div 7 =$ ⬜

Solve the problems.

80. $ 42.66
     −13.21
   $

81.   55¢
      −10¢
        ¢

82. $ 10.00
     +12.16
   $

83. Which mixed numeral shows how much pizza is left?
Circle the answer.

A. $1\frac{2}{3}$ B. $\frac{1}{3}$ C. $1\frac{1}{3}$

Name _____

Math Skills Test

84. What time does the clock show? **Circle the answer.**

3:00   10:15   2:30

85. What time does this clock show? **Circle the answer.**

9:15   7:15   6:45

86. What time does this clock show? **Circle the answer.**

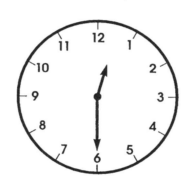

12:30   6:30   12:15

87. Which clock shows 11:10? **Circle the answer.**

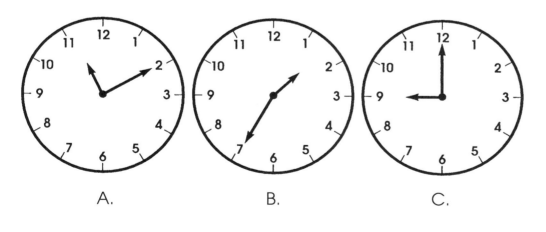

A.   B.   C.

Solve the problems.

88.   2176
    + 944

89.   66
    − 19

90.   910
    − 66

91.   232
    x 4

92.   65
    x 7

93.   22
    x 6

94. 4 ⟌ 52

95. 6 ⟌ 84

Name _____

Math Skills Test

PART THREE: GEOMETRY, MEASUREMENT, & GRAPHING

Write the letter of the figure that matches each of these terms:

   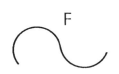 

_____ 96. point

_____ 97. line segment

_____ 98. parallel line segments

_____ 99. angle

_____ 100. triangle

Write the letter of the figure that matches each of these:

_____ 101. square

_____ 102. hexagon

_____ 103. triangle

_____ 104. circle

_____ 105. rectangle that is not a square

_____ and _____ 106. **Which 2 figures are congruent?**

_____ and _____ 107. **Which 2 figures are congruent?**

Name _____

Write the letter of the figure that matches each of these names:

A.   B.  C.   D.   E. 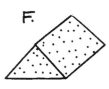 F.

_____ 108. cube

_____ 109. cone

_____ 110. sphere

_____ 111. pyramid

_____ 112. cylinder

_____ 113. prism

Circle the unit that would be best for measuring each of these.

114. juice in the glass ———— —— cup   gallon

115. water in the pool —— ———— pints   gallons

116. water in the jug ———— —— feet   liters

117. weight of cap ——  ———— kilograms   grams

118. weight of weight lifter ———  ——— kilograms   grams

119. weight of bug ——  ——— ounces   pounds

120. weight of shoes ———  —— cup   pounds

121. height of a building ——— ——— meters   centimeters

122. length of your thumb ——— —— inches   feet

Name _____

Math Skills Test

Circle the unit that is biggest.

123.	pound	ounce	ton	
124.	quart	cup	pint	gallon
125.	kilometer	centimeter	meter	
126.	gram	kilogram	milligram	
127.	yard	foot	inch	

Write the time that each clock shows.

_____128.

_____129.

_____130. Which clock shows 6:50?

A. 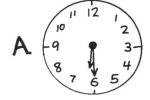 B. 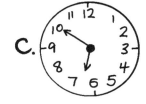 C.

_____131. How much money is shown here?

Use the menu to find the amounts of money.

_____132. 2 hot dogs, 1 soda—how much?

_____133. 1 taco, 1 pizza, 1 soda—how much?

_____134. 2 tacos, 2 sodas—how much?

Hot Dog . . $1.00
Pizza $2.00
Taco $1.00
Soda $1.00

Name _____

Fill in the blanks with the correct numbers.

135. _____ ounces = 1 pound

136. _____ cups = 1 quart

137. _____ grams = 1 kilogram

138. _____ inches = 1 foot

139. _____ centimeters = 1 meter

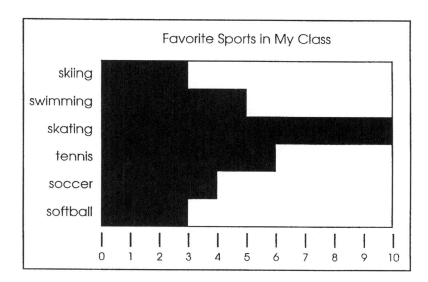

Favorite Sports in My Class

Use the graph at the right to answer the questions.

_____ 140. Which sport has 6 votes?

_____ 141. How many votes are for skating?

_____ 142. Which sport has 1 less vote than swimming?

_____ 143. Which 2 sports got the same number of votes?

_____

Use the graph at the right to answer the questions.

_____ 144. Write the location of the .

_____ 145. What is at (4, 3)?

_____ 146. Where is the ?

_____ 147. Where is the ?

_____ 148. What is at (1, 3)?

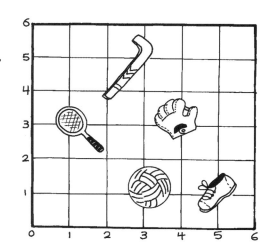

Name _____

Math Skills Test

Skills Test Answer Key

Language Arts Skills Test

1. c, m, l
2. w, g, n
3. l, z, d
4. b, rr, l
5. t, g, r
6. tr, ch
7. dr
8. sp
9. ck
10. ng
11. sh
12. ch
13. mp
14. ll, bb, dd, ss, ll
15. thumb, comb, wrong, ghost
16. yes, yolk, yodel
17. silly, myself, Monday, money
18. 1, 4, 2, 3, 5
19. 5, 4, 1, 2, 6, 3
20. o, a, o
21. o, a, o
22. i, e
23. o, a
24. witch, shut, whistle, thunder
25. groan, right, late
26. frown, cloud, mouth, loud
27. ed
28. ing
29. ing
30. ed
31. re, dis, un, mis, im
32. ly, ous, less, able, ment
33. happy
34. strange
35. drink
36. hope
37. appear
38. Circle snake and lion.
39. Circle bird, fish, crab, and tent.
40. Circle rose, cake, nose, and bike.
41. iceberg 2, rhinoceros 4, alligator 4, crocodile 3, elephant 3, tornado 3, hurricane 3, helicopter 4
42. chilly-frosty, easy-simple, mad-angry, awful-terrible, difficult-hard
43. trunk
44. bow
45. bat
46. beginning—ending, late—early, interesting—boring, empty—full, never—always, grumpy—happy
47. Answers will vary.
48. boxes, lunches, elephants, scorpions, bushes, glasses
49. 's added to all three
50. Circle: texas, september, halloween, tuesday. Underline: t in texas, s in september, h in halloween, and t in tuesday
51. b
52. c
53. c
54. hollered
55. Beware
56. He tried to run, he grabbed, he pulled, and he hollered. Allow any of these.
57. Any 3 of these: muck, wet, thick, gooey, glue
58. Answers will vary. Careless is a possibility.
59. 3, 1, 4, 5, 2
60. Answers will vary.
61. hollered and shouted
62. over and under
63. the helicopter motor
64. He ran away while the lion was laughing.
65. a long time ago
66. tricky
67. painful
68. powerful
69. Answers will vary.
70. Answers will vary—something about each person having something to offer, no matter how small.
71. 1980
72. hundreds
73. no
74. 60, 3 billion
75. 31,000
76. Volcanoes can be very destructive.
77. The author wanted to teach about volcanoes and tell how destructive they can be.
78. zipper, hugging
79. puddle, million, laugh
80. afraid, appear
81. graph, cotton, friend
82. absent
83. crayon
84. size
85. giraffe
86. friend
87. weigh
88. believe
89. piece
90. ou
91. oo
92. ea
93. ia
94. ee
95. oa
96. ai
97. ui
98. oi
99. candies
100. boxes
101. donkeys
102. mice
103. teeth
104. families
105. geese
106. judge, fudge, hedge, ridge, ledge
107. caught, slipped, grabbed, enjoyed
108. triangle
109. rewrite
110. untie or retie
111. submarine
112. mistake or retake
113. none, once, people, forty, ocean, voice
114. road, hoarse, threw, woulds, hoarse shoo, creak, brake, tow
115. moter
116. memary
117. questun
118. tomato sauce
119. sugar cookies
120. cheese pizza
121. lettuce salad
122. banana pie
123. hamburgers
124. quite
125. which
126. tried
127. giraffe, ant, goose, rooster, parrot, raccoon
128. five hundred
129. fifty-five
130. thirty-eight
131. third
132. nineteen
133. should
134. Wednesday
135. every
136. broken
137. little
138. before
139. people
140. February
141. Forty Million Dollars Found in Garbage
142. Ladder Falls on Animal Doctor
143. Mrs. Clown afternoon, trick, merry-go-round, Friday, laughter
144. Easter, Mexico, Boston, Thursday, Texas
145. swing, leaping, tricks, tricked, roar, laugh, grabbed, flying, clown
146. a. box around it
     b. √ in front
     c. line under it
147. Circled
148. Not circled
149. Circled
150. Circled
151. Not circled
152. Two brave clowns
153. A nervous Gino
154. climbed all over their barrel
155. grab those balloons before they float away
156. Allie Clown 112 Fun Street Central City, Iowa
     Abby Apricot 2222 Laughter Lane Cow's Ear, Illinois 60001
157. Dear Abby,
     You won't believe the news! The carnival came to our town last Thursday. Molly and I rode the roller coaster seven times. We bought cotton candy four times. Guess what happened when I went to see the circus acts? They invited me to be in the show! They gave me the job of fire-eater. It isn't all that hard—just a little hot!
     Love, Allie

158. we'll
159. they're
160. won't
161. Don't miss the carnival! See the most amazing things! We have clowns, acrobats, and jugglers. Eat delicious treats. (or !) You can play lots of fun games. There are 25 great rides. (or !) Thursday, October 20, 2015 Central City, Iowa
162. Just then the circus show started.
163. c
164. See that student has completed all sections of the question.

Social Studies Skills Test

1. neighborhood
2. law
3. service station
4. police station
5. transportation
6. C
7. E
8. D
9. A
10. B
11. mayor
12. city or town council
13. groceries
14. D
15. custom
16. needs
17. C and D
18. rent
19. orange juice
20. bread
21. sweater
22. cheese
23. India
24. Bolivia
25. France
26. United States
27. the Congress
28. the first airplane was flown
29. Kennedy was

president
30. the Statue of Liberty
31. A, 3
32. A, 1
33. B, 3
34. B, 1
35. C, 3
36. C, 1
37. A, 2
38. C, 2
39. B and C
40. A, B, and D
41. west
42. no
43. drugstore
44. 2
45. grocery store
46. C
47. D
48. B
49. A
50. A
51. N
52. W
53. E
54. N
55. S
56. C
57. A
58. D
59. E
60. F
61. B
62. E
63. B
64. W
65. E
66. B
67. Texas
68. Europe
69. Boston
70. Chicago
71. Canada
72. Mexico
73. B, 4
74. B, 2
75. C, 3
76. D, 2
77. 50
78. South
79. West
80. scale
81. island
82. west
83. continent
84. ocean
85. title
86. compass

Science Skills Test

1. e
2. c
3. d
4. a
5. b
6. f
7. h
8. i
9. g
10. j
11. B
12. E & G
13. A
14. H
15. A
16. d
17. b
18. e
19. a
20. c
21. A & C
22. E & G
23. B
24. A
25. A
26. b
27. d
28. c
29. e
30. a
31. A
32. F
33. A
34. D
35. A
36. A & B
37. D, E, & F
38. C
39. E
40. D
41. A
42. D
43. C
44. C
45. D
46. A
47. F
48. B
49. B
50. F
51. B
52. D
53. A
54. e
55. a
56. d
57. c
58. b

Math Skills Test

1. third
2. no
3. turtle
4. 47
5. 326
6. 610
7. 7,216
8. d
9. c
10. d
11. fifty nine or fifty-nine
12. 103, 193, 237, 273, 333
13. 94, 72, 67, 39, 36
14. 79
15. 439
16. 806
17. 2,500
18. 48
19. 102
20. $17.75
21. 93
22. 2, 0
23. 80
24. 230
25. 890
26. 500
27. 800
28. Upside down mushroom with 3 spots
29. 17
30. DE
31. $1\frac{2}{3}$
32. d
33. no
34. no
35. Monday
36. yes
37. 428
38. 10, 100, 14
39. 7
40. 5
41. 7
42. 8
43. 60
44. 70
45. 230

46. 500
47. B
48. B
49. A
50. B
51. A
52. 595
53. 7955
54. 233
55. $\frac{2}{4}$
56. $\frac{3}{5}$
57. $\frac{3}{6}$
58. $\frac{2}{8}$
59. $\frac{2}{5}$
60. 18
61. 5
62. 7
63. 27
64. 32
65. 6
66. 80¢
67. 21¢
68. 111
69. 4.5
70. 58
71. 187
72. B
73. C
74. 7
75. 2
76. 5
77. 7
78. 9
79. 5
80. $29.45
81. 45¢
82. $22.16
83. A
84. 10:15
85. 6:45
86. 12:30
87. A
88. 3120
89. 47
90. 844
91. 928
92. 455
93. 132
94. 13
95. 14

96. B
97. C
98. A
99. E
100. D
101. E
102. F
103. B
104. A
105. C
106. A and D
107. B and C
108. D
109. B
110. A
111. E
112. C
113. F
114. cup
115. gallons
116. liters
117. grams
118. kilograms
119. ounces
120. pounds
121. meters
122. inches
123. ton
124. gallon
125. kilometer
126. kilogram
127. yard
128. 12:25
129. 4:45
130. C
131. 77¢
132. $3.00
133. $4.00
134. $4.00
135. 16
136. 4
137. 1000
138. 12
139. 100
140. tennis
141. 10
142. soccer
143. skiing and softball
144. (3, 1)
145. mitt
146. (2, 4) or (3, 5)
147. (5, 1)
148. racquet

Skills Test Answer Key

Skills Exercises Answer Key

20—There are many beginning and ending consonants and blends in these phrases. See that student has circled at least one beginning and one ending consonant or blend in each phrase.

21—There are many middle consonants in these phrases. See that student has circled at least one in each phrase.

page 22

camel	m
riding	d
fuzzy	zz
settle	tt
sinking	nk
clothing	th
desert	s
freezing	z
rodent	d
burrows	rr
viper	p
largest	rg

page 23

lizard follows path: tricky, trade, treat, tree, trap, track, train, try, trouble, trim

snake follows path: start, stork, stone, sticky, sty, stormy, strange, stump, stop, stuck, strong. The lizard has the shortest path.

page 24

1. stick, slick
2. smile
3. scarf
4. swat, squat, scat, slat, spat
5. sniff, stiff, spiff
6. squirrel
7. skate, slate, state
8. spray, stay, sway
9. snail
10. swim, slim, skim
11. spoon, swoon
12. slip, skip, snip
13. skunk, stunk, spunk

14. sleep, sweep, steep
15. smash, slash, squash, stash
16. scoop, snoop, stoop, swoop, sloop
17. swing, sling, sting
18. stop, slop

page 25

1. clown, crown, frown, brown, drown, blown
2. blue, glue, clue, true
3. write, trite
4. bring, cling, fling, wring, sling
5. clog, frog
6. float, bloat, gloat
7. glass, crass, class, brass
8. plain, drain, train, brain
9. slippery
10. crate, plate, slate
11. creek, sleek
12. dry, cry, sly, fry, try, wry, pry
13. slip, clip, trip, flip, drip, blip
14. pride, slide, bride, glide
15. wrong
16. crow, plow, flow, slow, brow, glow
17. slick, prick, trick, click, flick, crick
18. stop, plop, crop, drop, flop, prop, slop

page 26

Blue icebergs: chip, bush, math, chin, thumb, shop, catch, wish, birch, with

Check to see that the path goes near the blue icebergs.

Circle ng endings on wing, sang.

Circle nk ending on mink.

Circle ck endings on sock, stuck, duck.

Circle lk ending on milk.

Circle st beginning and ending on stuck, worst.

Circle mp ending on jump.

Circle sk beginning and ending on risk, skin, brisk.

Circle sc beginning on scale, scoot.

page 27

jump	scream
crash	trick
float	prowl
swim	drink
strike	

page 28

Answers may vary some.
1. worry
2. sunny
3. chilly
4. cotton
5. giggle
6. wedding
7. funny
8. terrific

page 29

Lines connect to draw a hermit crab in a shell.

page 30

1. rain
2. jungle
3. parrot
4. banana
5. monkey
6. jaguar
7. canoe
8. leaf
9. vine
10. river
11. anaconda

page 31

Path should follow: run, sun, bull, red, trip, fall, rip, skip, hop, mud, flop, flick, stop

page 32

Check drawing to see that student has followed directions.
Long vowel sounds are:
1. bow, hair
2. smile, face
3. kite, air
4. kite
5. ice, cream, cone
6. nose
7. cape, green
8. rose, each
9. cupcake

page 33

drone, rate, cage, cake, page, stale, smile, dine, slope, ate, mate, page, cape, June, cone, white, rose, ape, plate, rage

page 34

These may be written in a different order.
1. goofy
2. looking
3. moose
4. loose
5. deep
6. woods
7. Look
8. see
9. feet
10. foot
11. needs
12. cool
13. pools
14. food
15. feed
16. toadstools
17. beetles
18. too
19. zoo
20. free

There are 20 different words with double vowels.

page 35

Words to be circled:
beast
be
related
These
seek
egrets (3 times)
feet
the (10 times)
eat
meal

page 36

Follow path: tow, low, know, mow, show, grow, snow, flow

page 37

Answers may vary some.
1. pain
2. caught
3. friendly
4. deadly
5. out, eat
6. heat
7. meat, moat
8. ouch
9. beat, boat, bait
10. meal, mail

11. poison
12. retreat
13. mouth
14. glue
15. hours, hairs, hears
16. teach, touch
17. about
18. against

page 38

1. playful (ay)
2. Take (a—silent e)
3. afraid (ai)
4. tail (ai)
5. Wave (a—silent e)
6. Aim (ai); straight (ai)
7. Hey (ey); away (ay)
8. Escape (a—silent e); late (a—silent e)

page 39

1. boat
2. loud
3. beach
4. rain

page 40

Y as consonant:
yes	yodeled
yellow	yank
Yeti	yelled
yummy	yikes

Y as vowel:
try	easily
snowy	yummy
lucky	silly
today	fly

page 41

walk	plumber
knob	wren
stalk	write
climb	lamb
know	knead
crumbs	limb
wrist	comb

page 42

possible treasures:
teeth	silver
books	worms
shoes	oysters
marbles	spoons
shells	sand
bottles	gold
coconuts	bones
cookies	candy
mud	diamonds
	jewels

laundry

page 43

The turtle with ed got the farthest.

1. ing
2. ed
3. ing
4. ed
5. ed or es
6. ing
7. s
8. ed

page 44

1. Pre
2. Re
3. mis
4. pre
5. dis
6. un
7. re
8. re

page 45

1. ible
2. ly
3. less
4. ous
5. ful
6. ish
7. ant; ly
8. ness
9. tion
10. ment

page 46

1. retired
2. restful
3. friendly
4. beautiful
5. restless
6. unhappy
7. disappointed

page 47

1. usual
2. appear
3. poison
4. quiet
5. strange
6. peace
7. large
8. believe
9. cold
10. power

page 48

1. stop
2. danger
3. work
4. agree
5. blame
6. fine
7. neighbor
8. care
9. tame
10. friend

page 49

1-syllable: to, swamp, Don't, fall, out, of, the, You, might, lose, your, hat, in, This, wild, has, teeth, him, would, be, an, we, should, now, want
2-syllables: Welcome, canoe, little, river, Taming, Perhaps, exit, wrestle
3-syllables: Mosquito, explorers, dangerous
4-syllables: alligator
6-syllables: impossibility

page 50

3-syllable words: rapidly, powerful, waterspouts, anywhere, underground, dangerous, tremendous, tornado

page 51

1. isn't
2. Who's
3. couldn't
4. aren't
5. you're
6. shouldn't
7. We'll
8. They're
9. You've
10. We've
11. don't
12. You'll
"Boom" is the word that appears.

page 52

1. They'll
2. She'll
3. I've
4. you'll
5. Don't
6. You'd
7. We'll
8. It's

page 53

Answers will vary.

page 54

Color these areas: because, right, which, ramp, people, scare, through, there, write, when, quiet, friend, scream, where, animal, thought, worst, leaves, thumb, through, believe
Answer to puzzle is: mosquitoes

page 55

1. wring
2. ate
3. pear
4. sew
5. sail, sea
6. scent, too
7. write
8. blew

page 56

Down
1. reigned
3. sales

4. blew
5. plane
9. here
10. dew
Across
2. pairs
5. pare
6. tale
7. way
8. sea
10. dear
11. knew

page 57

1. Africa
2. Dr., Kenwick
3. Ashland, Oregon, National, Forensic, Laboratory
4. New, Zealand
5. Saturday, Spanish
6. April, Mexico
7. United, States, Florida

page 58

All spaces colored gray except: dishes, wishes, foxes, branches, glasses, lunches, boxes

page 59

Add 's to each animal name in 1–8.

page 60

Answers will vary.

page 61

Answers will vary. Check to see that student has written words that do mean the opposite of those in 1–10.

page 62

Synonyms:
bright—brilliant
look—watch
fast—quick
journey—trip
sparkle—twinkle
cold—chilly
Antonyms:
old—new
distant—close
daylight—darkness
exciting—boring
return—leave

page 63

1. wave
2. sink
3. coast
4. star
5. jam
6. drop

page 64

1. foods
2. games or sports
3. school subjects
4. countries
5. diseases, illnesses, or sicknesses

page 65

Check to see that all words are circled.

page 66

Answers will vary. Check to see that student has written words that have to do with heat or cold.

page 67

Answers will vary. Check to see that words student writes use the letters provided.

page 68

Circled titles:
Mighty Math
Time to Read
Find Out About Plants
Write Here

page 69

1. Rule 2
2. closely
3. Rule 8
4. Rule 7
5. Raise your hand
6. Completed neatly and turned in on time
7. On the book table
8. Never

page 70

Check to see that student has matched the correct animal with his or her name tag.

page 71

Circled words: brushes, palette, paper, crayons, paint, easel, pencils, tempera, markers
Boxed words: tuba, piano, tambourine, clarinet, xylophone, violin, harmonica, saxophone, drum, guitar, keyboard
There are 11 musical instruments.
There are 9 art supplies.

page 72

Check to see that the following spaces are colored: #1, #2, #4, #5, #6, #9.

Picture should say: Good for you.

page 73

1. b
2. b
3. c
4. a
5. b
6. b
7. b

page 74

1. Three
2. apples
3. fish
4. butterfly
5. ball
6. lemonade
7. Answers will vary.

page 75

1. apples
2. lemonade
3. pizza
4. no
5. cups
6. no
7. yes
8. yes
9. three
10. carrots

page 76

Crossed-out words:
potato
pencil
microscope
notebook
hamburger
forks

page 77

1. sandwiches
2. 26
3. pizza
4. 8
5. 9
6. 20
7. pizzas
8. 10

page 78

1. c
2. Check to see that student has drawn something in the circle.
3. Answers will vary.

Skills Exercises Answer Key

page 79

Check to see that student has drawn the objects in the appropriate places. Main idea: This school is strict.
Answers may vary.

page 80

Answers will vary.

page 81

Answers will vary.

page 82

Check to see that student has filled in the blanks in this order: ball, day, hit, great, high, into, fence, window, run

page 83

1. We are studying addition and subtraction.
2. The problems are on page 21.
3. There are 22 problems in all.
4. The assignment is due tomorrow.
5. Let's study together.

page 84

1. c
2. a
3. b
4. c
5. a
6. a

page 85

1. Friday
2. Pauli
3. equipment manager
4. lemonade
5. by the creek
6. sunny
7. the team lost

page 86

Check to see that student has named each creature correctly. Answers to questions will vary.

page 87

Answers will vary.

page 88

Letters circled are:
1. B
2. F
3. P

4. S
5. B
6. C
7. R
8. Answers will vary.

page 89

Check to see that student has matched the talents to the correct students.

page 90

1. lizard
2. thick
3. pink and yellow
4. slowly
5. Answers will vary.

page 91

Words circled are: milk, hairbrush, fire, rock, ice cream, cotton

page 92

(Answers may vary.)
1. Down the Slide
2. Fun on the Seesaw
3. Flossie Likes to Swing
4. Time for the Game

page 93

Answers will vary.

page 94

Look at student drawings to see that they have followed directions correctly. There are 2 crabs.

page 95

1. about a raft trip
2. fun
3. A Wet and Wild Ride

page 96

1. cherry
2. pickle
3. tomato
4. corn
5. worm

page 97

Answers will vary.

page 98

#1 ll—dollar, swallow, million, follow, balloon, umbrella
#2 nn—connect, tennis, penny, cannot, running, funny
#3 ss—possible, scissors, guessing, messes, lesson

#4 bb—dribble, rabbit, bubble, cabbage, ribbon
#5 pp—happen, appear, clapped, hopping, zipper
#6 ff—office, different, ruffle, fluffy, sniffle
#7 gg—wiggle, soggy, hugging, goggles, muggy, giggle
#8 mm—drummer, swimmer, humming, yummy, summer, trimmed
#9 dd—fiddle, puddle, sudden, middle, muddy
#10 rr—correct, parrot, carry, tomorrow, arrow
#11 tt—cotton, button, matter, swatting, batted
#12 zz—fuzzy, buzzing, fizzle, jazzy, quizzes

page 99

1. magic
2. surprise
3. circus
4. circle
5. crazy
6. size
7. absent
8. cloudy
9. giant
10. gym
11. jelly
12. giraffe
13. eyes
14. tease
15. catch
16. color
17. cool
18. city
19. crayon
20. gentle

page 100

Sections containing these words should be colored:
lime, wife, tickle, lonely, halves, puzzle, froze, uncle, gone, scramble, cure, glue, cattle, ounce, maze, able, bottle, tone, argue, shine, ripe, lonesome, homework, beetle, shake

page 101

Words that should be circled in red:
lie, veil, vein, weight, their, piece, grieve,

brief, eight, freight, believe, pie, reign, sleigh, die, neighborhood
1. height
2. weird
3. either
4. neither
5. foreign
6. ceiling

page 102

The correctly spelled words are:
sassy, fussy, hissing, sausage, sword, Mississippi, disease, scissors, sneeze, necessary, snooze
These should be colored green. They form a snake.

page 103

1. color
2. photo
3. shampoo
4. studio
5. double
6. cocoon
7. blood
8. octopus
9. baboon
10. motor
11. trio
12. gorilla
13. fool
14. people
15. mosquito
16. poem
17. opposite
18. memory
19. solo
20. raccoon
21. forget
22. lasso
23. cotton
24. tomato
25. doctor
26. volcano
27. piano
28. taco
29. loose
30. odor

page 104

Words in the quilt should be:
Row 1 quiz, quiet, squirt, queen
Row 2 quill, squirrel, quarrel, square
Row 3 quake, quartet, squeeze, quarter
Row 4 quack, squirm, quit, squeak
Row 5 quick, question, squash, quotient

page 105

1. Wednesday
2. wonderful
3. waffle
4. whisper
5. awful
6. whole
7. wicked
8. whistle
9. except
10. exact
11. expect
12. mixture
13. extra
14. exciting
15. yolk
16. yawn
17. yesterday
18. rhyme
19. syrup
20. crazy
21. mystery
22. prize or size
23. zipper
24. dozen
25. freeze
26. squeeze
27. fizzy
28. cozy
29. lazy
30. yellow
31. jazz
32. zero
33. weather
34. wow

page 106

1. tremendous, ridiculous, outrageous
2. explosion, dictionary, exceptional, multiplication
3. restaurant, somersault
4. earthworm, underground, superhuman, extraterrestrial
5. Mississippi

page 107

1. mouse
2. phone
3. tiny
4. inch
5. open
6. many
7. which or witch
8. every
9. very or vary
10. when or win
11. would or wood
12. busy
13. just
14. first
15. fifth

346 **Skills Exercises Answer Key**

Copyright © 2016 World Book, Inc./ Incentive Publications, Chicago, IL

16. even
17. use
18. deer or dear
19. also
20. talk
21. maybe
22. burn or born or barn
23. buy or by or bye
24. often
25. ounce or once
26. none or nun or noon
27. was
28. could or cold
29. answer
30. won't

page 108
1. Rainy Weather Causes Problems
2. Amazing Grizzly Bear Visits Area
3. Awful Storm Hits Mountain
4. Circus Coming Tomorrow
5. Bigfoot Appears in State Park
6. Beavers Build Huge Dam
7. Crab Completes Difficult Climb
8. Raccoon Caught Stealing Food

page 109
1. Disneyland
2. California
3. New York City
4. Golden Gate Bridge
5. Mexico
6. Atlantic Ocean
7. Pacific Ocean
8. Florida
9. Australia
10. Canada
11. Washington, D.C.
12. Milky Way Galaxy
13. Grand Canyon
14. South America or Africa
15. Rocky Mountains
16. Chicago
17. Alaska
18. Mount Everest
19. South Pole
20. Europe
21. Africa
22. Antarctica

page 110
1. b
2. b
3. c
4. c
5. a
6. a
7. c
8. c
9. b
10. a
11. a
12. c
13. b
14. a
15. c
16. b
17. c
18. b
19. a

page 111
A. Sunday, Monday, Tuesday, Wednesday, Thursday, Friday, Saturday
B. January, February, August, September, November
C. 1. Christmas or Hanukkah
2. Valentine's Day
3. Thanksgiving
4. Fourth of July
5. Mother's Day
6. Presidents' Day

page 112
There are twenty-seven rabbit children.
A. one million
B. one thousand
C. five hundred
D. one hundred one
E. thirteen
F. forty
G. fifty-five
H. seventy-seven
I. thirty-eight
J. nineteen
K. fourteen
L. eighty
M. sixteen
N. sixty-seven
O. second
P. fifth
Q. third
R. ninth

page 113
A. Lizard
B. Grasshopper
C. Porcupine
D. Kangaroo
E. Monkey
F. Elephant
G. Giraffe
H. Raccoon
I. Turtle
J. Eagle
K. Rabbit
L. Parrot
M. Rattlesnake
N. Gopher
O. Mule
P. Zebra

page 114
There are 23 correct words including the example done for students. Correct words that should have a hook & line drawn to them:
accident
careful
drawer
bacon
empty
voice
uncle
music
somebody
recess
next
quiet
length
just
kitchen
heart
wrong
gladly
ocean
odor
taught
hundred
fever

page 115
Wrong words listed below, as well as color which student should use for square.
a. yellow: anamals, arownd
b. red: basball, batheing, becuz
c. blue: important
d. blue: diferent
e. yellow: mountins, usally
f. red: finaly, sudenly, musik
g. blue: clotheing
h. blue: probaly
i. yellow: sombody, regalar
j. red: eigher, wether, laddar, famus
k. blue: pleeze
l. yellow: togethar, trubble
m. blue: docter
n. red: sience, friend, resess
o. yellow: suger, cotton

pages 116–117
page 116—See that student has chosen nouns to name things pictured.
page 117—See that student has chosen verbs represented in the picture.

page 118
1. friend
2. umbrella
3. zebra
4. zoo
5. yaks
6. kitchen
7. iguana
8. tongue
9. teeth
10. eggs
11. nose
The surprise is a fuzzy kitten!

page 119
Mrs. Clown, Bellview School, Monday, October, Valentine's Day, Dallas, Texas, Rizzo, Main Street, Brooklyn Bridge, Milton, Colorado River, Thanksgiving, Friday, Leo, July

page 120
mice
bunnies
bears
knives
cameras
butterflies
puppies
turtles
fish (or fishes)
glasses
radios
monkeys
ducks
pennants
hippos

page 121
1–8. Add 's to all blanks.

pages 122–123
Down
1. teased
2. scratch
3. tickles
9. tumbled
10. roll
13. toss
Across
4. reach
5. flip
6. shake
7. skip
8. chatter
11. sobs
12. jump
14. flop
15. gobble

page 124
Answers will vary. See that student has written complete sentences.

page 125
Rings around 2, 3, 5, 6, 9, 10; Total 6. See that student has correctly fixed the run-ons.

page 126
Answers may vary somewhat.
1. Is that Ellie on the high wire?
2. Is it true that the elephant can fly?
3. Can Ellie juggle pies?
4. Does Ellie know how to ride a unicycle?
5. Did the elephant jump through a ring of fire?
6. Did Ellie eat all the cotton candy?

page 127
Sentences that should be checked are: 2, 3, 4, 5, 6, 8, 10, 11, 12 See that student has added periods to the end of these sentences.

page 128
1. The, Long, Beach, California—100¢
2. Zelda, Chester—50¢
3. Have, Screaming, Eagle—75¢
4. I, Valentine's, Day—75¢
5. The, Central, City, February—100¢
6. The, United, States—75¢
7. Did, Monday, Tuesday, Wednesday—100¢
8. Lolly, Molly, Cannonball, Saturday—100¢
9. Did, Polly, Cannonball, July—100¢
10. Someone—25¢
Total $8.00

347

page 129

Answers will vary. See that student has written a contraction in each space and that the sentence makes sense.

page 130

Answers may vary.
1. "Can we go faster?" asked Bubbles.
2. The engineer shouted, "All aboard! Ride the Circus Town Express."
3. "Do we stop in Kalamazoo?" wondered Mrs. Clown.
4. Danno said, "This choo-choo is my favorite ride."
5. "We like to go through tunnels," hollered the twins.

page 131

Students should color in most of the ducks.
1. Ellie ate peanuts, cotton candy, and a funnel cake.
2. Did you want to ride the Octopus?
3. Oh, no! Now it's raining!
4. Did the clown lose her nose?
5. Hurry! The show is starting! (or .)
6. Please don't feed the monkeys! (or .)
7. Mop, Pop, and Glop are clowns.
8. The elephants stole the peanuts. (or !)
9. Watch out for the tiger!
10. Could you tame a lion?
11. I can't wait to see the fire-eater! (or .)
12. Well, I think I have the tickets.

page 132

See that student has written words in every category.

page 133

See that student has complete poster including all the information asked.

pages 134–135

See that student has completed both pages, collecting ideas and using some for the writing on page 47.

page 136

See that student has described and illustrated a trick.

page 137

See that student has finished story in a way that is complete and makes sense.

pages 138–139

See that student has adequately completed all tasks.

pages 144–145

1. 3
2. 3
3. 2
4. northeast
5. Jefferson
6. Jefferson and Tenth
7. 5
8. The Smiths
9. south
10. Miss Trip
11. yes
12. none

pages 146–147

1. 9   9. 15
2. 4   10. 11
3. 3   11. 23
4. 22   12. 5
5. 8   13. 2
6. 17   14. 14
7. 19   15. 21
8. 24   16. 10

page 148

Answers will vary.

Students may give one or more answers for each. Possible answers are:
1. 1, 2, 3, 4, 7, 10, 13
2. 1, 2, 3, 4, 5, 7, 8, 9, 12
3. 1, 2, 3, 4, 5, 6, 10, 13
4. 2, 4, 5, 6, 7
5. 11, 12
6. 8, 9, 11, 12
7. 5, 6
8. 2, 4, 8, 9, 11, 12
9. 2, 4, 6
10. 8, 9, 12
11. 8, 9, 11, 12
12. 10, 13

page 149

Check to see that lines have been drawn to appropriate signs. Students' own sign designs at bottom will vary.

page 150

Answers will vary.

page 151

1. 22%
2. 9%
3. 13%
4. 17%
5. parks
6. police
7. garbage collection
8. fire department

page 152

1. library
2. fire department
3. police
4. parks office
5. water services
6. ambulance
7. post office
8. garbage collection
9. animal control
10. power company

page 153

Laws are:
Wrong Way
Do Not Enter
Private Property
Yield
One Way
Stop
Slow
Speed Limit 55

page 154

Answers will vary.

page 155

Answers may vary.
Needs: crackers, cans of soup, raisins, apples, tent, canteens (water), hat, gloves, socks, clothing

page 156

1. mechanic
2. gardener
3. babysitter
4. veterinarian
5. teacher
6. doctor
7. waiter or waitress
8. lifeguard
9. builder
10. judge

page 157

Answers will vary. See that student has colored 5 things and has circled 5 things.

page 158

Real Needs: 2, 3, 6, 7, 10, 11

page 159

Answers may vary, depending on interpretation of the jobs!
Goods path—red—farmer, auto maker, baker, artist, shoemaker, cook, tent maker, builder, gardener
Services path—green—librarian, doctor, janitor, piano teacher, animal trainer, auto salesperson, grocery store clerk, mayor, president, waiter, plumber, banker, police officer, fire fighter, baseball player

page 160

Answers will vary.

page 161

Money cannot buy friendship or love (# 5 and 9).

page 162

1. $2,850
2. $300
3. $600
4. $300
5. $60
6. $150
7. $300
8. $240
9. $300
10. $300
Answers will vary.

page 163

1. baseball cap
2. $10
3. no
4. Answers will vary.

page 164

1. D   5. A
2. B   6. H
3. E   7. F
4. G   8. C

page 165

1. cow—dairy—ice cream
2. tomatoes—cannery—pizza parlor
3. sheep—loom & spinning—wheel—hat & gloves
4. trees—lumberyard—house
5. apples—bakery—apple pie

pages 166–167

The correct map is # 1. Check to see that the map includes some representation of all items in their correct places.

page 168

Check to see that student has colored the map correctly.

page 169

1. #2   3. #1
2. #3   4. #2
Carl needs map #3 to find Maple Street.

page 170

The correct cave is the one in the far southeast corner (lower right).

page 171

1. N
2. NW
3. N
4. S
5. NW
6. Pelican's
7. Crocodile's
8. Turtle's
9. no
10. yes
11. Turtle's

page 172

Check to see that student has followed the directions accurately.

page 173

1. egg—brown
2. turtle shell—green
3. hive—yellow
4. tree—orange
5. cactus—green box
6. Fido's house & straw nest—brown with circle

Milk is delivered to the turtle shell, Fido's house, and the straw nest.

Skills Exercises Answer Key

pages 174–175
1. yes
2–3. Look to see that students have traced and colored these correctly.
4. yes
5. no
6. yes
7. library
8. Bridge
9. Downtown
10. 3
11. workers at the Pencil Factory

page 176
See that student draws the correct candy in each space.

page 177
1. Cactus, Sagebrush, or Locoville
2–4. See that student has colored these features accurately.
5. 2
6. 2
7. twice
8. Dry Desert State Park

page 178
The delivery is for the rat family.

page 179
Check the symbol for each toy named.

page 180
Map 2 should be colored.

page 181
Check to see that the student has drawn the map according to the key with the 6 items in the correct places.

page 182
1. apple
2. lunch box
3. yes
4. no

page 183
1. 7
2. no
3. X on gym
4–6. Check for correct colors and path.

page 184
1. 4
2. yes
3. yes
4. 2
5. 5

page 185
1. yes
2. 1
3. no
4. 3
5. no
6. yes

page 186
Answers will vary.

page 187
Check for correct color and direction. Paths may vary.

page 188
1. 70
2. 10
3. 30
4. 20
5. 20

page 189
1. C, 2
2. F, 1
3. A, 3
4. E, 5
5. no
6. no
7. yes
8. yes

page 190
Check for placement.

page 191
1. D, 2
2. C, 6
3. C, 3
4. A, 3
5. D, 7
6. D, 5
7. A, 7
8. B, 4

page 192
Check to see that the student has colored the globe correctly.

page 193
Star on #2
1. Topographic Map
2. Road Map
3. Weather Map

pages 194–195
1. Check to see that student has traced route.
2–4. Answers will vary. Check to see that

the student has identified his or her own state and bordering states.

page 196
1. Nevada
2. Washington
3. Arizona
4. California
5. Idaho
6. Utah
7. Oregon

page 197
1–8. Check to see that the student has colored maps correctly.
9. 5
10. yes

page 198
1. 55   4. 2
2. 2   5. yes
3. 6   6. no

page 199
Grandma—Tent A—blue
Girls—Tents E & F—green
Boys—Tents B & C—orange
Miss Grizz—Tent D—red

page 200
1–5. Check to see that the symbols are positioned correctly.
6–8. Check to see that items are colored correctly.

page 201
1. Check for accuracy.
2. no
3. 3
4. no
5. 1
6. yes

page 202
1. no
2. yes
3. yes
4. ship
5. fish symbol
6. 4

page 203
Check to see that the map is colored correctly.

page 204
1. 20
2. 80
3. 40
4. 50
5. Minnow Pond

page 205
1. pancakes
2. pizza
3. honey
4. berries
5. pizza & honey
6. Answers will vary.

page 206
1. Grandma's House
2. 35
3. 45
4. 15
5. Polar Bear Movies and Choco-Hut Ice Cream Store

page 207
Maps will vary.

page 211
1. roots
2. trunk
3. leaves
4. flower
5. cone
Check to see that students have added roots, leaves, and flower to the plant and trunk, roots, and cones to the tree.

page 212
Check that students have adequately depicted the stages of the cycle.

page 213
1. fruit
2. crown
3. outer bark
4. inner bark
5. cambium layer
6. trunk
7. sapwood
8. heartwood
9. roots

page 214
1. B   5. D
2. F   6. C
3. H   7. G
4. E   8. A

page 215
Across
1. carbon
2. sunlight
3. stomata
4. oxygen
5. leaves

Down
1. chlorophyll

page 216
Red Circle—insects: 1, 3, 4, 6, 8, 11
Blue Box—arachnids: 2, 5, 9, 12

page 217
Animals with backbones: rabbit, ostrich, squirrel, bird, snake, crocodile, bear, elephant, frog, turtle, pig, shark, person

pages 218-219
BIRDS
• feathers
• warm-blooded
• most fly
• wings

FISH
• fins
• breathe only with gills
• scales
• shark picture

AMPHIBIANS
• live on land or water
• cold-blooded
• smooth, moist skin
• frog picture

MAMMALS
• monkey picture
• hair or fur
• give milk to young
• babies grow inside mothers

REPTILES
• cold-blooded
• scaly, dry skin
• alligator picture
• snake picture

page 220
Bird Cage: snake—Reptiles
Fish Tank: cat—Mammal House
Mammal House: alligator—Reptiles
Reptiles: bird—Bird Cage
Amphibians: rabbit—Mammal House

page 221
1. segments
2. burrow
3. bristles
4. darker
5. pointed
6. castings
7. muscles

page 222
The home is a cactus. The animal is a lizard.

Skills Exercises Answer Key

page 223

1. C	5. D
2. C	6. H
3. A	7. D
4. D	8. M

pages 224–225

Students should add the following:

To desert—cactus, lizard, rattlesnake, camel

To grassland—lion, elephant

To coniferous forest—pine tree, owl, moose, wolf

To rain forest—monkey, parrot, palm tree

To pond—beaver, turtle, frog, fish

To ocean—whale, starfish, fish, crab, coral

page 226

1. producers
2. predator
3. consumers
4. decomposer
5. prey
6. food chain
7. community
8. scavenger

page 227

The producers are all plants.

The consumers are all animals.

Predators are owl, fox, ladybug, and fish.

page 228

Examples of pollution pictured are:
- airplane exhaust
- factory fumes
- car, truck, and boat fumes
- pollution into water from factory
- tractor spraying
- airplane noise

page 229

1. Pollution
2. waste
3. recycle
4. litter, trash
5. noise
6. oil
7. poison
8. exhaust, air
9. Acid

page 230

1. sun—yellow
2. moon—purple

3. Earth—blue & green

page 231

1. A
2. B
3. spins

page 232

See that pictures are correctly numbered.

page 233

Answers may vary. Discuss possibilities with students.

Unsafe situations:
- broken window
- broken ladder
- paint
- dog
- matches
- bicycle
- car
- electrical wires
- ball going into street
- lightning

page 234

Check to see that student pictures are appropriate to the season.

page 235

Check to see that student has colored temperatures correctly.

page 236

Check to see that students accurately label body parts.

page 237

Check to see that students accurately label body parts.

page 238

The coloring will vary.

page 239

1. fish
2. fern
3. frog
4. lizard
5. dinosaur
6. dragonfly

pages 240–241

See that pictures are drawn in the correct areas.

page 242

1. A
2. D
3. G

4. M
5. Q

page 243

See that student has matched the correct term to the correct picture.

page 244

1. K	7. F
2. C	8. I
3. L	9. A
4. B	10. E
5. D	11. G
6. H	12. J

page 253

The numbers out of order are:
1. 37
2. 600
3. 133 or 134
4. 103
5. 450 or 500
6. 26
7. 85
8. 234
9. 124
10. 564

page 254

Scores: Gus 6
Gordy 3
Gail 4
Gabby 4
Gipper 2

1. Gus
2. Gipper
3. Gus
4. Gipper

page 255

1. <		6. <
2. >		7. <
3. >		8. >
4. <		9. >
5. >		10. <

pages 256–257

1. <	a. 1
2. >	b. 24
3. >	c. 2
4. >	d. 18
5. <	e. 3
6. =	f. 11
7. >	g. 4
8. <	h. 3
9. <	i. 7
10. >	j. 6
11. <	k. 4
	l. 5
	m. 3

page 258

1. 23	6. 30
2. 88	7. 88
3. 47	8. 16
4. 26	9. 88
5. 16	10. 30

page 259

red balls: 32, 123
blue balls: 14, 11
purple balls: 90, 111
brown ball: 66
orange ball: 29
green balls: 84, 50
yellow ball: 76
pink ball: 45

page 260

1. pennies; 2¢
2. dimes; 60¢
3. quarter; 25¢
4. quarters; $1.00
5. dime; penny; 11¢
6. nickels; 10¢

Ben found the most money.

page 261

1. less
2. less
3. less
4. more
5. less
6. more

pages 262-263

1. second
2. fifteenth
3. sixth
4. seventh and eighth
5. bug
6. sixteenth
7. fifth and thirteenth
8. no
9. tenth
10. third

For 11-20, check student pages to see that the creatures and objects are colored or drawn as instructed.

page 264

Slurpy 95
Bog...............445
Muck............540
Quirk.............950
Grunt.........5,000
Muppy 905
Biff................. 45
Oozy........... 420
Dip.................54
Sloppy..........590
Flossie........4,000
Finn..............509

page 265

1. 62,000
2. 620
3. 602
4. 62
5. 6,200
6. 440
7. 404
8. 33

9. 33,000
10. 330
11. 4,400
12. 2,666
13. 444

page 266

Check student drawings to see that numbers are connected in this order:

Annie: 16, 22, 27, 45, 50, 54

Chester: 604, 640, 644, 649, 694, 696, 699, 700

Robby: seventeen, eighteen, twenty-three, fifty, fifty-one

Betty: 40, 44, 49, 64, 72, 76, 90

Gary: 214, 226, 232, 240, 288, 294, 322 Gary Grape did not cross the finish line.

page 267

1. 5
2. float
3. sunglasses (or hat)
4. 1
5. yes
6. bug spray
7. no
8. pail and shovel
9. sunglasses
10. 3 hats
11. yes
12. chair and towel

page 268

1. Maniac Mouse, 280 oz.
2. Big Al Alligator, 50 lb.
3. Slippery Sheila, 3,560 lb.
4. Dinah the Destroyer, 3,400 lb.
5. Beetle Brain, 70 oz.
6. Bug Eyes, 100 oz.
7. Ferocious Flamingo, 510 oz.
8. Perilous Polly, 280 oz.
9. Big Bad Bosco Bear, 990 lb.
10. Sam the Squeeze, 1,030 lb.

page 269

Missing numbers from the chart are:
Abdomen Lifts—
17 minutes
Rest—
23 minutes
(Note: The pattern is:

add 1 to first number to get 2nd, add 2 to 2nd number to get 3rd, add 3 to 3rd number to get 4th, add 4 to 4th number, and so on.) Other missing items are:

$$\begin{array}{r} 5 \\ + 13 \\ \hline 18 \end{array}$$

- B. 53 + 6 = 59
- C. 24 − 11 = 13
- D. 15 + 15 = 30
- E. 15 + 40 = 55
- F. 45 + 54 = 99

page 270

- A. 23 (all others are even numbers)
- B. 37 (All other numbers have 2 as final digit.)
- C. 26.8 (All other numbers are fractional numbers.)
- D. 5,333 (All other numbers are decimal numerals.)
- E. 3,404 (All other numbers have only 3 and 0 as digits.)
- F. 45 − 11 = 34 (All other equations have 11 as the answer.)
- G. 32 + 30 = 62 (All other equations have 2 exact numbers added together)

page 272

Hockey stick is the lost equipment.

page 273

Game 1 38
Game 2 43
Game 3 ....50 (Best)
Game 4 29
Game 5 50
Game 6 27
Game 7 68
Game 8 46
Game 9 15
Game 10 38
Game 11 40

page 274

1. 92 yellow
2. 32 blue
3. 177 red
4. 35 blue
5. 86 yellow
6. 35 blue
7. 50 striped
8. 123 red
9. 49 blue
10. 76 yellow

page 275

1.	68	6.	29
2.	54	7.	172
3.	227	8.	79
4.	106	9.	888
5.	288	10.	22

page 276

1.	1,336	6.	1,632
2.	1,336	7.	1,503
3.	1,092	8.	952
4.	981	9.	984
5.	2,166	10.	934

Answer: Steph Curry

page 277

1.	8	7.	4
2.	9	8.	9
3.	27	9.	8
4.	16	10.	5
5.	9	11.	12
6.	8	12.	49

pages 278-279

1. $248.83
2. $40.05
3. stick; $6.17
4. yes
5. 110.00
6. elbow pads and stick
7. $259.95
8. $103.83
9. $129.93
10. $26.46

page 280

1. $\frac{3}{6}$ 6. $\frac{2}{12}$

2. $\frac{5}{12}$ 7. $\frac{1}{6}$

3. $\frac{1}{6}$ 8. $\frac{4}{6}$

4. $\frac{5}{6}$ 9. $\frac{2}{6}$

5. $\frac{2}{6}$ 10. $\frac{1}{6}$

page 281

Rocky—$1\frac{1}{4}$

Ernest—$1\frac{2}{3}$

Bruiser—$2\frac{5}{6}$

Jess—$1\frac{1}{2}$

Kujo—$2\frac{3}{4}$

Bud—$1\frac{1}{6}$

Bruiser ate the most. Bud left the most.

pages 282–283

1. dentist and practice
2. June 17, June 26
3. 2 weeks and 4 days
4. practice and a game
5. Ellie's swim party
6. June 21
7. a game
8. Thursday, June 25
9. 3
10. 3
11. 3 weeks
12. 5
13. Wednesday, June 10
14. 11 days
15. 1st week in June

page 284

Jan - 311
Jamie - 80
Jerri - 7
June - 0
James - 621
John - 43
Julie - 156
Janet - 409
Jenny - 254
Justin - 4010

page 285

1. 1,612
2. 15,047
3. 806
4. 2,014
5. 310,923
6. 41,446
7. 1,137
8. 62,520
9. 41,446
10. 15,047

page 287

1. 2
2. 2
3. 10 (9 without waistband)
4. 3
5. no
6. 2
7. 4

page 288

Answers will vary. Check student pictures to see that shapes are colored correctly.

page 289

1. 5
2. 2
3. 3
4. 5
5. 2

page 290

Check student pictures to see that correct shapes are in each flag.

page 291

1. B and C
2. cone
3. cylinder
4. cone
5. G
6. D and J
7. cylinder
8. yes

page 292

A — F
B — H
C — E
D — I

page 293

Measurements are approximate.
1. 26 cm
2. 17 cm
3. 17 cm
4. 20 cm

page 294

1. 6 cm
2. 8 cm
3. 7 cm
4. 6 cm
5. 9 cm
6. 5 cm
7. 11 cm

page 295

1. $3\frac{1}{2}$ in.

2. $4\frac{1}{4}$ in.

3. $2\frac{1}{2}$ in.

4. $4\frac{3}{4}$ in.

5. $2\frac{1}{2}$ in.

6. 4 in.

page 296

Answers will vary.

page 297

1. $\frac{1}{2}$ L
2. 1 L
3. 20 L
4. 300 L
5. 7 L
6. 10,000 L
7. 300 L
8. 5,000 L

page 298

Fred   45¢
Happy   55¢
Wart   99¢
Toady   55¢
Rikki   28¢
Legs $1.00
Color Legs.

page 299

1. $50
2. $7
3. $3
4. the savings amount is too much
5. no; 5¢
6. 40¢

pages 300–301

1. 1 week, 1 day
2. Tuesday
3. after
4. swim class
5. 2 weeks
6. June 21
7. 1 week, 2 days
8. 2 days
9. 1 week, 2 days
10. 1 night

page 302

1. no
2. D
3. C
4. E or F
5. no
6. no
Color up to 160° (hot chocolate).

page 303

1. Frost Tea
2. 13
3. 3
4. 1
5. Quik-Gulp and Slug-Ade
6. 1
7. 6
8. Slug-Ade

page 304

1. 3:15
2. 6:30
3. 1:15
4. 12:00
5. Check clocks for accuracy.

Skills Exercises Answer Key